Guilt, Shame and Juvenile Delin

Guilt, Shame and Juvenile Delinquency

A symbolic interactionist analysis

Arne De Boeck

Boomjuridisch
Antwerpen

eleven

Published, sold and distributed by Eleven
P.O. Box 85576
2508 CG The Hague
The Netherlands
Tel.: +31 70 33 070 33
Fax: +31 70 33 070 30
e-mail: sales@elevenpub.nl
www.elevenpub.com

Sold and distributed in USA and Canada
Independent Publishers Group
814 N. Franklin Street
Chicago, IL 60610, USA
Order Placement: +1 800 888 4741
Fax: +1 312 337 5985
orders@ipgbook.com
www.ipgbook.com

Boom Juridisch Antwerpen
ISBN 978-94-6451-116-1
ISBN 978-94-6451-216-8 (e-book)
NU824
D/2023/15251/16

GPRC
Guaranteed
Peer Reviewed
Content
boekenvak.be/gprc

Eleven is an imprint of Boom uitgevers Den Haag.
ISBN 978-90-4730-165-3
ISBN 978-90-4730-166-0 (e-book)

I dedicate this work to the memory of my father

Acknowledgements

Writing this book and the PhD dissertation on which it is based would not have been possible without the support, encouragement and inspiration provided by many.

I first want to thank my supervisor Prof. Dr Stefaan Pleysier, who gave me the opportunity to work at the Leuven Institute of Criminology, first as a teaching assistant and later as a doctoral researcher. Stefaan, I have felt your trust and belief in me and this project since day one. Your support has been extremely valuable, and it has been a joy and privilege to work with you. My gratitude extends to my co-supervisor Prof. Dr Johan Put for his ever-positive attitude and his encouragement throughout the years.

I also wish to thank the members of my examination committee: Em. Prof. Dr Lode Walgrave, Prof. Dr Lieven Pauwels and Prof. Susan McVie. Their valuable suggestions and comments have helped me to improve this work. An additional thank you to Lode for being on my guidance committee, to Lieven for the inspiring discussions we had at the ESC conference in Sarajevo, and to Susan for hosting me as a visiting postgraduate student at the University of Edinburgh.

I was fortunate to be surrounded by many wonderful colleagues who made the Leuven Institute of Criminology such a pleasant and stimulating work environment. Thank you Bruna, Colinda, Diederik, Danique, Elke R., Elke V. H., Ellen, Elli, Ena, Evi, Huma, Loes, Manuela, Mattias, Maud, Mirko, Monique and others.

To my friends Louis, Mattias and Bram: thank you, not only for your continuous support but also for being a great source of fun and distraction from academic life. Thanks as well to all my other friends near and far, especially the 'Brusseleirs'.

I express my deepest gratitude, respect and love to my parents who gave me all the opportunities in life to succeed. I want to thank my mother in particular for being strong when times were hard, and my sister for being the honest and positive person that she is. I also want to thank the family of my girlfriend for their support: Judith, Senne and Laura.

My largest debt of gratitude goes to my girlfriend Hanne. Hanne, working on this book has demanded so many sacrifices from you, and I will forever be grateful. Thank you for bearing with me (and my mood swings), I know it was not easy.

Last but not least, to my children Ludovic and Yaëlle: you are the roots that keep me grounded. Thank you for reminding me of the things that matter most in life.

I dedicate this book to my father, who has taught me the value of hard work in life. I know you would have been proud of me.

Table of Contents

Introduction

No serious account of human behaviour, including criminal behaviour, can ignore emotion. Emotions are an intrinsic part of human nature; they highlight what is meaningful to us and motivate us to deal with important events in our lives (Frijda, 1986, 2007). In fact, so strong is the motivational force of emotions that they tend to 'override other concerns, other goals, and other actions' (Frijda, 2007, p. 16). As a consequence, human beings are often led by their emotions, sometimes for good, but sometimes for ill.

The motivational qualities of emotion have not gone unnoticed to criminologists. Indeed, few criminological theories explain crime without referring, at least implicitly, to emotions or closely related constructs. Strain theory argues that people are pressured into crime by negative emotions such as anger and frustration that result from blocked goals and other negative life events (Agnew, 1992; Merton, 1938). Social learning theory recognises the function that 'pleasant feelings' serve as reinforcers of both legal and illegal behaviour (Akers, 2009, p. 68). In deterrence and social control theory, the inhibitory emotion of fear – that is, fear of legal sanctions and fear of social disapproval, respectively – plays an important but often overlooked role (Hirschi, 1969; Pickett et al., 2018). Reintegrative shaming theory predicts that societies that shame offenders in a reintegrative way will have less crime, because reintegrative shaming induces guilt and builds conscience (Braithwaite, 1989). Actually, even rational choice theorists have incorporated emotions into their models as potential costs and rewards associated with offending (Grasmick & Bursik, 1990). Drawing upon these and other theories, criminologists have empirically identified several emotions that are associated with offending, ranging from anger and pride to fear and shame (e.g. Ahmed et al., 2001; Carmichael & Piquero, 2004; Pickett et al., 2018; van Gelder et al., 2014).

This book focuses on two emotions that should be of particular importance to criminologists: guilt and shame. Both guilt and shame are generally viewed as 'moral' emotions that discourage people from behaving immorally, while also encouraging reparative actions and self-improvement following moral failures and transgressions (Harris, 2003; Nelissen et al., 2013; Tangney et al., 2007; Turner & Stets, 2006). Recent reviews of the empirical literature largely support this view (Braithwaite, 2020; Schalkwijk et al., 2016; Spruit et al., 2016). Based on a comprehensive meta-analysis of 25 studies, Spruit et al. (2016) found that higher levels of guilt and shame are associated with less involvement in general and violent delinquency. Interestingly, it has also been found that girls anticipate higher levels of guilt and shame than boys for engaging in delinquent activities (Blackwell, 2000; Svensson, 2004; Svensson et al., 2013). Recent research suggests that these gender differences might play a crucial role in explaining the gender gap in delinquency (Rebellon et al., 2015, 2016). In sum, current evidence indicates that the emotions of guilt and shame should be fully integrated into criminological theory and research.

However, while criminologists have done a good job of empirically studying guilt and shame, the relationship of both emotions with offending remains under-theorised and, hence, poorly understood. One problem is that guilt and shame have not been sufficiently integrated into existing criminological theories of crime causation. Theories such as Sykes and Matza's (1957) theory of neutralisation, Braithwaite's (1989) theory of reintegrative shaming or, more recently, Wikström's (2010) situational action theory, all refer to guilt and shame, but only in passing, without much conceptual elaboration or theoretical integration. In 2001, Ahmed, Harris, Braithwaite and Braithwaite revised and expanded reintegrative shaming theory to include the concepts of guilt and shame (the emotions that shaming processes are hypothesised to elicit) (Ahmed et al., 2001). But this revised theory focuses mainly on emotions experienced *post*-offending (i.e. as a part of the reaction to crime) and does not clearly address how guilt and shame may dissuade people from offending in the first place.

A second problem is that despite being classified by many as 'social emotions' (Hareli & Parkinson, 2008; Tangney et al., 2007), there is limited knowledge of the social factors that influence guilt and shame in relation to offending behaviour. Indeed, criminological studies have predominantly drawn on individual-psychological models of guilt and shame, thereby neglecting insights from sociological theories of emotion (Dippong & Fitch, 2017). Yet if we want to fully understand social influences on crime and delinquency, we must deal with the social bases of crime-related emotions. In addition, a sociological approach to emotions could help to explain the social origins of gender differences in guilt and shame and thereby shed light on the gendered nature of social control.

The aim of this research is to contribute to a better understanding of the role of guilt and shame in the explanation of delinquency. To this end, I first develop a theoretical framework for:

a. understanding how prospective or forward-looking forms of guilt and shame can dissuade people from engaging in delinquency.
b. identifying and understanding the social factors that may influence prospective guilt and shame for engaging in delinquency.

Second, drawing upon this framework, I develop a set of hypotheses about the social factors that may contribute to individual and gender differences in prospective guilt and shame. I then empirically examine these hypotheses with an analysis of survey data from a sample of 856 adolescents in the Belgian city of Genk.

The theoretical framework of this research is established by integrating differential social control theory (Heimer & Matsueda, 1994), a symbolic interactionist theory of delinquency, with a complementary symbolic interactionist theory of emotion (Shott, 1979). Both theories draw upon Mead's (1934) concept of the role-taking self. Role-taking, as Mead famously explained, is the uniquely human capacity to respond to one's own oncoming gestures and actions in the same way, or in a similar way, as others would. This capacity makes it possible for human beings to become conscious of the meaning of their gestures and actions and thereby to become self-reflexive. It also enables them to imaginatively rehearse possible lines of action (before acting), to inhibit those that would have negative consequences and self-implications, and to facilitate those that would have the opposite effect. In short, role-taking enables self-monitoring and self-regulation in relation to others.

Drawing upon Mead, Heimer and Matsueda's (1994) differential social control theory specifies different role-taking processes that influence the likelihood that individuals will engage in delinquency. For example, the likelihood of delinquency should decrease when individuals take the role of significant others and anticipate others' disapproval of such behaviour. On the other hand, the likelihood of delinquency should increase when individuals hold delinquent views of themselves from the standpoint of others (e.g. as 'badasses' or 'troublemakers'). However, like Mead, Heimer and Matsueda did not pay attention to emotions that may arise in connection with role-taking experiences. Following Shott (1979), I argue that role-taking enables people to anticipate (and even pre-feel) negative self-evaluative emotions such as guilt and shame when they consider taking actions that are socially disapproved. Such prospective or forward-looking forms of guilt and shame act as warning signals indicating that a given action alternative poses an identity threat, thereby motivating people to take a different course of action. In sum, in this book I show how we can make sense of the delinquency-inhibiting effects of prospective guilt and shame by integrating them as role-taking mechanisms in differential social control theory.

By conceptualising guilt and shame as 'role-taking emotions', the theoretical framework also provides an approach to understanding the social nature of these emotions. As Heimer and Matsueda (1994) argue, role-taking is not a random process. Young people are likely to adopt the perspective of significant others and reference groups with which they identify. Depending on the normative orientations of these persons and groups, role-taking may either increase or decrease prospective guilt and shame for choosing a delinquent line of action. Drawing upon this framework and the broader criminological literature, I identify and discuss several social factors that may influence prospective guilt and shame during adolescence: religiosity and religious affiliation, relationships with parents and teachers, affiliations with delinquent friends, reflected appraisals of self from the standpoint of others, and traditional gender role norms. In the empirical part, I examine the relationships between these social factors and prospective shame-guilt in a sample of adolescents and young adults. I also examine whether some of these social factors might contribute to gender differences in guilt and shame.

This book is divided into eight chapters. In the **first chapter**, I discuss the nature of guilt and shame, identify the main differences between them and describe how they differ from other, related emotions such as embarrassment, humiliation and remorse. In doing so, I lay the groundwork for the **second chapter**, in which I present a narrative review of the empirical literature on the relationship of guilt and shame to delinquent behaviour. This review provides support for the inhibiting effects of anticipated and prospective feelings of guilt and shame on delinquency. In the **third chapter,** I discuss the limitations of existing theoretical approaches to (prospective) guilt and shame in the criminological literature. I then propose an alternative theoretical framework that builds on Mead's (1934) theory of the self, the symbolic interactionist analysis of the self-conscious emotions by Shott (1979), and the symbolic interactionist theory of delinquency developed by Heimer and Matsueda (1994). In the **fourth chapter**, I use this theoretical framework to generate hypotheses about the social factors that may contribute to individual and gender differences in prospective guilt and shame for engaging in delinquency. In the **fifth chapter**, I describe the data, measures and methods that were used in this study to empirically test the proposed hypotheses. In the **sixth chapter**, I present descriptive statistics for all variables used in the analysis. I evaluate the dimensionality and measurement properties of the scales through confirmatory factor analysis. In the **seventh chapter**, I report the results of a series of multivariate regression analyses to examine the relationships between different social factors and prospective shame-guilt for engaging in two different types of delinquency: shoplifting and retaliatory violence. I also report the results of a multiple mediation path analysis to examine whether the proposed social factors could play a mediating role in the relationship between gender and prospective shame-guilt. In the **final chapter,** I summarise the main findings of this study and discuss their broader significance. I also identify some of the key limitations of the data and methods that were used, and I make suggestions for future avenues of research.

1 The Place of Guilt and Shame among the Emotions

> Shame can understand guilt, but guilt cannot understand itself.
> (Williams, 1993, p. 92)

In this chapter, I discuss the nature of guilt and shame, identify the main differences between them and describe how they differ from other, related emotions such as embarrassment, humiliation and remorse. In doing so, I lay the groundwork for the next chapter, in which I review the literature on the relationship between guilt, shame and delinquency. I begin this chapter with a brief and general discussion of what emotions are before focusing in more detail on the specific emotions of guilt and shame.

1.1 What are emotions?

Although there is no consensus on the definition of emotions, theorists generally agree that they are complex mental and bodily states consisting of multiple interrelated components: cognitive, motivational, somatic, expressive and subjective-experiential (Frijda, 1986; Moors, 2009; Scarantino, 2016; Scherer, 2005; Scherer & Moors, 2019; Thoits, 1989). Each component tells us something about the function of emotions for the individual.

First, emotions have a *cognitive* component; they involve evaluations or appraisals of the significance of an event for the individual's needs, goals and concerns. Emotions therefore reflect what people care about and what matters to them. They are, to use the words of Frijda (1986), 'relevance detectors'. Second, emotions have a strong *motivational* force; they involve states of action readiness. Action readiness should not be understood as a readiness for a specific behaviour, but rather as a readiness to achieve a particular goal in interaction with the environment (e.g. to protect oneself in fear or to relate to others in happiness) (Deonna & Scherer, 2010). Third, emotions have a *somatic* component in that they involve neurophysiological responses (e.g. changes in muscle tone, rate of respiration, or heart rate). Together, the motivational and somatic components prepare and support the individual to take action to deal with the emotion-eliciting event or situation. Fourth, emotions have an *expressive* component, consisting of distinctive facial, vocal and/or gestural signals. This component serves an important communicative function (e.g. tears assist in communicating sadness; a lowered head assists in communicating shame). The *subjective-experiential* component, finally, refers to the emotion as it is felt or experienced by the individual. It is the conscious reflection of all components. The central representation of the emotional experience in the individual's consciousness enables monitoring the emotion and determining its meaning. Both of these cognitive processes in turn allow for so-called emotion-regulation, which has the function of organising an adaptive response.

Aside from listing these five diagnostic features, theorists have identified and defined emotions by distinguishing them from other affective phenomena (Ben-Ze'ev, 2001; Hacker, 2017; Moors, 2009; Scherer, 2005). Typically excluded from the class of emotions are purely physical sensations without cognitive-evaluative content such as feeling cold or pain (Moors, 2009). Short-term affective disturbances such as feeling startled or surprised are not considered emotions 'because they do not involve motives for action, as many emotions do, but rather temporarily *inhibit* motivated action' (Hacker, 2017, p. 14). Emotions have also been distinguished from moods, emotional dispositions/traits and sentiments. These distinctions call for a few words of explanation.

The boundary between moods and emotions is not sharp. In fact, to the person experiencing them, moods and emotions may feel very much the same. Nevertheless, there are some features that distinguish emotions from moods, the most frequently cited of which are the intentionality and the duration of the experience (Beedie et al., 2005). To start with the first, emotions need a specific intentional object; that is, they are always directed at something (Hacker, 2017; Parkinson et al., 1996). One cannot feel guilty or ashamed without feeling guilty or ashamed *about something*. This is different for moods, which can be unfocused. One can feel joyful or depressed without feeling joyful or depressed about anything in particular. Of course, moods *may* have objects (Hacker, 2017). For instance, one may feel depressed at the prospect of winter. Still, the grasp of a mood extends beyond its object, and, therefore, moods are always more diffuse than emotions. Indeed, a winter depression typically influences multiple aspects of one's life for longer periods of time. This brings us to the second distinguishing feature: unlike emotions, moods must last for a while (Hacker, 2017; Scherer, 2005). One may feel a sudden flash of anger or shame, but one cannot feel depressed or bored for only a couple of seconds.

Emotions can be further distinguished from emotional traits or dispositions (Ben-Ze'ev, 2001; Hacker, 2017; Scherer, 2005). Whereas an emotion is a temporary state that occurs on a given occasion and in relation to a particular event, an emotional trait refers to the tendency of an individual to experience certain emotions more frequently or to be more prone to react with certain emotions across different situations. A person who is fearful, for instance, is distinctively sensitive to potentially threatening or dangerous features of their environment and is therefore prone to experience fear more frequently and/or more intensely than others. Vice versa, however, experiencing a few episodes of fear does not necessarily imply that one is a fearful person. Unlike emotions, emotional dispositions or traits can be considered as an important aspect of an individual's personality.

Finally, emotions have to be distinguished from sentiments such as love, hate or grief (Ben-Ze'ev, 2001; Hacker, 2017). Sentiments, also referred to as 'enduring' or 'persistent' emotions, typically last for longer periods of time. Unlike emotions, they do not lapse when we fall asleep or lose consciousness. One's grief about the loss of a loved one, for instance, typically persists through periods of sleep. Under the right circumstances, it is possible that emotions turn into long-term sentiments. For example, an episode of guilt over a serious mistake may transform into a sentiment of guilt that burdens one for life. Having a sentiment of guilt, in turn, will likely lead to further episodes of guilt in the future. Still, what characterises sentiments is not so much the frequency of their outbursts, but their continued, if sometimes latent, existence. Sentiments have a dispositional nature, and in this way they resemble emotional traits. Unlike emotional traits, however, they always have a specific intentional object. Indeed, sentiments such as love, hate, hostility or grief are always directed towards particular persons or objects. Ben-Ze'ev (2001) nicely illustrates the differences between emotions, emotional traits and sentiments in the following paragraph:

> A tendency to anger, which is an affective trait, is the disposition to get angry irrespective of the situation. Hostility toward someone, which is a sentiment, is the disposition to get angry with this person whether or not we are provoked by an offensive action. Anger at someone who hurts us is an example of an emotion. We may always be hostile toward that person, but we only get angry when provoked. (p. 83)

1.2 WHAT KIND OF EMOTIONS ARE GUILT AND SHAME?

Emotion theorists have not only distinguished emotions from other affective phenomena, they have also identified subcategories within the class of emotions. The emotions of interest in this work – guilt and shame – have variously been classified as 'self-conscious', 'social' and 'moral' emotions. Each of these labels tells us something about the nature of guilt and shame.

1.2.1 Self-conscious emotions

Within the field of psychology, shame and guilt are typically classified as 'self-conscious emotions'. This classification, proposed by Michael Lewis, is based on whether emotions depend on the development of a specific cognitive ability: the ability to represent the self

(Lewis, 2007, 2016). Using this criterion, Lewis divides the emotions into two broad groups. The first group, referred to as 'primary' or 'basic' emotions, emerges very early in human development and requires little cognitive ability. This group includes emotions like anger, fear, sadness and joy. The second group of emotions, referred to as the 'self-conscious' emotions, emerges only with the development of more advanced cognitive skills. More specifically, at around the age of 15 to 18 months, children start to form a self-concept (i.e. the idea of a 'Me'). According to Lewis, this cognitive achievement enables them to experience a first set of self-conscious emotions: empathy, jealousy and non-evaluative embarrassment. These emotions involve self-awareness, but no self-evaluation. After another year, at around the age of 30 to 36 months, a second, more sophisticated set of 'evaluative' self-conscious emotions emerges: shame, guilt, pride, hubris and evaluative embarrassment. These emotions require not only that children are in possession of a self-concept but also that they have internalised a set of standards, rules and goals (SRGs) and that they have acquired the capacity to evaluate themselves against these SRGs. According to Lewis (2007, 2016), people will experience guilt and shame when they see themselves as responsible for failing to meet or follow their SRGs.

1.2.2 Social emotions

Lewis' classification rightly emphasises the distinct status of the self in guilt and shame as an object of attention and evaluation. At the same time, his approach has been criticised for neglecting the distinctively *social* nature of the self-conscious emotions (Draghi-Lorenz et al., 2001; Zahavi, 2014). Lewis focuses almost exclusively on the intrapsychic aspects of guilt and shame. His work leaves the impression that these emotions are solely a matter of an individual's own negative self-evaluation. At most, he acknowledges that the standards, rules and goals in terms of which individuals evaluate themselves are learned from others (Lewis, 2016). However, this is not and cannot be what makes guilt and shame *distinctively* social, for most if not all human emotions can be shaped by standards, rules and goals that are socially learned (Deonna & Teroni, 2011). Indeed, what disappoints, saddens or angers me, or fills me with joy, might very well be anchored in socially acquired values.

Although all emotions can be influenced by social factors and, therefore, are social in some way, the self-conscious emotions are social in a fundamental way. What sets them apart is that they '*necessarily* depend on other people's thoughts, feelings or actions, as experienced, recalled, anticipated or imagined at first hand, or instantiated in more generalised consideration of social norms or conventions' (Hareli & Parkinson, 2008, p. 131). This stands in contrast to basic emotions such as anger and fear, which can be elicited in relation to the world of things, without a social dimension ever coming into play (Draghi-Lorenz et al., 2001). Indeed, one can get angry for hitting one's head against the doorway and one can get scared by the sound of a thunderstorm, but one would not often experience guilt or shame in relation to doorways or thunderstorms.

To emphasise the social nature of guilt and shame is not to deny their self-evaluative nature; it is to emphasise that the self-evaluative processes involved in both emotions have an important social dimension (Baldwin & Baccus, 2004; Baumeister et al., 1994; Harris et al., 2004; Zahavi, 2014). This social dimension is obvious in those cases (arguably the majority of cases) where guilt and shame arise in direct response to the thoughts, feelings or actions of other persons. But even in 'private' experiences of guilt and shame, when specific others are not factually present or explicitly imagined, there is always a 'more generalized consideration of social norms or conventions', to use the words of Hareli and Parkinson (2008, p. 131). The dimension of the self that gets evaluated in guilt and shame, then, is not the private self, but the *intersubjective* self or the self in relation to others (Montes Sánchez, 2015).[1]

1.2.3 Moral emotions

Guilt and shame have not only been classified as self-conscious and social emotions but also as moral emotions (Haidt, 2003; Parrott, 2019; Svensson et al., 2017; Tangney et al., 2007; Teroni & Bruun, 2011; Turner & Stets, 2006). Now, there are different ways in which emotions in general, and guilt and shame in particular, can be classified as 'moral'.

First, moral emotions can be defined as those emotions that are elicited by violations of moral norms (Svensson et al., 2017; Turner & Stets, 2006). Research suggests that moral violations such as lying, hurting others and stealing are indeed important elicitors of guilt and shame (Keltner, 1996; Tangney, Miller, et al., 1996). At the same time, it seems that guilt and shame are not inherently moral in this sense, as they can be elicited by non-moral failures and shortcomings as well. Think for instance of breastfeeding guilt (towards one's infant) or shame related to mental health issues or intellectual disabilities.

Second, emotions can be said to be moral (as opposed to non-moral) insofar as they imply a moral evaluation of some sort (Parrott, 2019). Guilt is typically viewed as a moral emotion in this sense because it implies an appraisal of the self as responsible for a harm or wrong (Miceli & Castelfranchi, 2018; Montada, 1993; Teroni & Bruun, 2011). As regards shame, many scholars seem to agree that this emotion implies a non-moral (or morally neutral) appraisal of the self as 'inadequate' or 'flawed' (Deonna et al., 2012; Miceli & Castelfranchi, 2018; Olthof et al., 2004).

1 This is why Reddy (2003) prefers to speak of 'self-other-conscious emotions' rather than simply 'self-conscious emotions'.

Third, emotions can be regarded as moral (as opposed to immoral) in virtue of their prosocial action tendencies (Haidt, 2003). Guilt is generally considered to be a moral emotion in this sense, because it motivates reparative behaviour such as confessing, apologising or making amends (Tangney et al., 2007). There is more controversy regarding the moral nature of shame, as some of its action tendencies include a desire to hide or withdraw from social interactions (Tangney et al., 2007). As will be discussed later in this chapter, however, shame has other action tendencies such as the desire to self-reform that are undeniably morally relevant. In a related sense, it is possible to think of guilt and shame as 'moral' because of their inhibitory effects. That is, the prospect of feeling guilty or ashamed may deter individuals from engaging in immoral behaviour (Svensson et al., 2017; Tangney et al., 2007). Later in this book I will discuss the inhibitory effects of guilt and shame in more detail.

Fourth and finally, emotions can be considered moral (as opposed to immoral) to the extent that their manifestations are judged as 'morally appropriate' in a particular context. Indeed, we often praise or blame people on the basis of their emotional reactions, and we see these reactions as indicative of their values and their (moral) character. Parrott (2019) refers to this as the 'situational morality' of emotions. Research indicates that wrongdoers who express feelings of guilt or shame are perceived more positively than those who express no emotion (Ferguson et al., 2007; Stearns & Parrott, 2012). Ferguson et al. (2007) even found that people who responded with *both* guilt and shame to their wrongdoing were evaluated as more moral by others than people who responded only with guilt or only with shame.

1.3 What are the differences between guilt and shame?

If both guilt and shame are self-evaluative, social and moral emotions, then what differentiates them? Theorists and researchers from a variety of disciplines have proposed distinguishing criteria (Elison, 2005; Gilbert, 2003; Harris, 2003; Miceli & Castelfranchi, 2018; Tangney, Miller, et al., 1996; Teroni & Deonna, 2008). In this section, I will discuss the three most widely used criteria and the evidence supporting them. The first criterion concerns the nature of the situation that elicits guilt and shame, the second concerns their evaluative focus, and the third concerns the action tendencies they are associated with.

1.3.1 Public versus private

According to a longstanding view, shame and guilt can be differentiated in terms of the nature of the social context that elicits them (Ausubel, 1955; Benedict, 1946; Mead, 1937; Smith et al., 2002; Wallbott & Scherer, 1995). Following this view, shame is a public emotion because it is elicited by the disapproval of other people, whereas guilt is a private emotion because it is generated by one's own conscience. In short, shame is the emotion of external sanction; guilt, the emotion of internal sanction. Although this view of shame and guilt is popular, the evidence supporting it is not compelling enough to accept it unquestioningly.

Several studies have examined the validity of the public/private distinction by looking at the role of public exposure in shame and guilt. If shame is the more public emotion, then one might expect to find that shame is more likely to occur in the presence of others. However, the few studies that have tested this hypothesis have not confirmed this expectation. In a frequently cited study, Tangney, Miller, et al. (1996) found that both guilt and shame typically occurred in the presence of others and only occasionally when participants were alone. Similarly, Ellsworth and Tong (2006) found no differences between guilt and shame in terms of their social context; other people were almost always involved. In another study, Smith et al. (2002) used an experimental design to examine more closely the role of public exposure in guilt and shame. Participants were presented with several hypothetical scenarios in which the public exposure of failures and transgressions was manipulated. Their results suggest that shame (but not guilt) is more intensely felt when one's transgressions are exposed to others. Crucially, however, Smith et al. (2002) also found that public exposure is not necessary for shame and that both guilt and shame can be experienced either publicly or privately.

Other studies have focused on the role of others' actual or imagined reactions in guilt and shame, rather than on their mere physical presence. Also on this point, however, the empirical evidence is mixed, with different studies reaching different conclusions. Wicker et al. (1983) asked participants to recall personal guilt and shame experiences and to describe them on the basis of 34 items. One of these items asked participants to rate on a bipolar scale whether the negative evaluation was coming more from themselves or more from others. For both guilt and shame, average ratings were near the midpoint of the scale, suggesting that both internal and external evaluations may play an important role in the elicitation of these emotions. In a large cross-cultural study, Wallbott and Scherer (1995) examined whether respondents ascribed the cause of their guilt and shame experiences to internal or external factors. They found that shame experiences were triggered significantly more often by other people's (re)actions than were guilt experiences. A more recent cross-cultural study of shame and guilt reactions conducted in Belgium and Peru by Fontaine et al. (2006) further complicates matters. They found that perceptions of others as reproaching were more closely related to shame than to guilt, although the difference was relatively small. Furthermore, they observed that concerns about falling short of others' expectations were more central to the experience of guilt than to the experience of shame. Other studies too have shown that the (imagined) reactions of others can play an important role in the elicitation of guilt (Giner-Sorolla & Espinosa, 2011; Parkinson & Illingworth, 2009; Solak et al., 2017).

Still, it could be argued that shame is more 'public' or 'social' than guilt because even though both can be triggered by others' (actual or imagined) reactions, only shame can arise without evaluating oneself negatively (Ausubel, 1955). Put differently, in shame, but not in guilt, we may be more concerned with how we appear in the eyes of others than with our own standards. Yet again, the (scarce) evidence does not seem to strongly support this view. In the earlier-mentioned study by Wicker et al. (1983), one item asked participants whether they were more concerned with how others viewed them or with how they viewed themselves. The rating of this item did not differ much across shame and guilt. Furthermore, the mean rating was near the midpoint of the scale, suggesting that guilt and shame involve a mix of both personal and social concerns (i.e. they are simultaneously both inner- and other-oriented). The study by Tangney, Miller, et al. (1996), also mentioned earlier, included a similar item. Although they found that participants focused more on others' thoughts (as opposed to their own thoughts) about themselves in shame than in guilt, the difference was too small to constitute a fundamental difference.

In addition to these empirical studies, several philosophers of emotion have convincingly argued that one cannot feel guilty or ashamed in the eyes of others without feeling guilty or ashamed in one's own eyes (Deonna et al., 2012; Miceli & Castelfranchi, 2018; Taylor, 1985; Williams, 1993; Zahavi, 2014). As Miceli and Castelfranchi (2018) put it:

> In fact, others' evaluation and one's self-evaluation may diverge, either because one may not share the evaluative standards of one's 'judges' or because, while sharing their standards, one may believe that their evaluations are mistaken in that no actual fault has been shown according to those standards. We suggest that in both the above cases the disapproved person will not experience shame (and certainly not guilt), but other possible feelings – fear of the consequences of the negative evaluation; disappointment and resentment for having received an 'undeserved' evaluation; helplessness, elicited by the perceived inability to modify others' judgment; or, most notably, embarrassment, which implies no necessary negative self-evaluation, but mere discomfort at exposure. (p. 718)

In sum, there is not enough evidence to suggest that either the nature of the situation (private vs. public) or the source of the negative evaluation (self vs. other) constitutes a *fundamental* difference between guilt and shame. Consequently, the reputation of shame as an emotion that motivates 'blind conformity' in order to avoid social disapproval seems unwarranted (see Harris, 2011, for a similar conclusion). Of course, this does not exclude that, at the phenomenological level, feeling exposed may be more typical of shame than of guilt experiences (Katz, 1999; Miceli & Castelfranchi, 2018; Wicker et al., 1983).

1.3.2 *Self versus behaviour*

Perhaps the most popular approach to distinguish between guilt and shame is to contrast their evaluative focus (Lewis, 1971; Tangney & Dearing, 2002). The basic idea is that those who feel guilty evaluate their behaviour negatively (e.g. 'I *did* a bad thing'), whereas those who feel ashamed evaluate their whole self as fundamentally flawed (e.g. 'I *am* a bad person'). Thus, following this approach, the difference between guilt and shame is not to be found in the nature of the situations that elicit them, but in the way these situations are construed by the individual. The same failure or transgression, then, can elicit either guilt or shame depending on where one's attention is focused: on what kind of person one is (in shame) or on what one did or did not do (in guilt).

Evidence supporting the self/behaviour distinction has been reported in various studies using both qualitative and quantitative methods (e.g. Karlsson & Sjöberg, 2009; Lindsay-Hartz et al., 1995; Niedenthal et al., 1994; Tangney & Dearing, 2002; Tracy & Robins, 2006). In an early study, Lindsay-Hartz (1984) used a phenomenological method to analyse the structure of participants' experiences of guilt or shame. She found that shame typically involves a more transformative focus on the self than guilt. She concluded that in shame 'we feel we *are* small and worthless,' but in guilt 'we only feel *as if* we are a bad person' (Lindsay-Hartz, 1984, p. 695, emphasis in original). In other words, those who feel guilt (but no shame) accept that they did something bad without fully accepting or believing that they truly are a bad person. In a similar but more recent phenomenological study, Karlsson and Sjöberg (2009) concluded that 'guilt falls under the mode of *doing*,' whereas shame 'has to do with one's mode of *being*' (p. 352). An ingenious study by Niedenthal et al. (1994) presented participants with various shame- and guilt-eliciting situations and then asked them how they would try to undo these situations. They found that participants were more likely to mentally undo aspects of the self ('If only I weren't…') in dealing with shame experiences than in dealing with guilt experiences. In dealing with guilt experiences, they were more likely to mentally undo their behaviour ('If only I hadn't done so and so'). In a series of studies based on recalled emotional experiences and hypothetical vignettes, Tracy and Robins (2006) found that participants reported shame rather than guilt when they attributed failures (e.g. doing badly on an exam) to more stable and uncontrollable features of the self (e.g. low ability that cannot be remedied through effort).

Other studies, however, have cast doubt on the value of the self/behaviour distinction. One of the 34 items in the earlier mentioned study by Wicker et al. (1983) asked participants to rate on a bipolar scale whether they felt unhappy with themselves in general or with their behaviour only. For both guilt and shame, the mean rating was close to the midpoint of the scale. The study by Tangney, Miller, et al. (1996), also discussed earlier, included a similar bipolar item, asking respondents whether they blamed their 'personality and self' or rather their 'actions and behaviour'. Again, for both guilt and shame, the mean rating was close to the midpoint of the scale. In their cross-cultural study, Fontaine et al. (2006) found that guilt was associated not only with behaviour-focused reactions but also with self-focused reactions. All in all, then, it seems that guilt can involve being critical of one's self and that shame can involve being critical of one's behaviour.

Although these results appear conflicting, they can be reconciled if we adopt a more nuanced understanding of the self/behaviour distinction. In fact, Lewis (1971) originally expressed her view on the distinction as follows:

> The experience of shame is *directly* about the self, which is the focus of evaluation.... In guilt, the self is *negatively evaluated in connection with something*, but is not itself the focus of evaluation. (p. 30, emphasis added)

Thus, what Lewis proposed is not a clear-cut distinction between an evaluation of one's self (in shame) and an evaluation of one's behaviour (in guilt). What she argued is that both emotions involve a negative self-assessment, the difference lying in the nature of the focus on the self: direct in shame versus indirect in guilt. Hence, 'guilt involves *less* experience of the self than shame' (Lewis, 1971, p. 34, emphasis added). This is different from arguing that guilt is *exclusively* concerned with one's behaviour or that shame is *exclusively* concerned with one's self. Therefore, findings that feelings of guilt can involve self-focused reactions or that feelings of shame can involve behaviour-focused reactions do not necessarily invalidate the self/behaviour distinction. The crucial point, as several phenomenological studies have shown, is that the focus on the self is more direct, more pervasive and more transformative in shame than in guilt (Karlsson & Sjöberg, 2009; Katz, 1999; Lindsay-Hartz, 1984). Indeed, a recurring theme in these studies is that 'shame carries the sense that there is revealed an undeniable truth about the self' (Katz, 1999, p. 150). Guilt, by contrast, does not fundamentally threaten one's self-identity.

Miceli and Castelfranchi (2018) have recently advanced another relevant distinction between guilt and shame that is compatible with the foregoing considerations. They too emphasise that both emotions involve a negative self-evaluation, but they argue that the self-evaluation is of a different kind: shame involves an evaluation of the self as 'inadequate', whereas guilt involves a self-evaluation of 'responsible harmfulness'. That is, people who feel guilty see themselves as responsible for an adverse outcome or state of affairs.[2] Hence, 'guilt relates to the self as an agent' (Miceli & Castelfranchi, 2018, p. 721). In shame, by contrast, the focus of the self-evaluation is not one's agency or responsibility but on one's state of inadequacy. In other words, whereas guilt focuses on one's *ability* (to cause, or prevent, a negative outcome), shame focuses on one's *inability* (to be the right kind of person) (Gilbert et al., 1994; Katz, 1999). As Miceli and Castelfranchi emphasise, this is not to say that ashamed people never see themselves as responsible for the things that happen to them. It is only to say that it is not necessary to consider responsibility issues in order to feel ashamed. This could explain why physical defects, mental illnesses or intellectual disabilities are far more likely to elicit shame than guilt (Olthof et al., 2004; Smith et al., 2002).

As a final nuance to the self/behaviour distinction, several shame theorists and researchers have convincingly argued that shame does not necessarily involve a negative evaluation of the *whole* self (Deonna et al., 2012; Gausel et al., 2016; Gausel & Leach, 2011; Miceli & Castelfranchi, 2018). Indeed, feelings of shame can be confined to some specific dimension of the self. For instance, when a person feels ashamed for failing a mathematics exam (despite having studied a lot), this may reflect a perceived incapacity to be a good student and not – or at least not necessarily – a perceived incapacity to be a good person overall. Put differently, there are different aspects of selfhood, or different identities, which need not all be damaged by the negative evaluation of shame. In the moment of shame, however, people tend to take a part of themselves to be the whole of who they are, as phenomenological studies have shown (Karlsson & Sjöberg, 2009; Lindsay-Hartz, 1984). This is why shame typically *feels* as a global or holistic experience. But this is different from saying that shame always involves a negative assessment of the self in its totality (with all its features and identities).

To sum things up, the self/behaviour distinction highlights an important difference between the experience of guilt and shame. Both guilt and shame are self-evaluative emotions, but the focus on the self is more direct, more pervasive and more transformative in shame than in guilt. What is revealed in shame is perceived as a truth about oneself (Karlsson & Sjöberg, 2009; Katz, 1999). Furthermore, guilt and shame imply different kinds of negative self-evaluations. In shame, the self (or a part of the self) is negatively evaluated as inadequate or flawed. In guilt, the self is negatively evaluated as an actual or potential wrongdoer.

2 It is important to emphasise that one can *perceive* oneself as responsible for an untoward outcome or state of affairs without actually *being* responsible (in the sense of being morally responsible or accountable). For instance, a man who is infertile can feel guilty for not being able to fulfil his wife's desire for children, although he knows that he is not at fault.

1.3.3 *Adaptive versus maladaptive action tendencies*

A third way to capture the difference between guilt from shame is to contrast their action tendencies. According to a popular view in psychology, guilt is an adaptive emotion that motivates prosocial behaviour, whereas shame is a maladaptive emotion that motivates self-defensive behaviour (Tangney et al., 2007). In support of this view, researchers have observed that guilt is more strongly associated with a tendency to apologise, make amends and restore damaged relationships, whereas shame is more strongly associated with a tendency to cover up or hide things, withdraw from the situation and avoid others (Schmader & Lickel, 2006; Sheikh & Janoff-Bulman, 2010; Tangney, 1995; Tangney & Dearing, 2002; Tangney, Miller, et al., 1996). Tangney and Dearing (2002) explain these contrasting action tendencies by reference to the self/behaviour distinction. In their view, 'it is much easier to change a bad behaviour than to change a bad self' (Tangney & Dearing, 2002, p. 45). Because it is so difficult to change who one is as a person, shame easily leads to self-defensive action tendencies.

However, this view of guilt and shame is too one-sided. New evidence suggests that there is no one-to-one relationship between these emotions and specific action tendencies. Rather, it seems that action tendencies can vary greatly depending on contextual factors. Starting with guilt, some recent studies have found that it does not always produce reparative or prosocial behaviour but may also result in self-punishment (Inbar et al., 2013; Nelissen & Zeelenberg, 2009). Self-punishment, for instance, by depriving oneself of pleasures or even by hurting oneself physically, is most likely when circumstances make it difficult or impossible to undertake reparative actions (Nelissen & Zeelenberg, 2009). Research by Nelissen (2012) suggests that guilt-induced self-punishment may still serve an adaptive social function in that it acts as a 'sign of remorse' towards those before whom one feels guilty. Inbar et al. (2013) conclude that guilt activates a desire to 'balance the scales' and that this can be done either through other-serving or self-destructive behaviour.

Recent research has also painted a more nuanced picture of shame, suggesting that people do not necessarily react self-defensively when they feel ashamed. For example, de Hooge and colleagues observed that participants who were experimentally induced to feel shame expressed a stronger desire to affiliate with others (de Hooge et al., 2018) and a stronger willingness to engage in cooperative behaviour (de Hooge et al., 2008). In another experimental study, Gausel et al. (2016) found that shame felt in response to a recalled or imagined moral failure predicted various prosocial motivations (e.g. a desire to repair the damage, compensate the victim and communicate contrition). Such findings underscore the role of shame in the maintenance of social cohesion. In explaining their findings, de Hooge et al. (2018) and Gausel et al. (2016) both argue that shame motivates people to restore their damaged self-image and that engaging in prosocial behaviour is one way of doing this. In line with this explanation, studies have found that shame is more closely associated with a desire for self-change and self-improvement than guilt (Leach & Cidam, 2015; Lickel et al., 2014; Niedenthal et al., 1994). According to Deonna et al. (2012), this gives shame a greater moral value than guilt:

> In respect of the moral quality of the action tendencies belonging to the two emotions, guilt may well be more closely correlated with a tendency to make up for wrongdoing. This is only a very narrow part of what can be considered morally valuable behavior, however. Those self-regarding aspects of shame that entail a motivation to improve ourselves suggest a greater moral value for shame. In a word, guilt, as it were, treats only the symptoms of our moral defects; it is only concerned with the defects in our actions. The self-reforming tendencies associated with shame, in contrast, treat the cause; in shame we often focus on the faults in our character that dispose us to misbehave. (p. 184)

The divergent findings on shame's action tendencies raise an important follow-up question: when does shame lead to withdrawal and avoidance tendencies and when does it lead to prosocial tendencies and self-improvement? Research suggests that it largely depends on the *perceived reparability* of the failure or shortcoming that is the source of shame (Cibich et al., 2016; de Hooge et al., 2011; Leach & Cidam, 2015). That is, when the failure or shortcoming in question is perceived as repairable, shame is more likely to motivate prosocial behaviour and/or self-reform. However, when this failure or shortcoming is perceived as difficult or even impossible to repair, shame is more likely to motivate avoidance behaviour and social withdrawal. According to de Hooge et al. (2011), avoidance behaviour serves to protect the self from further damage.

To sum things up, it is unwarranted to conclude that guilt is an adaptive emotion and that shame is a maladaptive emotion. Both guilt and shame can elicit prosocial behaviour (e.g. approach or reparative actions). In addition, shame can elicit a strong desire to change or improve the self. However, both emotions also have a dark side. When it is impossible to undo or repair the damage that one has caused, guilt can lead to self-punishment (e.g. by denying oneself pleasure). As regards shame, it can motivate people to socially withdraw and avoid others, especially when its cause is perceived as uncontrollable or unchangeable.

1.3.4 Some additional remarks on the shame-guilt distinction

Whereas guilt and shame are distinct emotional states, they are not mutually exclusive. Quite the contrary, several studies have found that feelings of guilt are frequently accompanied by some measure of shame, especially in cases of moral wrongdoing (Harris,

2003; Karlsson & Sjöberg, 2009; Olthof et al., 2004; Schmader & Lickel, 2006). As Sabini and Silver (1997) explain, there is a 'natural connection' between guilt and shame in such cases. That is, the appraisal of oneself as responsible for a harm or wrong (i.e. a self-appraisal associated with guilt) easily leads to the perception of oneself as a (morally) inadequate person (i.e. a self-appraisal associated with shame). Braithwaite and Braithwaite (2001, p. 9) even suggest that the blending of guilt and shame may be inevitable in relation to offending: 'a person cannot experience guilt about a criminal wrong without this spilling over into feeling ashamed of oneself as a person.' Because of the natural connection between them, it may not always be easy, or even meaningful, to attempt to separate guilt from shame in criminological research (Harris, 2003). Of course, there are other contexts in which guilt and shame are less likely to co-occur and, therefore, easier to distinguish. For instance, guilt should be minimal compared to shame in the context of 'non-moral' flaws (e.g. intellectual or physical disabilities) (Olthof et al., 2004).

The fusion of guilt with shame may not only be difficult to avoid but also serve important functions in some contexts. According to Williams, we need shame 'to understand how a certain action or thought stands to ourselves, to what we are and to what realistically we can want ourselves to be' (Williams, 1993, p. 93). In other words, shame reveals a connection between our deeds and our self-identity that is absent in 'pure' guilt. Hence Williams' enigmatic, but otherwise insightful claim that 'shame can understand guilt, but guilt cannot understand itself' (Williams, 1993, p. 93). In light of shame's capacity to motivate self-reform, Braithwaite and Braithwaite (2001) have argued that 'shame-infused' guilt can be a very valuable experience in a criminal justice context. According to them, it may not be enough for (serious) offenders to merely feel guilty about their actions; they should also feel a need to change the kind of person they are in some important ways (without believing that they are evil beyond repair). Finally, Sabini and Silver (1997) doubt whether 'shame-free' guilt is painful enough as a disincentive to prevent people from doing immoral things. They suggest that guilt needs the 'bite' of shame, as a more intense self-criticism, to be a powerful inhibitor.

1.4 How do guilt and shame compare with other, closely related emotions?

Apart from guilt, shame has two other prominent relatives: embarrassment and humiliation. Sometimes these emotions are treated as varieties of shame (Scheff, 2003). However, although experiences of embarrassment and humiliation may overlap in some respects with those of shame, there are important distinctions between them. Embarrassment can best be described as a self-conscious emotion that involves discomfort over one's appearance to others (Deonna et al., 2012; Katz, 1999; Zahavi, 2014). Or, as

Robbins and Parlavecchio (2006) put it: 'embarrassment is the feeling that accompanies the perception of an unwanted exposure or revelation' (p. 329). Hence, embarrassment is an emotion that always requires the actual presence of an audience (or, at least, an audience that is believed to be present). In this respect, it differs significantly from shame and guilt, which can be experienced in solitude. In support of this distinction, research by Tangney, Miller, et al. (1996) has found that respondents' experiences of embarrassment occurred almost universally in public, whereas a substantial proportion of their shame and guilt experiences occurred in solitude.

A second and perhaps more crucial difference between embarrassment and shame is that embarrassed people do not construe their actions as revealing anything negative about who they *really* are as a person (Deonna et al., 2012, p. 116). Actually, embarrassment may not involve a sense of flaw at all. One can feel embarrassed merely for being an unwanted object of public attention or scrutiny. Also, events that would elicit embarrassment in the presence of others (e.g. farting, picking one's nose, snoring etc.) may be considered normal or even enjoyable when they occur in private. To reiterate, the concern in embarrassment is with the *appearance* of the self only. Ashamed people, by contrast, evaluate themselves negatively, regardless of whether others are watching (Deonna et al., 2012; Ferguson, 2010; Miceli & Castelfranchi, 2018). Like embarrassment, shame can be triggered by the reactions of others in a given social situation. Unlike embarrassment, however, shame transcends the immediate situation. That is, shame highlights what is believed to be a *core* flaw of the self, one that has the potential to negatively affect one's relationships with any set of others (Katz, 1999; Zahavi, 2014).

Humiliation can be described as the painful, self-conscious feeling that accompanies the perception of being unjustly put down, degraded or ridiculed by others (Elison & Harter, 2007; Elshout et al., 2017; Leidner et al., 2012). Humiliation resembles embarrassment in that it is also fundamentally an audience-involving emotion. What is particular to humiliation is that the audience is perceived as having hostile intentions (Elison & Harter, 2007). Humiliation also resembles shame in that both emotions involve a sense of personal devaluation and social isolation (Elison & Harter, 2007; Elshout et al., 2017; Leidner et al., 2012). The crucial difference is that people who feel shame acknowledge their flaws and blame themselves, whereas people who feel humiliation focus on the unfair treatment received from others (Elison & Harter, 2007; Gilbert, 1997). Or to use the words of Klein: 'people believe they deserve their shame; they do not believe they deserve their humiliation' (Klein, 1991, p. 117). In support of this, research has found that humiliation involves stronger feelings of other-directed blame and outrage than either shame or embarrassment (Elshout et al., 2017; Leidner et al., 2012). Because of this, humiliation may not only motivate avoidance behaviour, as shame and embarrassment do, but also motivate aggressive behaviour (Fernández et al., 2015; Silfver-Kuhalampi et al., 2015). Shame and humiliation are sometimes conflated in the literature, leading to inaccurate interpretations of the relationship between shame and aggression or violence (Deonna et al., 2012). In the criminological literature too, several studies have identified 'shame' as an important, or even the primary, cause of violence (Gilligan, 2003; Ray et al., 2004; Websdale, 2010). Upon closer inspection, however, what is meant by 'shame' in these studies is actually in most cases a feeling of humiliation inflicted by an external act of shaming.

Finally, one other emotion that has often been listed together with guilt and shame is remorse. Remorse can be seen as a specific form of regret (Proeve & Tudor, 2010; Warr, 2016). Regret, in turn, can be described as the negative feeling we experience when we realise or imagine that an alternative action or decision would have produced a better outcome (Zeelenberg, 1999). What differentiates remorse from other instances of regret is its moral content. That is, remorse does not merely consist in deep regret about a certain deed but also include the belief that one was wrong in doing what one did (Hacker, 2017; Sussman, 2018; Taylor, 1996). Regret, by contrast, is compatible with acceptance of what has been done. For instance, one can regret not having gone on holiday with one's friends and still believe that staying with one's sick spouse was the right thing to do.

Remorse is sometimes seen as part of the guilt experience (Tangney, Stuewig & Hafez, 2011). However, several differences between them have been highlighted in the literature (Proeve & Tudor, 2010; Sussman, 2018; Taylor, 1985, 2002; Van Stokkom, 2002). First, whereas both guilt and remorse involve feeling responsible for a wrong or harm, remorse has a narrower scope of application. More specifically, unlike guilt, remorse only applies to intentional actions that have already been completed. Hence, one can feel guilty, but not remorseful, for a wish or desire on which one did not act, and one can feel guilty, but not remorseful, for an involuntary error that caused harm. Second, guilt is self-directed and self-evaluative, whereas remorse (like regret) is more exclusively focused on one's actions and their consequences. In remorse, as Taylor (1985) puts it, 'the agent does not see herself as burdened or stained by her wrongdoing' (p. 100). In partial support of this, Proeve (2001) observed that undergraduate students rated their experiences of regret and remorse as less self-conscious than their experiences of guilt and shame. Fisher and Exline (2006), in turn, found that remorse was positively associated with accepting responsibility but not with self-condemnation.

1.5 Conclusion

In this chapter, I have presented a general picture of the emotions of guilt and shame. These two emotions have more in common than is sometimes recognised. They belong to the same family of emotions that are self-conscious, self-evaluative and self-critical. Also, they are both deeply social in nature. Unlike the so-called basic emotions such as anger and fear, guilt and shame are always directly or indirectly connected to the thoughts, feelings or actions of other people. Put differently, in guilt and shame we evaluate ourselves not from a purely personal or private perspective but from the perspective of our engagements with others.

Although both guilt and shame involve a negative self-evaluation, the nature and content of their evaluative focus on the self is different. Shame involves a more direct and more pervasive focus on the self than guilt – that what is revealed in shame is perceived by the subject as an essential truth about the self. In guilt, by contrast, the self is evaluated more indirectly, that is, in relation to an action or omission that caused (or could cause) a negative outcome. Furthermore, guilt and shame imply different kinds of self-appraisals. In shame we evaluate ourselves (or a part of ourselves) as inadequate or defective, whereas in guilt we evaluate ourselves as (potential) harm- or wrongdoers.

Guilt and shame are complementary rather than alternative or even conflicting emotional experiences. Especially in cases of moral wrongdoing, guilt and shame are likely to co-occur. In such cases, there is a natural connection between the two emotions. That is, an appraisal of oneself as responsible for a serious harm or wrong (an appraisal that predicts guilt) may easily give rise to a self-appraisal of inadequacy (appraisals that predict shame). The co-occurrence of guilt and shame is theoretically interesting because guilt helps individuals to acknowledge responsibility for a wrongdoing while shame pushes them to reflect more deeply about who they are and what they may need to change about themselves. Nevertheless, there is a dark side to both of these emotions as well. When their causes are perceived as irreparable, guilt and shame can lead to self-harm, avoidance behaviour and social withdrawal.

Guilt and shame are both of great interest for criminologists, not only because they give negative feedback *after* norm violations but also because they can prevent people from transgressing norms in the first place. That is, individuals may anticipate emotional outcomes when considering immoral behaviour and try to avoid painful emotions such as guilt and shame. Furthermore, when it comes to motivating compliance with (moral) norms, guilt and shame have a considerable advantage over other, closely related emotions such as embarrassment and remorse. Unlike embarrassment, guilt and shame do not depend upon the actual discovery of the wrongdoing in question by others. Unlike remorse, which can only be felt for one's past acts, guilt and shame can also be felt about contemplated future acts of moral rule-breaking.

2 The Relationship of Guilt and Shame to Crime and Delinquency: a Review of Research

> Young people should be prone to the feeling of shame, because they live by feeling and therefore commit many errors, but are restrained by shame.
> (Aristotle, Nicomachean Ethics, Book IV)

Over the past decades, a considerable amount of research has been conducted on the relationship of guilt and shame to crime and delinquency. In this chapter, I present a narrative review of this body of work. This review shows that the research literature is rife with different ways of defining and measuring guilt and shame, leading to diverging results. However, the results are not necessarily contradictory. In fact, different measures capture different forms or aspects of guilt and shame, not all of which are related to offending in the same way.

2.1 Approach and selection of studies

In 2016, Spruit et al. conducted a meta-analysis on the relationship between guilt, shame and delinquency. They synthesised data from 25 studies and found that higher levels of guilt and shame were associated with less involvement in both general and violent delinquency. Nevertheless, shame was less strongly related to delinquency than guilt was. Considering the mixed findings in the literature, the authors did not regard the evidence for the protective effects of shame as very conclusive.

The narrative review presented here is intended to complement the meta-analysis by Spruit et al. (2016) and overcome some of its limitations. Most importantly, this meta-analysis synthesised data from a wide range of studies without discussing key differences in the definition and measurement of guilt and shame. Understanding these differences is important, because different measures tap into different forms and aspects of guilt and shame. In addition, quite a few relevant studies were not included in the meta-analysis because they failed to meet the inclusion criteria. Understandably, qualitative studies were excluded as they do not provide the quantitative evidence that is needed for a meta-analysis. Yet, qualitative studies have generated valuable insights, especially regarding the role of guilt and shame in the process of desistance from crime.

Several criteria guided the selection of studies for the present review. First, only studies that examined the relationship of guilt and shame to crime and delinquency were included (including studies that examined violence as a separate outcome). Studies that focused on noncriminal forms of deviant behaviour (e.g. absenteeism, bullying, alcohol abuse etc.) or on a more general category of problem behaviour (e.g. externalising behaviour, antisocial behaviour etc.) were excluded. Second, only studies that used self-report measures of guilt and shame were included. Research indicates that it is difficult to identify and differentiate cognitively complex emotions such as shame and guilt on the basis of observational measures (Consedine et al., 2003; Tangney & Dearing, 2002). Finally, studies that examined guilt and shame in clinical populations were also excluded (e.g. Crocker et al., 2016). Relevant quantitative as well as qualitative studies published until 2019 are reviewed.[3] The studies included can be cross-sectional or longitudinal, and they can be based on community or offender samples.

This review is divided into two sections, corresponding to the two main approaches to measuring self-reported guilt and shame: the experience-based approach and the scenario-based approach. This division is meaningful because experience-based measures and scenario-based measures capture different things (Tignor & Colvin, 2017). Experience-based measures capture actually *experienced* feelings of guilt and shame (i.e. experienced either currently or in the past). Scenario-based measures, in contrast, are conjectural and capture *anticipated* feelings of guilt and shame in hypothetical situations. Because they capture propensities instead of actual experiences, scenario-based measures are often interpreted as measures of 'guilt- or shame-proneness'. As will become clear at the end of this review, both experienced and anticipated emotions can influence delinquent behaviour in their own way.

2.2 Actually experienced feelings of guilt and shame

Several studies have examined how actual experiences of guilt and shame are associated with involvement in crime and delinquency. These studies have used different experience-based measures that capture different forms of guilt and shame. More specifically, looking at the range of measures used, at least three distinct forms can be identified:

1. Frequent or persistent feelings of guilt and shame, measured without reference to an immediate precipitating event (also referred to as *generalised guilt and shame*).

3 The electronic databases PsycINFO, Web of Science, Google Scholar, JSTOR, Scopus, ScienceDirect Academic Search Premier, SpringerLink and DOAJ were searched using the following key words: shame, guilt, humiliation, embarrassment, moral emotions, self-conscious emotions, in combination with crime, criminal, offend*, delinq*, violen*, aggress*. These keywords were also translated in Dutch.

2. Feelings of shame that are related to specific domains of the self, such as one's body or one's intellectual abilities (also referred to as *domain-specific shame*).
3. Feelings of guilt and shame that are connected to specific events or situations in people's lives (also referred to as *event-related guilt and shame*).

I will discuss each of these in turn.

2.2.1 Generalised guilt and shame

Some experience-based measures capture what Kim et al. (2011) refer to as 'generalised' guilt and shame. These measures assess the frequency with which individuals experience guilt and shame – either generally or during a particular period of time – without reference to the specific situations in which these emotions arise or the events that elicit them. In other words, these measures assess the tendency to experience guilt and shame across different situations or contexts. So far, only two studies have examined whether individuals who frequently experience guilt and/or shame are more likely to engage in crime and delinquency (Hosser et al., 2007; Tibbetts, 2003). In both studies, guilt was hypothesised to reduce delinquency (given its associations with prosocial behaviour and reparative action tendencies) whereas shame was hypothesised to increase it (given its associations with social withdrawal tendencies and alienation).[4]

The first study by Tibbetts (2003) used the Personal Feelings Questionnaire 2 (PFQ-2; Harder & Zalma, 1990) to examine the associations between guilt, shame and delinquency in a sample of college students. The PFQ-2 is a global adjective checklist that contains ten shame-related affective descriptors (e.g. 'feeling embarrassed', 'feeling ridiculous', 'feeling humiliated', 'feeling laughable') and six guilt-related affective descriptors (e.g. 'feeling mild guilt', 'feeling intense guilt', 'feeling regret', 'feeling remorse'). Subjects are asked to rate how frequently they *generally* experience each feeling on a 5-point scale ranging from 'never' to 'continuously'. Tibbetts found that PFQ-2 guilt and shame, despite being well-correlated among themselves ($r = 0.61$), had different patterns of association with self-reported delinquency. As hypothesised, generalised shame was associated with higher levels of delinquent behaviour, whereas no evidence was found for an association between generalised guilt and delinquency. Nevertheless, the results should be interpreted with caution. Tibbett's study is cross-sectional and gives us little insight into the direction or nature of the relationship between shame and delinquency. Generalised shame may contribute to delinquency or result from it. Furthermore, questions can be raised about

4 A discussion of the different action tendencies associated with guilt and shame can be found in the previous chapter.

the content validity of the FPQ-2 shame scale, which uses affective descriptors that reflect not only shame but also related emotions such as embarrassment and humiliation.

The second study by Hosser et al. (2007) used a stronger, longitudinal design to examine whether the frequency of guilt and shame experienced during a prison term influenced recidivism after release. They repeatedly interviewed 1,243 adolescent and young adult offenders in six German youth prisons. During each interview, participants were asked to report the frequency with which they had experienced 'shame' and 'guilt' over the past seven days (on a 4-point scale ranging from 'not at all' to 'very often'). Although feelings of guilt and shame were moderately correlated (Kendall's $\tau = 0.35$), they were differently associated with recidivism after release. Specifically, the recidivism rate was *lower* among those who reported frequently experiencing guilt during their prison term, whereas it was *higher* among those who reported frequently experiencing shame. These effects held even when controlling for other well-established risk factors for recidivism, such as age, length of imprisonment, intelligence, self-reported drug addiction, offence seriousness and parents' criminal history.

Taken together, both studies suggest that generalised shame, but not guilt, may be a risk factor for delinquency and recidivism. The link between generalised shame and recidivism might in part be explained by the fact that generalised shame is 'often associated with beliefs that negative personal characteristics are not susceptible to change' (Sekowski et al., 2020, p. 668). However, what is true of generalised shame is not necessarily true of shame in general. As will become clear later in this review, episodic or event-related shame (i.e. shame which is not necessarily persistent or generalised but tied to specific events or situations) can have quite different effects on delinquency and recidivism.

2.2.2 *Domain-specific shame*

A second type of measure captures feelings of guilt and shame in particular domains or contexts. The Experience of Shame Scale (ESS) developed by Andrews et al. (2002) is a commonly used scale that measures the extent to which individuals experience domain-specific shame. More specifically, the ESS assesses shame about three particular aspects of the self: 'characterological shame' (comprising shame about personal habits, manners, the sort of person one is and personal ability), 'behavioural shame' (comprising shame about doing things wrong, saying stupid things, and failures) and 'bodily shame' (comprising just this kind of shame). Each form of shame is measured using three related items, addressing not only an experiential element (e.g. 'have you felt ashamed of...?') but also a cognitive element (e.g. 'have you worried about what other people think of...?') and a behavioural element (e.g. 'have you tried to cover up or conceal...?'). Subjects have to rate these items on a 4-point Likert-type scale ranging from 'not at all' to 'very much'. The ESS does not assess guilt, but Andrews et al. (1998, p. 51) notes that shame and guilt are likely to be confounded when assessing behavioural shame.

The ESS has been used in a number of studies to examine the relationship of shame to anger, aggression and violence. Several shame theorists have argued that some individuals may cope with their shame feelings by shifting blame to others, a process that might lead to anger and aggression (Elison et al., 2014; Gilligan, 2003; Scheff & Retzinger, 1991). Consistent with this hypothesis, some cross-sectional studies have indeed found an association between domain-specific shame and higher levels of reactive anger (i.e. anger in response to criticism) (Farmer & Andrews, 2009; Hejdenberg & Andrews, 2011; Keene & Epps, 2016; Milligan & Andrews, 2005). However, there is currently little evidence to suggest that either characterological, behavioural or bodily shame is related to violent delinquency. Owen and Fox (2011) compared a sample of 40 violent and 40 nonviolent institutionalised young offenders, but found no substantial differences between both groups in terms of either characterological, behavioural or bodily shame. In a study of 400 undergraduate students, Keene and Epps (2016) found no evidence for an association between the ESS and either verbal or physical aggression. Finally, in a community sample of 380 Italian adults, Velotti et al. (2017) even found that characterological shame was (weakly) associated with lower levels of physical aggression among males and lower levels of verbal aggression among females. The authors conclude that shame may have adaptive consequences: 'feeling ashamed about a previous aggressive behaviour can have the positive consequence of inhibiting the same behaviour in the future' (Velotti et al., 2017, p. 181).

2.2.3 Event-related guilt and shame

A third measurement approach involves asking respondents about the feelings of guilt and shame they experienced in response to specific events or situations in their lives. Naturally, the focus here is on studies that have examined feelings of guilt and shame in response to criminal acts. Recent research indicates that even serious offenders sometimes feel guilty or ashamed about their actions. Leclerc and Lindegaard (Leclerc & Lindegaard, 2018; Lindegaard et al., 2014), for instance, interviewed 76 incarcerated male robbers and 553 convicted male sex offenders to examine their affective experiences immediately before, during and after criminal events. Emotions such as guilt, shame and regret were hardly ever felt immediately before or during the process of committing the crime. But about one in five robbers and almost half of the sexual offenders admitted that they had experienced these emotions afterwards. A question that naturally arises in this context is whether feelings of guilt and shame about past criminal behaviour reduce the likelihood of reoffending in the future. Some preliminary answers to this question can be derived from a number of qualitative and quantitative studies on desistance and recidivism.

In one of the first qualitative studies on the topic, Leibrich (1996) interviewed 48 petty offenders who were on probation and in the process of desistance from crime. She found that 'shame was the thing which most often dissuaded people from offending' (Leibrich, 1996, p. 297). Leibrich adopted a broad notion of shame, encompassing three emotional experiences she identified in the narratives of the offenders: the public humiliation they felt in court, the personal disgrace they suffered before significant others, and private remorse. Of these three shame-related experiences, Leibrich described private remorse as the 'most painful and most enduring in its effect'. In a comparable study, Jensen and Gibbons (2002) interviewed a sample of 20 serious offenders who had served lengthy prison sentences and who had, on average, been out of prison for six years at the time of the interview. Again, shame was mentioned by several respondents as a major factor in their desire to stop offending. Jensen and Gibbons (2002) identified experiences similar to those described by Leibrich (1996), including public humiliation, shame/embarrassment before loved ones, and a more private form of remorse. Humiliation, which resulted from the public stigmatisation of offenders in the community, made it harder to go straight. Shame and remorse, on the other hand, typically involved accepting responsibility for the crimes, rather than blaming others, and paved the way for rehabilitation.

A more detailed picture of the emotional trajectories of desistance emerges from a longitudinal qualitative study by Farrall and Calverley (Calverley & Farrell, 2011; Farrall & Calverley, 2006). The study involved an original sample of 199 probationers, which included male probationers as well as female probationers; the probationers were interviewed at three points in time over the course of two years, and a follow-up subsample of 51 probationers were interviewed a fourth time almost five years later. Given the considerable degree of overlap and frequent co-occurrence of guilt and shame, Farrall and Calverley grouped both emotions together in the discussion of their results. They found that guilt and shame did not only play a role at the start of the desistance process, prompting the decision to go straight, but also, and perhaps even more so, at more advanced stages of the process, when respondents had already managed to stay (largely) crime-free for several years. In fact, it was often through feelings of guilt and shame about their past actions that 'desisters' fully realised the strength of their new commitments. These feelings informed them of the growing distance between their identities as 'would-be non-offenders' in the present and their identities as 'offenders' in the past. Farrall and Calverley (2006) also identified a causal pathway through which guilt and shame contributed to the desistance process. Specifically, they found that *retrospective* guilt and shame feelings about the suffering caused to loved ones and direct victims triggered and nourished *prospective* guilt and shame feelings at the thought of reoffending. Respondents who still felt tempted to offend described how anticipated guilt and shame feelings had a strong deterrent effect on them. In this way, guilt and shame further motivated the process of desistance.

Although the aforementioned studies provide insights into the role of guilt and shame in the desistance process, they also have limitations that prevent firm conclusions from being drawn. First, the studies by Leibrich (1996) and Jensen and Gibbons (2002) are cross-sectional and rely on respondents' retrospective accounts of what initially motivated them to stop offending. It is well-known that such (biographical) accounts are subject to all sorts of (memory) biases and underrate the importance of other, unknown factors. Second, the studies by Leibrich (1996) and Farrall and Calverley (2006) do not contain a systematic comparison of successful and less successful desisters in terms of their emotional trajectories. Jensen and Gibbons (2002) did make such a comparison, albeit in a rudimentary way, and found that about half of their respondents successfully desisted without reporting shame. While acknowledging the possibility that some of their respondents may have underreported their feelings of shame, Jensen and Gibbons interpreted their results as indicating that 'shame is a sufficient, but not a necessary, condition for going straight' (Jensen & Gibbons, 2002, p. 220). Finally, both Leibrich (1996) and Jensen and Gibbons (2002) identify a powerful form of shame that they then describe as 'private remorse'. Yet, there are significant differences between shame, which is self-directed and self-evaluative (like guilt), and remorse, which is more focused on one's actions and their consequences (like regret). Of course, it is likely that participants experienced a mix of guilt, shame and regret/remorse (see Murphy & Harris, 2007). Nevertheless, a better conceptualisation of the relevant emotions would have made it easier to interpret the results.

The effects of offence-related shame and guilt on reoffending have also been examined in quantitative studies. In a cross-sectional study, Murphy and Harris (2007) collected survey data from a group of 652 tax payers who had been caught and punished for engaging in illegal tax evasion by the Australian Tax Office (ATO). They used a measure comprised of 5 Likert-type scale items to measure offenders' feelings of shame and related emotions, such as embarrassment, guilt and regret/remorse ('I felt guilty,' 'I felt ashamed of myself,' 'I felt that what I had done was wrong,' 'I felt embarrassed' and 'I felt regret'). All items were strongly correlated and loaded on a single factor, suggesting that the participants in the study experienced a mix of these emotions in response to their transgression. Mediation analyses revealed an indirect association between the shame-related emotions and self-reported tax compliance. That is, feelings of shame, embarrassment, guilt and remorse predicted a desire to make things right, which in turn predicted tax compliance in the year following the enforcement experience. In another cross-sectional study, Tosouni and Connie (2008) examined 249 juvenile offenders who were referred to either restorative justice conferences or juvenile courts for property and/or violent crimes. They used the same measure as Murphy and Harris (2007) to assess offence-related feelings of guilt and shame. In both groups, higher levels of shame-guilt predicted lower intentions to break the law in the future.

The studies by Murphy and Harris (2007) and by Tosouni and Connie (2008) rely on cross-sectional data, which makes it difficult to establish the direction of causality. Stronger evidence for causal effects can be obtained using prospective longitudinal studies. In a Dutch study, Ferwerda et al. (2006) followed a group of 1,000 adolescents who were apprehended for a criminal offence and referred to a diversion program by the police. Adolescents who agreed to take part in the study were assigned either to the experimental group (who actually participated in the diversion program) or to the control group (who did not participate). Adolescents from both groups were interviewed twice: once at the time of their referral to the program (the pre-test) and a second time after six months (the post-test). To measure recidivism, the researchers examined police records over a one-year period following the initial referral to the program. There was little difference between the recidivism rates of those who participated in the program and of those who did not. Nevertheless, the study found that other factors – unrelated to the diversion program – predicted lower recidivism rates. Notably, in both groups, those who reported that they felt ashamed about their offence tended to commit fewer and/or less serious delinquent acts during the follow-up period.

In another longitudinal study, LeBel et al. (2008) interviewed 130 male property offenders immediately prior to their release from prison and questioned them about their feelings of shame and regret in relation to their past criminal careers. Only 22% of the sample reported that they felt ashamed, whereas over half (52%) indicated some form of regret over their criminal career, which they felt had not been worth the trouble it caused them. In the ten-year follow-up period, only 18% of the men managed to avoid reconviction and only 37% of them managed to avoid re-imprisonment. Contrary to what one would expect on the basis of the studies discussed so far, Lebel et al. (2008) did not find evidence for the effect of shame on the likelihood of re-conviction and re-imprisonment. Although its effect was only marginally significant, regret did substantially lower the odds of being reconvicted ten years later. This was the case even when controlling for age, race/ethnicity, prior convictions, time served and a number of social problems experienced immediately after release.

All in all, current research suggests that retrospective feelings of guilt and shame about past misdeeds may reduce the probability of reoffending and motivate desistance. At the same time, the data also suggest that such feelings are not necessary for desistance to occur. Finally, several studies discussed in this section confirm that guilt and shame are not mutually exclusive experiences; offence-related guilt tends to be accompanied by some measure of shame. In the context of specific moral transgressions, the distinction between guilt and shame may be less important than the distinction between shame-guilt and other feelings that may increase recidivism such as humiliation (Ahmed et al., 2001; Jensen & Gibbons, 2002; LeBel et al., 2008).

2.3 ANTICIPATED FEELINGS OF GUILT AND SHAME

Next to experience-based measures, researchers have also used scenario-based measures to assess guilt and shame. Scenario-based measures present respondents with hypothetical situations in which they must imagine themselves (e.g. breaking something at a friend's house or stealing something from a shop). Respondents are then asked about their expected level of guilt or shame. Thus, scenario-based measures capture *anticipated* rather than actually experienced feelings of guilt or shame. They are commonly used to assess an individual's *proneness* to feel guilt or shame. Crucially, being prone to guilt or shame does not necessarily imply that one frequently experiences these emotions. It only means that one is particularly sensitive to feeling guilty and ashamed if one were to find oneself in potentially guilt- and shame-inducing situations.

Within the category of scenario-based measures, a further distinction can be made between general and contextual measures. The former present respondents with a wide variety of hypothetical situations in order to assess their *general* proneness to guilt and shame (as a relatively stable emotional trait). The latter focus on anticipated guilt and shame states in specific contexts (e.g. in the context of crime and delinquency). In what follows, I first review research that has examined the relationhip of general guilt- and shame-proneness to crime and delinquency. I then turn to criminological studies that have investigated the inhibiting effects of anticipated offence-related guilt and shame states.

2.3.1 General guilt- and shame-proneness

Arguably the best known and most widely used measure of general guilt- and shame-proneness is the Test of Self-Conscious Affect (TOSCA) developed by Tangney et al. (2000; Tangney & Dearing, 2002). The TOSCA consists of 15 short scenarios depicting a wide variety of relatively minor failures and transgressions (e.g. failing an exam, standing up a friend or breaking something at work). These are not necessarily moral transgressions. In fact, it is not always clear whether the transgressions in the scenarios are intentional or accidental. Each scenario is followed by four statements representing possible ways of dealing with the situation. Two of these statements describe reactions defined as characteristic for either guilt or shame. The other two statements describe reactions that represent two other constructs: detachment and the externalisation of blame. Respondents are asked to indicate how likely it is that each statement would be true for them on a

5-point scale ranging from 'not at all likely' to 'very likely'. The scores are summed to produce total scores for guilt-proneness, shame-proneness, detachment and externalisation of blame.

Tangney and colleagues specifically designed their instrument to sharply differentiate between guilt- and shame-proneness. The TOSCA is based on the self-behaviour distinction between guilt and shame. According to this criterion, shame implies a negative evaluation of the whole self, whereas guilt implies a negative evaluation of a specific behaviour (see previous chapter for a detailed discussion). On Tangney's account, this difference sets the stage for different action tendencies: those who feel ashamed mainly want to escape the situation or hide from others, whereas those who feel guilty experience a desire to make things right (e.g. apologising, confessing). These elements – global negative self-evaluations and withdrawal action tendencies for shame, negative behaviour evaluations and reparative action tendencies for guilt – are clearly recognisable in the TOSCA statements. Consider for instance these two scenario's from the adolescent version of the TOSCA (Tangney & Dearing, 2002, appendix):

1. 'You walk out of a test thinking you did extremely well. Then you find out you did poorly.'

The shame statement is: '*I would feel stupid.*'

The guilt statement is: '*I would feel that I should have done better. I should have studied more.*'

2. 'You break something at a friend's house and then hide it.'

The shame statement is: '*I would avoid seeing that friend for a while.*'

The guilt statement is: '*I would think: "I need to either fix it or replace it."*'

Tangney and Dearing (2002) argue that being prone to guilt is more adaptive than being prone to shame, because 'it is much easier to change a bad behaviour than to change a bad self' (p. 45). They also argue that guilt should facilitate empathic processes and encourage people to be attentive to the negative consequences of their behaviour for others. Shame, by contrast, should interfere with empathic processes due to its egocentric focus on the self. In fact, according to Tangney and Dearing (2002), shamed individuals may sometimes become angry and even aggressive towards others in attempt to escape their painful feelings and regain a sense of control and self-esteem. Following this account, guilt-proneness is typically hypothesised to be associated with lower levels of violence and delinquency. Shame-proneness, by contrast, is typically hypothesised to be either unrelated or even positively related to these outcomes. What does the empirical evidence say?

The TOSCA has spurred a considerable amount of research on the intersection of psychology and criminology. The results overwhelmingly support the view that guilt-proneness as measured by the TOSCA is a protective factor, not only for delinquency in general (Martinez et al., 2014; Stuewig et al., 2015; Stuewig & McCloskey, 2005; Tangney, Stuewig & Hafez, 2011; Tangney, Stuewig, Mashek, et al., 2011; Tangney et al., 2014; Tibbetts, 2003, 2014) but also for violence and physical aggression in particular (Kivisto et al., 2011; Robinson et al., 2007; Roos et al., 2014; Stuewig et al., 2010; Tangney, Wagner, et al., 1996). The results are remarkably consistent across different age groups (children, adolescents and adults), across community and offender samples and across both cross-sectional and longitudinal designs. TOSCA guilt-proneness is associated with empathic processes (e.g. empathic concern and perspective taking). and research suggests that this may at least partly explain why guilt-prone people are less likely to be involved in crime and delinquency (Martinez et al., 2014; Stuewig et al., 2010; Tangney, Stuewig, Mashek, et al., 2011).

Although usually moderately to highly correlated with guilt-proneness, the results for shame-proneness are quite different. Specifically, once its shared variance with guilt-proneness is removed, shame-proneness appears to be mostly unrelated to both self-report and official measures of delinquency (Stuewig et al., 2015; Stuewig & McCloskey, 2005; Tangney et al., 2014; Tangney, Stuewig & Hafez, 2011; Tibbetts, 2003, 2014). Starting from the earlier-mentioned hypothesis according to which people may try to cope with their shame by acting out against others (Lewis, 1971; Tangney & Dearing, 2002), several studies have also examined the link between TOSCA shame-proneness and measures of physical aggression. These studies have produced mixed results. Only two cross-sectional studies found (weak) positive correlations between shame-proneness and self-reported physical aggression (Robinson et al., 2007; Tangney, Wagner, et al., 1996). In most other studies, no evidence was found for an association of shame-proneness with either self-report or observer measures of physical aggression and violent delinquency (e.g. Gold et al., 2011; Kivisto et al., 2011; Roos et al., 2014, 2015; Stuewig et al., 2010; Tangney et al., 1992).

These inconsistent findings may be due to the presence of different mediators and moderators that intervene in the relationship between shame-proneness and violent behaviour (Gold et al., 2011; Roos et al., 2015; Stuewig et al., 2010). A tendency to externalise blame to others for one's own failures and transgressions is generally considered to be one of the key mediators of this relationship (Gold et al., 2011; Stuewig et al., 2010; Tangney & Dearing, 2002). In one of the most extensive studies on this topic to date, Stuewig et al. (2010) collected data on shame-proneness and aggression among four different samples (college students, early adolescents, prisoners and at-risk youth in middle adolescence). In all four samples, shame-proneness was only *indirectly* related to self-reported physical aggression. Specifically, shame-proneness was positively associated with a tendency to externalise blame, which in turn was associated with higher levels of self-reported aggression.

Based on their own and others' research using the TOSCA, Tangney and colleagues (2007, p. 349) have concluded that 'guilt but not shame is most effective in motivating people to choose the moral paths in life.' In their view, we should embrace guilt as the moral emotion of choice and avoid shame or, at least, treat it carefully. However, there are good reasons to be cautious about these claims. To understand why, it is necessary to discuss some of the major criticisms that have been raised against the TOSCA in recent years (Deonna et al., 2012; Giner-Sorolla et al., 2011; Montes Sánchez, 2014; Nelissen et al., 2013). A thorough discussion of these criticisms is much needed, as criminologists studying guilt and shame frequently refer to TOSCA-based theory and research (e.g. Maxwell et al., 2017; Tibbetts, 2014).

First, the TOSCA has been criticised for being biased towards measuring the *adaptive* side of guilt and the *maladaptive* side of shame (Ferguson & Stegge, 1998; Luyten et al., 2002; Sabini & Silver, 1997). Indeed, as Luyten et al. (2002) have shown, most items in the TOSCA guilt scale represent mild and constructive responses to the events depicted in the scenarios (i.e. feelings of regret/remorse and reparative action tendencies). The TOSCA shame scale, by contrast, primarily consists of items that refer to problematic aspects of shame (i.e. low self-esteem, withdrawal action tendencies). As discussed in the previous chapter, however, both guilt and shame have adaptive as well as maladaptive features. Unfortunately, the maladaptive aspects of guilt (e.g. rumination, self-punishment) are underrepresented in the TOSCA guilt scale, whereas the adaptive aspects of shame (e.g. social approach behaviour, self-improvement motivation) are completely absent from the TOSCA shame scale.

A study by Cohen et al. (2011) empirically shows that the tendency to engage in withdrawal behaviours following transgressions represents the maladaptive side of shame and, by implication, that the TOSCA – which measures shame in terms of withdrawal action tendencies – exhibits a bias against shame. Cohen and colleagues developed the Guilt and Shame Proneness (GASP) scale, a scenario-based measure relatively similar to the TOSCA. Unlike the TOSCA, however, the GASP contains two separate subscales to measure shame-proneness: one that captures a tendency to make negative self-evaluations ('shame-NSE') and one that captures withdrawal action tendencies ('shame-withdraw'). Cohen and colleagues found that individuals with higher scores on the shame-withdraw subscale, but not individuals with higher scores on the shame-NSE subscale, tended to report more physical aggression, unethical business decisions, workplace delinquency and general delinquency. In fact, just like individuals high in guilt-proneness, individuals high in shame-proneness (defined as shame-NSE) were less likely to lie for monetary gain and less likely to make unethical business decisions. Cohen et al. (2011, p. 963) interpret their findings as suggesting that 'shame, like guilt, is a moral emotion.'

A second and perhaps more fundamental criticism of the TOSCA concerns its construct validity, that is, the degree to which its guilt scale actually captures a disposition to feel guilt and its shame scale actually captures a disposition to feel shame (Ferguson et al., 2007; Olthof et al., 2000; Sabini & Silver, 1997). Unlike most other measures discussed in this review, the TOSCA does not rely on the use of everyday emotion words such as 'guilty' or 'ashamed'. Instead, response options take the form of statements that represent particular experiences associated with each emotion.[5] However, this approach is not without problems. As Olthof et al. (2000) point out, 'there need not be a one-to-one correspondence between the particular experiential correlate that is referred to in the statement and the target emotion' (p. 55). For example, in one of the scenarios, respondents are asked to imagine that they accidently spilled wine on a new carpet at a co-worker's housewarming party. The guilt response is: 'you would stay late to help clean up the stain after the party.' One may wonder, however, whether this action tendency necessarily involves an emotion and, if it does, whether this emotion should necessarily be guilt (and not shame or a combination of both). Similarly, the negative self-evaluations represented in various TOSCA shame statements (e.g. 'I would feel irresponsible') are, as Andrews et al. (1998, pp. 48-49) observes, 'not exclusive to shame and may be experienced independently of shame'. In support of these criticisms, a recent study by Giner-Sorolla et al. (2011) found that the TOSCA guilt scale was unrelated to actual feelings of guilt (and self-conscious affect in general) and that the TOSCA shame scale was associated with a variety of negative emotions (and not only the specific emotion of shame).

In sum, the TOSCA is designed to measure two affective dispositions or personality traits that involve distinct ways of dealing with (relatively minor) failures and transgressions. These two traits are likely to implicate different affective components, but it is doubtful that they correspond one-to-one with either guilt or shame. Crucially, the prosocial nature of 'guilt-proneness' and the dysfunctional nature of 'shame-proneness' are partially built into the TOSCA and, thus, remain presupposed rather than tested. It is therefore not surprising that TOSCA-based research has consistently shown that 'guilt-proneness' is a protective factor for delinquency and that 'shame-proneness' does not have a delinquency-inhibiting effect. Given the above implications, researchers should be careful in drawing conclusions about the moral nature of guilt and shame from TOSCA-based research.

---

5 According to Tangney, most laypersons are unclear about the meaning of the terms 'guilt' and 'shame' (Tangney, 1996; Tangney & Dearing, 2002). However, research has found that even children (from the age of 9 and upwards) have sufficient knowledge of the meaning of terms of 'guilt' and 'shame' and are able to differentiate between them (Ferguson et al., 1991; Olthof et al., 2000).

2.3.2 *Anticipated offence-related guilt and shame*

Criminologists have developed their own scenario-based measures to assess anticipated guilt and shame (e.g. Grasmick & Bursik, 1990; Wikström et al., 2012). Like the TOSCA, these measures capture expected guilt and shame reactions to hypothetical scenarios. Unlike the TOSCA, however, they only use hypothetical offending scenarios (e.g. assault, vandalism, shoplifting etc.). Criminologists have developed two types of measures of anticipated guilt and shame: those that are crime-general and those that are crime-specific. The former measures the propensity to anticipate guilt and shame across different types of offences, and the latter measures anticipated guilt and shame states for engaging in specific offences.

a Crime-general measures

Crime-general measures assess anticipated guilt and shame feelings across a variety of hypothetical offending scenarios (e.g. theft, vandalism, assault etc.). To measure anticipated guilt, respondents are typically asked to indicate on a Likert-type scale to which degree they would feel 'guilty' if they were to commit the given act (e.g. Maxwell et al., 2017; Melde & Esbensen, 2011; Wikström et al., 2012). Shame is mostly operationalised as 'external shame', that is, the shame that occurs when a wrongdoing is detected by others. Correspondingly, respondents are typically asked how 'ashamed' they would feel if they had committed a given offence and significant others such as parents, friends or teachers found out (Svensson et al., 2013; Wikström et al., 2012). Respondents' ratings of the various guilt and shame statements are then summed or averaged to obtain a final score that represents their propensity to anticipate guilt and shame for engaging in delinquency. According to situational action theory (SAT), a relatively recent and influential criminological theory, the propensity to anticipate moral emotions such as guilt and shame is an important indicator of morality (Wikström, 2010; Wikström et al., 2012). More specifically, guilt and shame are assumed to function as 'moral filters' through which action alternatives are evaluated. They are hypothesised to make rule-breaking acts such as crime unthinkable for most people.

Both cross-sectional (Pauwels & Svensson, 2015; Svensson et al., 2013) and longitudinal studies (Coffman et al., 2014; Cole et al., 2014; Matsuda et al., 2013; Maxwell et al., 2017; Melde & Esbensen, 2011; Rebellon et al., 2016; Trivedi-Bateman, 2019) among samples of adolescents and young adults have found that individuals with a higher propensity to anticipate guilt report lower levels of delinquency. Moreover, the effects of anticipated guilt on self-reported delinquency remain strong, even when controlling for other important correlates such as parental monitoring, school bonding or peer delinquency. Several cross-sectional studies have also examined whether adolescents who are more inclined to anticipate shame in front of others report lower levels of delinquency

(De Buck & Pauwels, 2019; Pauwels & Svensson, 2015; Svensson, 2004; Svensson et al., 2013). In all of these studies, anticipated shame was associated with lower levels of self-reported delinquency. Again, these effects held when controlling for the effects of other important correlates of delinquency. Finally, it is worth mentioning that studies have found that female adolescents are more inclined than male adolescents to anticipate guilt and shame for engaging in delinquency (Rebellon et al., 2016; Svensson, 2004; Svensson et al., 2013). One study by Rebellon et al. (2016) also found evidence to suggest that gender differences in guilt may be a crucial factor in explaining the gender gap in delinquency.

So far, only three criminological studies have included measures of both anticipated guilt and shame (Pauwels & Svensson, 2015; Svensson et al., 2013; Trivedi-Bateman, 2019). These studies found moderate to high correlations between the two measures (r = 0.5, r = 0.72 and r = 0.67, respectively). This suggests that anticipated guilt and anticipated shame share much in common and that any subject who is likely to anticipate feelings of guilt is also very likely to anticipate feelings of shame before others (and vice versa). In two studies, both anticipated guilt and anticipated shame were associated with lower levels of delinquent involvement (Pauwels & Svensson, 2015; Svensson et al., 2013), although the effects of guilt were somewhat stronger than those of shame. In the study by Trivedi-Bateman (2019), anticipated guilt, but not anticipated shame, predicted lower levels of self-reported violence. However, the offending scenarios used to measure anticipated shame in this study involved property crimes (i.e. feeling ashamed in front of others if one is caught shoplifting or breaking into a car), so there was a mismatch between the shame measure and the delinquency measure.

Taken together, the above-mentioned studies strongly suggest that the propensity to anticipate moral emotions such as guilt and shame is a protective factor for delinquency.

b Crime-specific measures

Crime-specific measures assess anticipated guilt and shame states in relation to specific offences (e.g. theft or driving under influence) without assuming that individuals have a general propensity to anticipate guilt and shame across all types of offences. These measures have mostly been used in studies of rational choice/deterrence theory (e.g. Grasmick & Bursik, 1990; Rebellon et al., 2010; Tibbetts, 1997b). Deterrence and rational choice theories of crime assume that individuals take into account the anticipated costs and benefits of their actions and, consequently, that they will refrain from offending if the costs outweigh the benefits. From this perspective, guilt and shame are viewed as 'possible threats or costs, which are more or less certain and more or less severe, that reduce the expected utility of crime' (Grasmick & Bursik, 1990, p. 841).

Grasmick and Bursik (1990) were among the first criminologists to study the effects of anticipated emotions on criminal decision-making. They extended deterrence theory beyond its focus on the legal costs of crime, such as arrest or imprisonment, to include two emotional costs associated with offending: shame or guilt (they treat both terms as interchangeable) and embarrassment. According to Grasmick and Bursick, shame/guilt is a 'self-imposed sanction' felt by those who violate their internalised norms, whereas embarrassment is a 'socially imposed sanction' felt in response to the perceived disapproval of significant others. Grasmick and Bursik (1990) developed offence-specific measures of anticipated shame/guilt and embarrassment, tapping both the perceived *certainty* and *severity* of each. To measure the perceived certainty of shame/guilt, respondents were asked whether they would feel 'guilty' if they were to commit the offence in question. To measure the perceived certainty of embarrassment, respondents were asked whether people whose opinion they value 'would lose respect for them' if they were to commit the offence in question. Responses had to be given on a 4-point scale ranging from 'definitely would not' to 'definitely would'. To measure the perceived severity of both emotional costs, respondents were asked 'how big of a problem' feeling guilty and losing the respect of significant others, respectively, would create for their life. Responses had to be given on a 5-point scale ranging from 'no problem at all' to 'a very big problem'. Consistent with Becker's expected utility model (Becker, 1968), perceived certainty and perceived severity scores were multiplied to operationalise the threat of each emotional cost.

Many researchers have used the measures developed by Grasmick and Bursik to examine the deterrent effects of shame/guilt and embarrassment across different types of offending. They consistently found that those who perceive a higher threat of shame/guilt report lower intentions to offend in the future. This was the case for offences as varied as corporate crime, littering, tax fraud, petty theft, violations of campus policies, drunk driving and speeding (Blackwell, 2000; Elis & Simpson, 1995; Grasmick et al., 1991, 1993; Grasmick & Bursik, 1990; Mann et al., 2016; Nagin & Paternoster, 1993; Paternoster & Simpson, 1996; Spivak et al., 2011). Interestingly, in most of these studies, the deterrent effects of shame/guilt were found to be considerably stronger than those of legal sanctions (e.g. arrest and conviction). Despite being moderately correlated to one another, the deterrent effects of 'socially imposed' embarrassment were generally smaller (or even negligible) as compared to those of 'self-imposed' shame/guilt. It should be noted, however, that Grasmick and Bursik's measure of 'embarrassment' (i.e. 'Would most of the people whose opinions you value lose respect for you if you...?') is more a measure of expected social disapproval than a specific measure of embarrassment. As discussed in the previous chapter, the anticipated reactions of others are an important source of guilt and shame. It is likely, therefore, that anticipated social disapproval (i.e. what Grasmick and Bursik refer to as 'embarrassment') deters offending mostly indirectly, through its influence on anticipated shame/guilt. Indeed, a recent study has found that anticipated shame states largely mediate the effects of perceived social disapproval on the decision to offend (Allen et al., 2017).

Other researchers have criticised Grasmick and Bursik for not differentiating between shame and guilt and for measuring shame in terms of 'guilt feelings' (Rebellon et al., 2010; Tibbetts, 1997b). They have proposed alternative measures of anticipated shame. Before discussing these alternatives, however, it is worth noting that the criticism against the Grasmick and Bursik measure is probably overblown. As discussed previously, experiences of guilt and shame tend to be very highly correlated, especially when it comes to acts of moral wrongdoing (Harris, 2003; Olthof et al., 2004; Schmader & Lickel, 2006). Hence, when respondents indicate that they 'would feel guilty', this should not be taken to mean that shame would not be felt. Furthermore, anticipated guilt and shame states are hypothesised to have similar inhibiting effects on offending. Analysing them separately therefore may not be as important as some researchers have alleged.

Also examining the role of emotions within a rational choice model of offending, Tibbetts (1997b) proposed an alternative way of measuring shame. Drawing upon the self-behaviour distinction between guilt and shame, he argued that a shame measure should consist of items that represent 'global evaluations of the self, which typically are not involved in experiences of embarrassment or guilt' (1997b, p. 240). Accordingly, Tibbetts operationalised the perceived certainty of shame by asking respondents to estimate the risk that they would 'feel a loss of self-esteem' if they were to commit a given offence (even if no one else found out). Responses had to be given on an 11-point scale ranging from 'no chance' to '100% chance'. The perceived severity of shame was measured by asking respondents to indicate 'how big of a problem' this would create for their life. Responses had to be given on an 11-point scale ranging from 'no problem' to 'a very big problem'. Certainty and severity scores were multiplied to form a composite variable representing the perceived threat of shame.

Using this measure, Tibbetts and colleagues conducted a series of cross-sectional studies to examine the effects of anticipated shame states on students' future intentions to drive drunk, shoplift and cheat on exams (Tibbetts, 1997a, 1997b, 2014; Tibbetts & Herz, 1996; Tibbetts & Myers, 1999). Without exception, anticipated shame was associated with lower intentions to offend, even when taking into account prior levels of delinquency and other perceived costs (e.g. legal sanctions) and benefits (e.g. pleasure) associated with offending. Most of these studies focused on the deterrent effect of 'internal shame' (i.e. 'the risk and severity of losing self-esteem even if no one else found out'). In one study, Tibbetts (1997b) also examined the deterrent effects of 'external shame' (i.e. the risk and severity of losing self-esteem if the behaviour were detected by family or friends) on students' future intentions to shoplift and drive drunk. However, private and public shame states were so highly correlated ($r > 0.75$ in the case of drunk driving and $r > 0.80$ in the case of shoplifting) that it was impossible to estimate their unique effects.

Although the studies by Tibbetts and colleagues contribute to the empirical literature on the deterrent effects of shame, their approach to shame measurement raises some concerns. More specifically, this approach rests on the assumption that a loss of self-esteem necessarily indicates the presence of shame. However, the relationship between shame and self-esteem is not an exclusive one. That is, although shame is typically accompanied by a (temporary) loss of self-esteem, not every loss of self-esteem amounts to shame (Deigh, 1983; Miceli & Castelfranchi, 2018; Velotti et al., 2017). Moreover, some scholars have argued that guilt feelings, which are often fused with shame, may also involve a decrease of self-esteem, namely a decrease of one's *moral* self-esteem (Miceli & Castelfranchi, 1998). In sum, a loss of self-esteem may not only signify either shame or guilt or both, but potentially also something else. This makes it difficult to interpret Tibbett's measure unambiguously.

A second alternative state-based measure of anticipated shame was proposed by Rebellon et al. (2010). They defined anticipated shame as the 'emotion that a prospective criminal believes might result from a future crime if that crime were to be discovered by intimates' (2010, p. 989). Rebellon and colleagues studied the deterrent effects of external shame on the intention to engage in employee theft in a sample of university students. Accordingly, they asked respondents how 'ashamed' or 'embarrassed' they would be if their family and friends would discover that they had stolen money from an employer's cash register. Rebellon et al. (2010) found that higher levels of anticipated shame were associated with lower intentions to steal, even when taking into account other predictors of delinquency such as low self-control and differential association (i.e. exposure to delinquent peers). In a follow-up study, Rebellon et al. (2015) also found that female university students anticipated higher levels of shame for engaging in employee theft than male university students. Furthermore, anticipated shame accounted for a substantial portion of the gender gap in criminal intent, over and above the effects of other mediators such as self-control and exposure to delinquent peers.

One criticism that can be made of the shame measure proposed by Rebellon and colleagues is that it does not differentiate between shame and embarrassment. They measured anticipated shame by asking respondents how 'ashamed' or 'embarrassed' they would be if significant others found out that they had stolen money. As discussed in the previous chapter, however, shame and embarrassment are more different than alike. In fact, research has shown that embarrassment and shame have less in common than do guilt and shame (Harris, 2003; Tangney, Miller, et al., 1996). Embarrassment is more superficial than shame in the sense that it does not affect one's sense of who one *really* is as a person. In embarrassment, the concern is only with how one *appears* before others in a given social situation. Hence, unlike shame, embarrassment always requires the presence of an audience (Robbins & Parlavecchio, 2006; Tangney, Miller, et al., 1996).

In general, it can be concluded that criminological studies, regardless of whether they used crime-general or crime-specific measures of guilt and shame, have produced similar results. These results strongly suggest that both anticipated guilt and anticipated shame can prevent (young) people from getting involved in delinquent activities. This conclusion contrasts with the conclusion drawn from TOSCA-based studies that proneness to guilt, but not to shame, is a protective factor for delinquency. The diverging results are due to differences in the conceptualisation and measurement of shame. As discussed earlier, the TOSCA captures a propensity for maladaptive shame reactions in response to relatively minor failures and transgressions. Criminological measures, by contrast, capture a healthy, forward-looking sense of shame that is situationally appropriate. Finally, it is worth noting that most criminological studies have focused on the inhibiting effect of 'external shame' (i.e. the shame that we expect to feel when our wrongdoing is exposed to others). However, although it is true that the public exposure of a transgression may intensify shame, public exposure is neither necessary nor sufficient to elicit shame. It is not necessary because shame can be triggered merely by imagining the reactions of others. It is not sufficient, because we also have to (imaginatively) share the reactions of others to us in order to feel ashamed (Harris, 2011; Miceli & Castelfranchi, 2018; Zahavi, 2014). Hence, it would be a mistake to conclude, as some have (e.g. Svensson et al., 2013, p. 33), that the inhibiting effect of shame is based on the fear of being caught, whereas the inhibiting effect of guilt is based on internal moral beliefs. Both anticipated guilt and anticipated shame depend on a positive valuation of the moral standards and values in question.

2.4 CONCLUSION

The aim of this chapter was to provide the reader with a synthesis of the research literature on the association between guilt, shame and offending. As the review demonstrates, considerable attention has been directed at examining these associations, with evidence suggesting that a healthy sense of guilt and shame may play an important role in the prevention of crime and delinquency. Such a sense of guilt and shame appears to manifest itself in two distinct but related ways: first, in the form of *retrospective* guilt and shame about past misdeeds and, second, in the form of *prospective* guilt and shame about future acts of wrongdoing.

Both quantitative and qualitative studies suggest that episodic feelings of guilt and shame about past misdeeds may discourage reoffending and motivate desistance. The results of these studies also support the view that guilt and shame are complementary rather than mutually exclusive emotions. Especially in the context of moral transgressions, guilt and shame tend to co-occur. More research is needed to understand how these emotions potentially interact with each other to prevent reoffending. Although offence-related guilt reflects the acknowledgement of wrongdoing and the acceptance of responsibility, offence-related shame may be more important for illuminating and deepening the guilt one feels over a specific misdeed. That is, unlike pure guilt, guilt-fused-with-shame may motivate reflection about what the misdeed in question reveals about one's moral identity (Ahmed et al., 2001; Williams, 1993). Because of its unique connection to self-identity, shame could play a distinctive role in the desistance process as a motivator of self-reform (Lickel et al., 2014).

However, it has also become clear from this review is that it is important to distinguish between different forms of shame and, more specifically, between the (episodic) shame that accompanies guilt in response to particular acts of wrongdoing and the frequent or persistent experience of (generalised) shame. Psychological research has shown that shame can become problematic when experienced too frequently, too intensively or disproportionately relative to the situation (Cibich et al., 2016). Consistent with this, criminological research has found that individuals who struggle with persistent shame report higher involvement in delinquency (Tibbetts, 2003) and also that young offenders who frequently experience shame in prison are more likely to reoffend after release (Hosser et al., 2007). Problematic shame manifests itself in avoidance and withdrawal behaviour and is often associated with beliefs that the whole self is flawed beyond repair. Psychological measurement instruments such as the TOSCA are designed to capture the propensity for such maladaptive shame reactions. Unsurprisingly then, studies using this instrument have found no evidence that shame-proneness is a protective factor for delinquency and recidivism (e.g. Stuewig et al., 2015; Tangney et al., 2014).

Crucially, shame and guilt do not only provide feedback on past behaviour; they can also play a role in the decision-making process that precedes acts of wrongdoing. That is, when individuals consider doing something wrong, they may anticipate guilt and shame and, based on these warning signals, refrain from engaging in such behaviour. Criminological research has consistently found that individuals who are able to anticipate guilt and shame are less likely to be involved in crime and delinquency. Interestingly, it has also been found that women anticipate higher levels of guilt and shame than men and that these gender differences may explain a considerable portion of the gender gap in delinquency. In the next two chapters, I will focus more closely on anticipated or prospective guilt and shame. In the first place, I will discuss the integration of prospective guilt and shame in criminological theories of crime causation. Second, I will develop a theoretical framework for understanding both the social nature of guilt and shame and the social factors that may lead to individual and gender differences in prospective guilt and shame during adolescence.

3 Prospective Guilt and Shame: a Symbolic Interactionist Analysis

> The reference to other persons involved in the sense of self may be distinct and particular, as when a boy is ashamed to have his mother catch him at something she has forbidden, or it may be vague and general, as when one is ashamed to do something which only his conscience, expressing his sense of social responsibility, detects and disapproves; but it is always there. There is no sense of 'I,' as in pride or shame, without its correlative sense of you, or he, or they. (Cooley, 1902, p. 182)

Shame and guilt do not only provide feedback on past transgressive behaviour. With the help of prospective or forward-looking guilt and shame, people can avoid transgressing norms in the first place. As reviewed in the previous chapter, criminological studies have consistently found that those who anticipate feeling guilty and/or ashamed for committing wrongdoings are less likely to be involved in crime and delinquency (Grasmick & Bursik, 1990; Rebellon et al., 2016; Spruit et al., 2016; Svensson et al., 2013; Tibbetts, 1997b). In this chapter, I deal with a number of theoretical issues raised by these findings. The first issue concerns the precise role of prospective guilt and shame in the explanation of crime and delinquency. The second issue concerns the explanation of individual differences in prospective guilt and shame and especially the role of social factors and processes in explaining these differences. In the first section of this chapter, I discuss current attempts to address these two issues in the criminological literature. In the second section, I propose an alternative theoretical framework that builds on Mead's (1934) theory of the self, the symbolic interactionist analysis of the self-conscious emotions by Shott (1979) and the symbolic interactionist theory of delinquency developed by Heimer and Matsueda (1994).

3.1 Guilt and shame in criminological theory

3.1.1 Between utility calculation and moral filtering

Three major theories in criminology incorporate the role of guilt and shame in their explanation of crime: reintegrative shaming theory, rational choice/deterrence theory and situational action theory. Each of these theories has its own shortcomings.

The theory that most readily comes to mind when thinking about guilt and shame in the context of crime and justice is Braithwaite's reintegrative shaming theory (Braithwaite, 1989). In this theory, Braithwaite famously distinguished between two ways in which individuals can be disapproved of or 'shamed' for their wrongdoings: reintegrative and stigmatising. Reintegrative shaming involves communicating disapproval of a specific offence while maintaining respect for the person of the offender. Disintegrative or stigmatising shaming, by contrast, involves disrespectful disapproval of the person (and not just the deed) and their devaluation and social rejection. According to Braithwaite, shaming offenders in a reintegrative way prevents crime because it restores their social bonds while simultaneously building up their conscience, whereas stigmatic shaming further alienates them and thereby enhances their chances of reoffending.

In its original formulation, Braithwaite's theory addressed the relationship between the two types of shaming and crime without much discussion on the emotions that shaming practices were supposed to elicit. In a subsequent work, Braithwaite and Braithwaite (2001) refined reintegrative shaming theory with the help of Harris (2001) and Ahmed (2001). The revised theory proposes that the emotions of guilt and shame mediate the link between shaming practices and subsequent offending. Specifically, the theory assumes that offenders will almost inevitably feel some form of shame when they are confronted with their deeds, that the type of shaming they receive will influence their management of these feelings and that this in turn will affect their chances of reoffending. The theory predicts that reintegrative shaming 'is more likely to result in offenders acknowledging shame, feeling remorseful for what has happened, and making amends', whereas stigmatising shaming 'is more likely to result in offenders displacing shame and feeling anger towards others' (Harris, 2014, p. 4815). The former is expected to reduce the likelihood of subsequent offending and the latter to increase it (Braithwaite & Braithwaite, 2001, pp. 52-53). In short, the revised theory mainly discusses how different shaming practices influence (retrospective) feelings of guilt and shame after the fact (e.g. in court cases or restorative justice conferences). It does not discuss precisely how (prospective) guilt and shame may prevent individuals from engaging in criminal activities in the first place.

Deterrence and rational choice theories of crime assume that would-be offenders, just like anyone else, chose to do what they think is best for them (Becker, 1968; Cornish & Clarke, 1986). That is, they 'consider the costs and benefits of available alternatives, form expectations about the consequences of these alternatives, and choose the alternative that best satisfies their preferences' (Kroneberg & Kalter, 2012, p. 76). According to this perspective, individuals act in an outcome-oriented way and choose to commit crime when the anticipated benefits of doing so outweigh the anticipated costs. Deterrence and rational choice theorists conceive of guilt and shame as 'emotional costs' associated with offending (Grasmick & Bursik, 1990; Tibbetts, 1997a, 1997b). They argue that the prospect of feeling guilty or ashamed decreases the expected utility of crime, just like the prospect of legal sanctions (e.g. arrest or imprisonment) does. Accordingly, they hypothesise that, all else equal, individuals who anticipate feeling guilty or ashamed will be less likely to commit crime.

Attempts to integrate moral emotions in traditional rational choice and deterrence models are not without problems. Several scholars have convincingly argued that normative-affective factors such as guilt and shame cannot be seen as just one 'cost' among others in a rational utilitarian calculus (Elster, 1999; Etzioni, 1988; Kroneberg et al., 2010). Elster makes this point in the following way:

> If guilt were nothing but an anticipated or experienced cost, an agent whose guilt deters him from stealing a book should be willing to buy a guilt-erasing pill if it was sufficiently cheap. I submit that no person who is capable of being deterred by guilt would buy the pill. In fact, he would feel guilty about buying it. For him, taking the pill in order to escape guilt and be able to steal the book would be as morally bad as just stealing it. (Elster, 1999, p. 303)

Normative-affects factors are generally considered to play a distinctive role in the decision-making process in that they influence how other (non-normative) costs and benefits are perceived, evaluated and weighed against one another (Elster, 1999; Etzioni, 1988; Kroneberg et al., 2010). In other words, normative-affective factors influence the nature and occurrence of the trade-off itself. Under the influence of guilt and shame, people may follow a certain course of action without, despite, or even against, instrumental cost-benefit considerations. For instance, a person may feel morally compelled to return a lost wallet without stealing anything from it, even if the option of stealing is perceived as relatively easy, riskless and highly rewarding.[6]

A completely different take on the role of guilt and shame in crime causation can be found in Wikström's situational action theory (SAT). In SAT, internalised moral norms and the associated emotions of guilt and shame are seen as the key components of an individual's morality (Wikström, 2006, 2010; Wikström et al., 2012). The theory assumes that people's personal morals and the (perceived) moral norms of the settings in which they participate interact to constitute a 'moral filter'. This moral filter determines which action alternatives people perceive in a specific situation (i.e. the things they would consider doing). SAT argues that the reason why most people are law-abiding most of the

6 Rational choice theorists may counter that, even in this case, people still do what they believe is best for them in light of their moral preferences. Although this may be true, however, their decision-making models have no way of distinguishing between deontological deliberations guided by normative/affective factors (including considerations about possible consequences) and utilitarian deliberations guided *only* by a non-moral comparison of the causal consequences of different action alternatives.

time is *not* because they deliberately choose to refrain from crime (in consideration of the costs and benefits) but because a moral filter prevents them from perceiving crime as a viable action alternative in the first place. Thus, whereas rational choice models focus on the factors that influence people's *choices* between criminal and legal action alternatives, SAT shifts the focus to an earlier phase of the decision-making process and proposes that morality may preclude crime *categorically* from the range of options that is up for consideration. Or, as Messner (2012) puts it,

> morality serves as the first line of defence by effectively restricting the range of situations to which the decision-making processes that are well explicated in other criminological perspectives will be applied. (p. 9)

In sum, feelings of guilt and shame are not conceived of as perceived costs in a utilitarian calculus. Rather, as a component of the moral filter, they help to limit the process of utility calculation by ruling certain action alternatives out of bounds altogether. Essentially, SAT draws upon the idea that morality is not a matter of self-interest and that social order is only possible if certain values and norms cannot be subjected to utility calculations (see also Etzioni, 1988; Parsons, 1968).

Although SAT provides an interesting and valuable alternative to rational choice and deterrence theories, the role of guilt and shame in the theory is seriously underdeveloped (Brauer & Tittle, 2017). Little attention is given to the conceptualisation of guilt and shame beyond simple statements such as 'guilt refers to a person feeling bad about his/her actions; shame refers to a person feeling bad about his/her actions in front of others' (Wikström, 2010, p. 222). Furthermore, (anticipated) feelings of guilt and shame are only vaguely described as 'measures' or 'indicators' of the strength of an individual's morality (Wikström, 2006, 2010; Wikström et al., 2012). This leaves one wondering: what, if anything, is the precise function of these emotions in the moral filtering process? According to SAT, the moral filtering of action alternatives is either a fast, unreflective and even largely unconscious process, or a more deliberate process that takes the form of a moral judgement. But the role of guilt and shame in either of these two processes is never explicitly addressed. Overall, one is left with the impression that SAT sees emotions such as guilt and shame merely as *indicative of* rather than *functional for* morality.

To sum things up, rational choice and deterrence theories can be criticised for seeing guilt and shame as just one cost among others in a rational calculus, whereas reintegrative shaming theory and situational action theory can be criticised for failing to specify exactly how (prospective) guilt and shame may affect the decision-making process leading up to crime.

3.1.2 *Between internalisation and social disapproval*

What are the social factors that lead to prospective guilt and shame in relation to crime and delinquency? Despite recognising the fundamentally social nature of both emotions, criminologists have paid little theoretical attention to this question. Yet, the answer has important implications for understanding individual differences in prospective guilt and shame. What follows is a critical reflection on two different possible answers, the features of which will be somewhat exaggerated for the sake of comparison.

One way to address the question is by reference to the socialisation process, the essence of which consists in the *internalisation* of norms (e.g. Svensson et al., 2013, 2016). The following passage by Svensson and colleagues epitomises this line of thought:

> When the socialization process is completed, norms will be internalized and the individual will develop a moral sense of what is right or wrong. This leads the individual to feel ashamed in relation to significant others and feel guilty if he or she commits a particular type of crime.... On the other hand, if the socialization process is poor, internalization of norms and moral development will be adversely affected. This means that the individual will not feel shame or guilt when committing a crime. (Svensson et al., 2017, p. 236)

Although rarely explicitly defined, internalisation is generally understood as the process by which individuals come to adopt the norms of the groups or society in which they participate as their own. When moral norms are internalised, they are followed not because of social pressures or external sanctions but out of inner conviction (Campbell, 1964). It is widely accepted that internalisation occurs not only through long-term and/or close interactions with significant others in key social institutions such as the family and the school but also within peer networks and the wider community (Brody, 1982; Grusec & Hastings, 2015; Hardy et al., 2008; Svensson et al., 2016; Wikström & Sampson, 2003). Drawing upon learning theories, some criminologists have proposed more precise mechanisms through which the internalisation of norms presumably occurs (e.g. Akers, 1973; Wikström & Treiber, 2017). Situational action theory, for instance, has recently proposed that people internalise norms through 'moral education' (Wikström et al., 2012; Wikström & Treiber, 2017). Moral education encompasses three mechanisms: (1) direct instruction by others who communicate about the moral rules that apply in different settings, (2) observation of others' behaviour and the consequences thereof, and (3) 'trial and error', that is, trying out different lines of action and experiencing their consequences (Wikström & Treiber, 2017).

Although explanations of guilt and shame in terms of internalised norms are not wrong, they fail to do justice to the distinctively social nature of both emotions. This is so because they limit the role of others to that of teaching and transmitting rules and standards (i.e. moral education) (Baumeister et al., 1994; Miceli & Castelfranchi, 1998). Once these rules and standards have been learned and accepted, guilt and shame become a matter of people's private self-evaluations (i.e. the result of a purely intrapersonal process). After that point, social processes – namely, ongoing social interactions and relationships – are no longer or only marginally involved. In short, the traditional 'internalisation' perspective assumes that those who anticipate guilt and shame are well-developed moral persons who autonomously evaluate themselves against their own (socially acquired) standards.

As several authors have pointed out, however, the social features of guilt and shame go well beyond the fact that the moral standards by which individuals measure themselves are socially learned (Baumeister et al., 1994; Miceli & Castelfranchi, 1998; Montes Sánchez, 2015; Zahavi, 2014). Most if not all episodes of these emotions occur in a specific social context (Tangney & Dearing, 2002). People who feel guilty or ashamed typically have 'others in mind', be it as victims, judges or audiences (Rochat, 2009). The identity of these others and the nature of one's relationship with them are rarely if ever irrelevant. However strongly we may endorse honesty as a standard of conduct, lying to our parents is likely to elicit more guilt than lying to a total stranger. Indeed, guilt is often specific to particular relationships (Baumeister et al., 1994, 1994; Katz, 1999, p. 150). Similarly, shame is often felt in response to the actual or imagined disapproval of others whose opinion we value (Katz, 1999; Smith et al., 2002). This is not to deny the role of self-evaluation in guilt and shame; it is only to say that this self-evaluation has an important social dimension. In fact, there are good reasons to assume that this social dimension is all the more important during adolescence, a period of life characterised by 'heightened susceptibility to peer influence and hypersensitivity to social rejection' (Andrews et al., 2021, p. 109).

A completely different take on the issue of internalisation can be found in Hirschi's (1969) social control theory. In fact, Hirschi explicitly avoided using the concept of internalisation in explaining norm conformity. He argued that notions such as 'internalised norms', 'conscience' or 'superego' refer to relatively stable and enduring personality attributes and, therefore, create 'difficulties in explaining variations in delinquent activity over time' (Hirschi, 1969, p. 19). At a more fundamental level, Hirschi rejected the idea of internalisation because it would imply that a person eventually becomes a 'moral animal' with a genuine desire to follow rules, even in the absence of external pressures or controls (Hirschi, 1969, p. 5). This idea clashes profoundly with one of his theory's most basic assumptions, namely that, deep down, people remain fundamentally self-interested.[7] According to social control theory, norms only regulate externally; they do not become

7 Hence, Hirschi's theory is fully compatible with rational choice and deterrence theories of crime (Hirschi, 1986).

constitutive of the personality structure. In other words, social control theory assumes that people are natural deviants whose egoistic drives can be controlled but never fundamentally altered by the stakes they have in conformity. 'To violate a norm', Hirschi (1969) famously wrote,

> is to act contrary to the wishes and expectations of other people. If a person does not care about the wishes and expectations of other people – that is, if he is insensitive to the opinions of others – then he is to that extent not bound by the norms. (p. 18)

Thus, according to Hirschi, people follow norms mainly because they are afraid of the social consequences if they would break them. Hence, his theory predicts that those with strong social bonds will be less likely to engage in delinquency.

Some scholars have proposed to include guilt and shame in Hirschi's social control theory as mechanisms that explain why social bonds to conventional society produce law-abiding behaviour (Clay-Warner, 2014; Svensson, 2004). This is a defensible proposal as it takes seriously the idea that these emotions are fundamentally embedded in ongoing social relations rather than merely being the product of intrapersonal processes. At the same time, certain features of Hirschi's theory make it difficult to grasp the moral qualities of guilt and shame in a wholly satisfactory way. Specifically, having rejected the notion of 'internalisation', Hirschi's theory is left with little else than *fear* of social disapproval as the main psychological mechanism behind law-abiding behaviour (Lynch et al., 1992). In this respect, Hirschi's answer to his main research question (i.e. 'why do people *not* engage in delinquency?') is telling: 'there is much evidence that we would if we *dared*' (Hirschi, 1969, p. 34). Guilt and shame, however, are not merely the product of social disapproval and their inhibitory effects cannot be reduced to those of fear. This is so because the actual or imagined reactions of others will not elicit guilt or shame unless one reacts to oneself in a similar way (Harris, 2011; Lagattuta & Thompson, 2007; Miceli & Castelfranchi, 2018). Guilt and shame are emotions in which the self – and not only others – stands in judgement of itself. That is why they are called emotions of self-assessment (Taylor, 1985).

Another different problem with Hirschi's theory lies with its assumption that social bonds are inherently prosocial in their effects. Indeed, according to Hirschi, social bonds only work to *inhibit* delinquency but never to *facilitate* it. Social control theory implies that 'criminals are atomized actors unable to form trusting relationships' (Matsueda et al., 2020, p. 245). However, such a view is at odds with empirical evidence indicating that family ties and bonds of friendship are often the foundation of criminal associations (Kleemans, 2013; Van de Bunt et al., 2014; von Lampe & Ole Johansen, 2004). It is also at odds with one of the most well-established findings in the field of juvenile delinquency, namely that friends can encourage an individual's involvement in delinquent activities

(Brauer & De Coster, 2015; McGloin & Thomas, 2019; Warr, 2002). As Svensson et al. (2013, p. 24) note, with reference to the work of Warr (2002), 'individuals may anticipate feelings of guilt and shame for *non*-offending when they believe that offending is needed to demonstrate loyalty to friends and to prevent ridicule.' Hirschi's social control theory precludes this possibility.

In sum, the first account of guilt and shame, in terms of the internalisation of norms, can be criticised because it does not fully account for the distinctively social nature of these emotions. The second account of guilt and shame, in terms of social disapproval, can be criticised because it downplays the role of people's internal self-evaluations. What is needed is an alternative account that does not uncouple self-judgement from judgement by others.

3.2 A symbolic interactionist alternative

In the remainder of this chapter, I will propose an alternative framework for understanding: (1) the role of prospective guilt and shame in the explanation of offending and (2) the social nature and origins of (prospective) guilt and shame. This framework primarily draws upon the following three building blocks: (1) Mead's (1934) pragmatist theory of the self, (2) Heimer and Matsueda's (1994) differential social control Theory and (3) Shott's (1979) symbolic interactionist analysis of the self-conscious emotions. In what follows, I will discuss each of these three building blocks and I will try to integrate them into a single framework. As will hopefully become clear, this framework is able to transcend and encompass the different positions discussed earlier in this chapter.

3.2.1 *Mead's pragmatist theory of the self*

In the continuous flow of social life, people do many things in a spontaneous, almost automatic way, without much need for forethought or deliberation. They rely on habits and routines that have worked for them in the past. According to pragmatists such as George Herbert Mead (1934), people become self-conscious when their taken-for-granted ways of doing things are blocked or no longer adapted to the situation at hand. Only when faced with uncertainty of action or conflicts must individuals become self-conscious, redefine the meaning of the situation and consider possible action alternatives. What enables them to do this, Mead famously argued, is their capacity to take the attitude or role of the other. By this he means that individuals can evoke in themselves responses that are functionally similar to those they might evoke from others. In other words, individuals can see themselves and react to themselves as others would or could. It is only because they can respond to themselves in terms of the attitudes of others, Mead reasoned, that individuals can reflect on themselves as objects and grasp the social meaning of their own conduct.

For Mead (1934), the 'self' is a dynamic process that involves two alternating and complementary phases: the self-as-subject or the 'I' and the self-as-object or the 'Me'. The self becomes an object of awareness to the individual (i.e. a 'Me') when that individual takes the attitude of the other. In other words, 'the Me is the object formed of oneself from a socialized perspective' (Shibutani, 1991, p. 61). The self-as-subject or the 'I' is the seat of awareness and activity. It is that to which the 'Me' appears and that which reacts to the 'Me' by initiating a new course of action. This, in turn, calls out a new 'Me' which criticises or approves this initiative or points in the direction of yet another action alternative. In other words, the 'Me' has a mediating function in an ongoing process of action. It embodies the social meaning and consequences of a particular path of action for the self. Through an ongoing dialogue between the 'I' and the 'Me', individuals can correct and adjust their conduct in view of the virtual reactions of others and the self that is inscribed in them (i.e. a cybernetic process). This feedback cycle continues until individuals have selected an action alternative that resolves the problem at hand. Solutions or adjustments that have proven successful will, after sufficient repetition, turn into new habits. Importantly, solutions to problematic situations are not necessarily 'optimal' in the sense that they maximise, optimise or satisfice the individual's 'utility' (as in rational choice theory). As Gross (2009) writes:

> Pragmatism does not equate problem solving with the maximization of utility. To be sure, the situations humans experience as problems may involve utility maximization – for example, the need of businesses to generate revenue. But the kinds of problems of concern to pragmatists range much more widely and include all the difficulties humans or collective actors face in life, from the need to remain healthy to the need to find meaning and purpose in existence. To reduce these to the desire to maximize on a preference function is to ignore the phenomenological diversity involved in the experiencing of problem situations. (p. 367)

Mead realised that if people only assumed the attitude of specific others, their self and behaviour would always remain volatile, changing their colours as a chameleon does, with every interaction they engage in. If the self is to have a certain degree of unity and its actions a certain degree of consistency, some consolidation and generalisation of meanings must occur. Mead (1934) therefore proposed that people gradually move beyond adopting the attitude of specific others towards consolidating and adopting the attitudes that are common to the groups, organisations, communities and larger collectives in which they participate. Mead referred to these more comprehensive and encompassing perspectives as 'generalised others'. Families, schools, peer groups and cultural, political and religious communities can all serve as generalised others and give rise to a corresponding 'Me'. But generalised others can also be relatively abstract and difficult to identify, such as for instance when individuals interpret their own plans in terms of what 'responsible parents' or 'respectable people' should do. Here, the generalised other refers to a moral community of which the individual considers themselves to be a member. In modern, fragmented and diverse societies, individuals can adopt the perspective of multiple different generalised others. These can be embedded inside of each other or overlap or conflict. The unity of the self, then, depends on the extent to which the individual is able to synthesise the different 'Me's' corresponding to these generalised others into a coherent self-image. If this synthesis succeeds, Joas (1985) writes, 'then there originates the "self" as a unitary self-evaluation and orientation of action, that is nevertheless flexible and open to communication with a gradually increasing number of partners' (p. 118).

It is sometimes overlooked in discussions of Mead's work that the 'I-Me' dialectic does not only have an intersubjective but also a temporal basis (Joas, 1985; Matsueda, 2006; Mead, 1932). The 'Me' arises as individuals interpret their behavioural impulses in terms of a set of acquired social responses (i.e. an established generalised other). In other words, the specific 'Me' that emerges in the present, in the context of a problematic situation, has its roots in previous interactions, in the responses of others to similar actions in the past. Whereas the 'Me' is a function of the past, the responses of the 'I' are directed towards the future possibilities that flow from that past. Specifically, by drawing upon recollections of their past experiences, individuals can imaginatively rehearse alternative future paths of action, including the probable replies of others and their implications for the self. Thus, for Mead, self-reflection and deliberation involve a self that is spatiotemporally extended through a dynamic interplay between memory and imagination, both of which are used as epistemological resources to inform and structure one's actions in the present. As Cook (1993) writes:

> We can make sense of our immediate present only by fitting it into the larger context of where we have been and where we are going, of what we have done and what we are trying to do. We can intelligently direct present conduct only if we can relate it to what has happened in the past and to what is likely to happen in the future. (p. 148)

Choice and novelty play an important role in Mead's theory. How the 'I' will eventually respond to the 'Me', he writes, 'is more or less uncertain' (Mead, 1934, p. 176). The 'I' is not merely the seat of awareness and activity but also the seat of agency and creativity. While exhibiting varying degrees of novelty, however, the responses of the 'I' are never completely random because they arise in relation to a 'Me' which is a function of the past. Or, as Rock (1979) puts it more eloquently: 'The freedom of the "I" to produce novel "Me's" is constrained by the possibility of an enforced autobiographical constancy.' If the 'I' does react to the 'Me' in a sufficiently novel way, however, the structure and content of the next 'Me' will have to be readjusted so that it incorporates both the old and the new. The creative response of the 'I' to the 'Me' represents the agentic dimension of the self, the potential that individuals have to reconstruct themselves, to change their habits and create new meanings for the self. Thus, contrary to what is sometimes erroneously believed, Mead does not see the self simply as a passive reflection or uncritical accumulation of others' definitions, ascriptions, reactions or evaluations. On the contrary,

> with Mead's 'I' and 'me' distinction we have before us a self that contains a seat of novelty as well as a set of organized prior responses, a set of responses that comes not only from others but also results from one's own past novel reactions. (Aboulafia, 1991, p. 10)

Because of the conditioned freedom of the 'I', there are limits to social control.

Finally, two related points about Mead's theory of the self are worth emphasising, for they are often the source of confusion. First, the response of the 'I' to the 'Me' should not be interpreted as some kind of natural or biological response of the individual to a set of externally constraining social relations (Cook, 2013). As should have become clear from the previous paragraphs, both phases of the self are socially structured. Contrary to Hirschi, Mead's approach to society does not start with individual selves who are by their nature isolated and egoistic and who are then brought and held together by social forces (or 'bonds') external to them. Human nature, for Mead (1934), is *essentially* social because individuals can only become selves in the first place by adopting the attitudes of others with whom they are engaged in common activities. The 'I-Me' dialectic does not exist prior to the social process. Mead presupposes individuals,

> but only as biological organisms having certain socio-physiological capacities and tendencies to respond, not as self-conscious beings. The actual development of distinctively human mentality and personality in these organisms is held to be the product of social interaction (Cook, 1993, p. 167).[8]

8 Thus, when individuals act egoistically, it cannot be explained as a biological impulse that is uninhibited by social controls. Rather, individuals act egoistically when self-interested impulses acquire a social meaning – through interactions with other individuals – that validates or reinforces them and facilitates their expression in overt behaviour. In other words, egoistic behaviour is the expression of a social pattern within highly socialised individuals.

Second, at first sight, the 'I' and the 'Me' bear some resemblance to the Freudian concepts of the 'Id' and the 'Superego'. Upon closer inspection, however, the resemblance is seeming rather than real (Miller, 1973). Freud conceived of the human self as a battleground between the instinctual drives of the 'Id' and a set of social norms internalised in the 'Superego'. In Mead's model, by contrast, the 'I' and the 'Me' are mutually constitutive phases of the self that engage in an open dialogue and discussion. The 'I', as we have already seen, should not be seen as a biological impulse that is uncontaminated by social expectations. The 'Me', rather than merely being an internal censor or suppressor like its Freudian counterpart, is indispensable to the existence and the expression of the 'I'. To be sure, conflicts between the spontaneous 'I' and the self-reflective 'Me' may arise, but this is not necessarily the case. If conflicts arise, the 'I' can either willingly or more reluctantly defer to the authority of the 'Me' and abandon its plans. If the attitudes that are contained in the 'Me' fail to resolve the problematic situation, however, the 'I' may respond in a novel way and thereby reconstruct the old 'Me'. Because of the conditioned freedom of the 'I', there are limits to social control.

3.2.2 *Differential social control theory*

It is well-known that Mead's ideas about the self as a product of social action and social interaction have inspired the labelling theories of crime and deviance developed by Lemert (1951) and Becker (1963). Another, perhaps less well-known, criminological theory that uses Mead's ideas to explain delinquency is Heimer and Matsueda's differential social control theory (Heimer & Matsueda, 1994). This theory integrates ideas from social control, social learning and labelling theories based on a unified interactionist framework.

Drawing on Mead, Heimer and Matsueda (1994) argue that role-taking is the key individual-level mechanism that explains how social relationships influence delinquency. Like Mead, they assume that people often engage with the world in a habitual, non-reflective way. When habitual actions are hindered by conflicts or uncertainty, however, individuals take the role of the other to define the meaning of the situation and understand the self-implications of different possible action alternatives. This enables them to select an action alternative that sustains or reconstructs a self-image (or 'Me') that is meaningful for them in light of the virtual reactions of others. This 'Me' is then 'incorporated into the individual's memory and becomes part of the self to be called up in future interactions' (Heimer & Matsueda, 1994, p. 367). Heimer and Matsueda's differential social control theory specifies five processes based on role-taking that could affect the likelihood that individuals select a delinquent action alternative in a given situation: (1) views of oneself as either a conformist or a deviant from the perspective of others; (2) expectations of how significant others would react to delinquent behaviour; (3) one's own attitudes towards delinquent behaviour, shared by one's reference groups and incorporated into the self; (4) associations with delinquent peers; and (5) habitual delinquent response tendencies that one has acquired by repeatedly resolving past situations with delinquent solutions. Heimer and Matsueda (1994) call their theory *differential* social control theory, because they recognise that significant others and reference groups may differ in their normative orientations and, therefore, that role-taking can both inhibit and facilitate delinquent behaviour.

Differential social control theory incorporates variables from other mainstream criminological theories (social control theory, learning theory and labelling theory in particular) but explains their effects on delinquency by reference to the role-taking process. Being strongly attached to conventional others (e.g. parents or teachers), for instance, should prevent delinquency as this increases the likelihood that one will adopt these others' attitudes towards the self, anticipate their disapproval and consider the potential consequences for one's self-image (Heimer & Matsueda, 1994). However, one may also identify with delinquent peers, look at the self from their perspective and forecast their approval or even admiration in adopting a delinquent line of action. As Heimer and Matsueda state, 'the likelihood of delinquency will depend on the relative efficacy of the two kinds of groups' (Heimer & Matsueda, 1994, p. 369). Differential social control theory also incorporates insights from labelling theory through the concept of 'reflected appraisals' (Matsueda, 1992). Parents, teachers and peers, and later the juvenile justice system, may react to initial acts of deviance ('primary deviance') by labelling the person in question (rather than their deeds) as 'bad' or 'evil'. Such appraisals may set off a criminogenic transformation of one's identity, so that one comes to view oneself as a bad kid or a troublemaker. Specifically, differential social control theory predicts that reflected appraisals of the self as a 'rule-violator' may increase the likelihood of future deviant behaviour in line with these views (i.e. 'secondary deviance'). To put it differently, under certain conditions, informal and formal control efforts may amplify rather than reduce delinquency. A considerable body of evidence supports hypotheses derived from differential social control theory (Heimer & Matsueda, 1994; Matsueda, 1992; Matsueda et al., 2020; Walters, 2016).

3.2.3 *Guilt and shame as role-taking emotions*

Differential social control theory explains delinquency by reference to the role-taking process. It is, however, an overly cognitive theory. Heimer and Matsueda do not discuss the role of emotions in self-monitoring and self-regulation. Role-taking is conceived of as a purely mental, disembodied process. This is not so surprising given that Mead too neglected the role of emotions in his analysis of the role-taking self (Turner, 2009). Mead stressed the cognitive capacity of human beings, declaring that 'self-consciousness rather than affective experience … provides the core and primary structure of the self, which is thus essentially a cognitive rather than an emotional phenomenon' (Mead, 1934, p. 173). It was Charles Horton Cooley, another pragmatist and contemporary of Mead, who stated more explicitly that evaluations of the self from the standpoint of others may be accompanied by 'self-feelings'. Specifically, in discussing his notion of the 'looking glass self', he points out that 'the imagination of our appearance to the other person' and 'the imagination of his or her judgment of that appearance' coincides with 'some sort of self-feeling, such as pride or mortification [shame]' (Cooley, 1902, p. 152).

Drawing upon the insights of Mead and Cooley, Shott (1979) was among the first to make explicit the emotional dimension of the role-taking process. She argues that certain emotions, which she calls 'role-taking emotions', simply cannot occur without putting oneself into the perspective of others. Shott identifies a specific set of 'reflexive role-taking emotions', comprising shame, guilt, embarrassment and pride. These emotions are self-directed and involve 'considering how one's self appears to others or the generalised other' (Shott, 1979, p. 1324). Reflexive role-taking emotions differ from empathic role-taking emotions which are other-directed (e.g. feeling compassion for someone else) and from primary emotions such as anger and fear which can be aroused without role-taking (e.g. as when one gets scared of a spider). Shott argues that reflexive role-taking emotions such as guilt and shame facilitate social control through self-control. This is so because they motivate people to regulate their own behaviour in accordance with social and moral norms even when others are not watching. Or, as Gecas (2006) puts it, 'feelings of guilt and shame check and punish deviant behaviour, making the individual him- or herself an ever-present critic and censor of his or her own behaviour' (p. 85).

Shott's work is important for highlighting that it is not simply by *cognitively* taking the perspective of others that social control turns into self-control. Through the role-taking emotions, individuals literally *feel* a dimension of their self-identity that emerges from – and is at stake in – their engagements with others. Without the compelling nature of emotions, the capacity to role-take would lose much of its effectiveness for social control. To illustrate this point, Shott refers to the capacity of successful con men to accurately understand and exploit the thoughts and feelings of their victims without suffering any guilt or shame. In other words, what Shott illustrates here is that 'taking' the attitude of the other does not necessarily mean 'adopting' or 'appropriating' the standpoint of the other as one's own (Turner, 1956). Crucially, it is the latter form of role-taking that is involved in guilt and shame. Put differently, in guilt and shame, the evaluations that others (might) make of us infiltrate and influence our own self-evaluations.

Although Shott emphasises the connection between internal self-evaluations and the (anticipated) reactions of others, she does not discuss what kinds of reactive attitudes are relevant to guilt and shame. According to Williams, both emotions are associated with different kinds of reactive attitudes of others:

> What arouses guilt in an agent is an act or omission of a sort that typically elicits from other people anger, resentment, or indignation. What the agent may offer in order to turn this away is reparation; he may also fear punishment or may inflict it on himself. What arouses shame, on the other hand, is something that typically elicits from others contempt or derision or avoidance. This may equally be an act or omission, but it need not be: it may be some failing or defect. It will lower the agent's self-respect and diminish him in his own eyes. (Williams, 1993, pp. 89-90)

The internal self-evaluations that are characteristic of guilt and shame are the counterparts to these (anticipated) external reactions. In guilt, the actual or anticipated anger, resentment or indignation of others go hand in hand with an evaluation of oneself as a wrongdoer (i.e. perceiving oneself as responsible for a harm or wrong) (Ferguson et al., 2007; Miceli & Castelfranchi, 2018). In shame, the actual or anticipated contempt, derision or avoidance of others go hand in hand with a self-evaluation of being inadequate or unwanted (Ferguson et al., 2007; Miceli & Castelfranchi, 2018). Put differently, in guilt, the reactive attitudes of others draw people's attention to what they did or could have done to prevent something from happening (i.e. one's doing), whereas in shame, they draw people's attention to something negative about the kind of person they are (one's being). In partial support of these ideas, research by Giner-Sorolla and Espinosa (2011) found that respondents anticipated more guilt when they imagined receiving angry reactions from their peers than when they imagined receiving disgusted reactions. Imagining disgusted reactions evoked more shame than guilt. A recent study by Sunar et al. (2016) found similar links between anger and guilt on the one hand and between contempt/disgust and shame on the other. Nevertheless, more research is needed to examine the associations between different kinds of self- and other-reactions in guilt and shame.

The social nature of guilt and shame is obvious when they are elicited by the reactions of actual other people or when they involve explicit or conscious thoughts about others. But individuals can also anticipate and/or experience guilt and shame when they sit in judgement on themselves, without having any concrete evaluative other in mind (Baldwin & Baccus, 2004; Deonna & Teroni, 2011). In this respect, it is worth recalling Mead's argument that the self becomes integrated as individuals begin to assume the attitudes of 'generalised others' over and beyond those of specific others (Mead, 1934). More specifically, according to Mead, people consolidate and absorb the standards they believe are common to the groups, organisations, communities and cultures in which they participate. Crucially, the perspective of the generalised other is both *internalised*, in the sense of being adopted by the individual who derives self-images from it, and *externalised*, in the sense of being imputed to a diffuse and generally unidentified set of other people (e.g. 'religious people', 'those like me', 'real men') (Holdsworth & Morgan, 2007). Mead's concept of the generalised other helps to explain how even the most 'private' instances of guilt and shame – those that do not involve thoughts about concrete identifiable others – still have a social referent. In Williams (1993) words, 'the other' may be 'abstracted and generalised and idealised, but he is potentially somebody rather than nobody, and somebody other than me' (p. 84).

3.2.4 *The role of prospective guilt and shame in the explanation of delinquency*

Having conceptualised guilt and shame as role-taking emotions, thereby elucidating their social nature, the next step is to specify their role in the explanation of offending. This can be done by integrating the work of Shott with Heimer and Matsueda's (1994) differential social control theory. Recall that the focus here is on prospective guilt and shame, that is, feelings of guilt and shame that are anticipated or felt *prior* to action initiation.

As discussed earlier, Heimer and Matsueda (1994) follow Mead in assuming that much of our daily behaviour occurs in a relatively spontaneous and automatic way, that is, with little or no immediate forethought or deliberation. In familiar situations, people rely on previously acquired patterns of thought and action of which they are typically not conscious in the moment. Heimer and Matsueda would agree with those who argue that everyday conformity is often a matter of unthinking habits and routines, rather than of deliberate choice (Bottoms, 2002). Besides, not only conformity but also delinquency can become 'automatic, scripted and habitual' (Heimer & Matsueda, 1994, p. 358). Seasoned offenders may no longer deliberate the moral implications – or any other (non-moral) consequences – of their deeds, especially when they operate in familiar circumstances. When individuals follow or break rules in an unreflective or habitual way, self-regulatory mechanisms such as prospective guilt and shame do not come into play.

According to Mead (1934), individuals become self-reflective when their habitual responses are not adequate to deal with a new situation or when they experience conflicting response tendencies. In situations of uncertainty or conflict, individuals have to imagine and consider alternative future lines of action. Following Mead, Heimer and Matsueda (1994) argue that role-taking enables individuals to extend the self beyond the experience of the present. That is, through their role-taking capacities, individuals can mediate or interpret different impulses to act in terms of others' probable responses and thereby become conscious of their meaning and consequences for the future self. In other words, individuals have the capacity to generate self-images of how they would look from the perspective of concrete and/or generalised others if they were to act in this way or another. This capacity to imaginatively rehearse alternative future possibilities creates the possibility to choose some action alternatives over others in function of the self that is inscribed in them. Whether individuals will come up with a delinquent solution to overcome a problematic situation, then, will partly depend on whether they can see and accept themselves as the kind of person who might possibly do such a thing.

Heimer and Matsueda did not discuss the emotional dimension of the role-taking processes that affect offending behaviour. Yet, as Shott's (1979, p. 1324) analysis suggests, guilt and shame may be the pre-eminent role-taking emotions relevant to the explanation of delinquency. When individuals evaluate the meaning and consequences of their imagined actions in terms of others' probable responses (i.e. normative expectations), a self-image or 'Me' results. In prospective guilt and shame, this self-image is affectively laden, and it signals a threat to one's (ethical) identity (Harris, 2011). More specifically, prospective guilt and shame imply an affectively laden image of oneself as a potential wrongdoer and a (morally) inadequate person, both in the eyes of oneself and in the eyes of (generalised) others. Emotional self-conceptions of this kind provide people with motivation to steer their behaviour in a different direction. In sum, by enabling people to vividly 'pre-feel' or 'pre-experience' their future self, prospective guilt and shame motivate and make meaningful efforts at self-regulation in the face of delinquent temptations.

Crucially, however, prospective guilt and shame do not render people incapable of violating norms; that is, they do not prevent people from having deviant desires and they do not guarantee that people will live up to normative expectations. They only indicate that people will experience inner tension and conflict if they fail to live up to them. Finally, it is important to emphasise that prospective guilt and shame do not necessarily motivate law-abiding behaviour. This depends on the normative orientations of one's reference groups. A mobster who feels tempted to cooperate with the police to receive a shorter sentence may refuse to do so because he experiences forward-looking guilt and shame for betraying his associates.

3.2.5 *Prospective guilt and shame: conceptual clarifications*

Finally, before concluding this chapter, the concept of 'prospective' guilt and shame deserves some further elaboration. Actually, the word 'prospective' is ambiguous between two different meanings in this context: (1) the prospect of feeling guilty and ashamed and (2) feelings of guilt and shame at the prospect of some future event or behaviour. Both possibilities can be explained in more detail using the work of Miceli and Castelfranchi (2015). According to these authors, prospective emotions can take different forms.

In the first place, prospective emotions can take the form of anticipated emotions (Miceli & Castelfranchi, 2015). Anticipated emotions are those emotions that one expects to feel in the future as a consequence of engaging in a particular course of action. So, while imaginatively projecting oneself into a delinquent course of action, one may anticipate one's own feelings of guilt and shame. Anticipated emotions are purely cognitive mental states; they contain no affective content (Loewenstein & Lerner, 2003). Criminologists who study the inhibiting effects of guilt and shame within a deterrence/rational choice model typically restrict their focus to anticipated guilt and shame (i.e. *beliefs* about future guilt and shame states). Their models assume that people dispassionately trade off future guilt and shame states against other expected costs and benefits associated with offending (see Section 3.1.1. for a critique of the rational choice model).

Second, prospective emotions can take the form of 'anticipated and felt' emotions (Miceli & Castelfranchi, 2015). This possibility has been largely overlooked in the criminological literature. In this case, one experiences a 'foretaste' of the emotion one anticipates to feel at a later point in time. Specifically,

> first, one has just a cognition about the emotion one will experience, and then, representing oneself in the post-choice situation, one 'pre-feels' what one will (presumably) feel at that future time. (Miceli & Castelfranchi, 2015, p. 197)

So, while imaginatively projecting oneself into a delinquent course of action, one may not just anticipate guilt or shame but also *pre-feel* these emotions. The whiff of guilt or shame that is pre-felt does not amount to a full-blown guilt or shame experience but foreshadows what this experience is likely to be.

Whereas anticipated guilt and shame states are purely cognitive mental states, 'anticipated and felt' guilt and shame states are affectively laden. This additional feature is important because, as Gerrans and Kennett (2010, 2017) convincingly argue, effectively projecting one*self* into a future scenario, that is, vividly inhabiting this scenario and feeling its personal significance, requires infusing mental representations with affective content.[9] Differently put, images of the self in a future situation become personally meaningful insofar as they are accompanied by self-feelings. From this perspective, imagining oneself in a future situation and merely *thinking* about the guilt or shame one would experience without actually *feeling* these emotions would be a rather abstract and impersonal exercise. Whereas this type of imagination provides the subject with information, it does so in a motivationally neutral way. Guilt and shame states that are both anticipated and pre-felt

9 In fact, Gerrans and Kennett (2010, 2017) go as far as to argue that individuals who lack the ability to integrate mental simulations of possible futures with affective content, that is, individuals who cannot *feel* the future, have a diminished sense of self and are therefore compromised in their (moral) agency.

should have a stronger inhibitory effect on delinquency. Indeed, 'the cognitive anticipation of the emotional reaction, when tinged with an affective element, is experienced as more compelling, thereby acquiring a stronger motivating power' (Miceli & Castelfranchi, 2015, p. 198).

Actually, anticipated and felt emotions come in two variants according to Miceli and Castelfranchi (2015). There is the variant just described, in which the anticipatory representation of an emotion produces a pre-feeling of that emotion. But there is also a second variant, in which an anticipated behaviour *directly* elicits an emotional response, and this experienced emotion 'tells' the individual what they will probably feel when the behaviour materialises. In other words, here a feeling induces the anticipatory representation of an emotion rather than the other way around, as with the first variant. So, while anticipating a delinquent course of action, one may instantly feel guilty or ashamed about one's own intentions. These feelings, in turn, are the evidence on which one grounds their thoughts about the future guilt or shame states they will experience when following through with these intentions. When guilt and shame states are first felt and then anticipated, they fulfil a 'pre-monitory' function (Miceli & Castelfranchi, 2015). Both 'anticipated-and-felt' and 'felt-and-anticipated' emotions fit less well into traditional deterrence/rational choice models of offending because they are not merely expected consequences of the decision to offend. Rather, they are felt during the decision-making process itself, and they influence the state-of-mind in which the consequences of the decision are evaluated.

A final interesting possibility discussed by Miceli and Castelfranchi (2015) occurs when the anticipation of an emotion arouses the experience of an emotion that is qualitatively different from the one that is anticipated. In fact, it is sometimes assumed that the prospect of experiencing painful emotions such as guilt and shame induces *fear* in people and that 'the fear of experiencing these pains … is able to restrain individuals from engaging in crime' (Svensson et al., 2013, p. 33). However, it is a mistake to think that the 'deterrent' effects of anticipated guilt and shame are entirely explicable in terms of fear. This is so because guilt and shame, regardless of whether they are forward- or backward-looking, involve a self-evaluative component that is absent in pure fear. Given that, it is more plausible that the inhibiting effects of anticipated guilt and shame are buttressed by *pre-felt* guilt and shame rather than only fear. As Kristjánsson (2006) explains with respect to shame (but his reasoning applies equally well to the case of guilt):

> In forward-looking shame, I do more than experience an emotion of fear of what may/will happen if I follow a certain course of action or reaction; rather, I am filled with shame at the recognition that if I really found myself in the circumstances which I am imagining, I might, possibly, succumb to the temptation in question, for instance, that of betraying a member of my own

> family for financial gain. It is this forward-looking shame, this prior identification with the shame of the proposed action or reaction, which (among other things) deters me from ever doing such a vile thing; it is not only the fear that if I decide to betray my relative, I will feel bad about it afterwards. (p. 114)

3.3 CONCLUSION

The aim of this chapter was to develop a theoretical framework for understanding the social nature of prospective guilt and shame and their role in the explanation of crime and delinquency. Following Shott (1979), prospective guilt and shame were conceptualised as anticipatory self-evaluative reactions elicited through a process of reflexive role-taking. That is, they are negative evaluations of a future course of action, felt and directed towards oneself as a result of one's anticipation of the negative response of others towards oneself. These 'others' can be specific identifiable persons or groups (e.g. 'my friends'), but they can also extend to more abstract communities of which the person desires to be a part (e.g. 'real men'). Crucially, in prospective guilt and shame, we *share* the anticipated responses of others. That is, we react to ourselves as we believe relevant others would react to us. Prospective guilt and shame, then, are a matter not only of our own self-evaluations or the (anticipated) evaluations of others but also of the connection between both.

Prospective guilt and shame are important factors in explaining why people do not commit criminal or delinquent acts. Rather than being just one cost among others in a rational calculus or the mere by-product of internalised norms, they play a unique role in motivating self-regulation. Prospective guilt and shame are emotional self-conceptions that act as warning signals. They warn us that an intended behaviour may have important negative consequences for who we are, both in our own eyes and in the eyes of our reference groups. Prospective guilt and shame encourage us to steer our behaviour in a different direction, even when others are not looking.

The symbolic interactionist framework that is proposed here has important implications for understanding individual differences in prospective guilt and shame. More specifically, this framework emphasises the social origins of these differences. It invites us to look at the various perspectives through which individuals may view and evaluate themselves, and it directs us towards the social embeddedness of these perspectives. In the next chapter, I will draw upon this framework to formulate empirically testable hypotheses about the social factors that might contribute to individual and gender differences in prospective guilt and shame for engaging in delinquency.

4 Individual and Gender Differences in Prospective Guilt and Shame: Where Do They Come From?

> All kinds of groupings, with great variations in size, composition, and structure, may become reference groups. Of greatest importance for most people are those groups in which they participate directly – what have been called membership groups – especially those containing a number of persons with whom one stands in a primary relationship. But in some transactions one may assume the perspective attributed to some social category – a social class, an ethnic group, those in a given community, or those concerned with some special interest.
> (Shibutani, 1955, p. 565)

A growing body of empirical research indicates that prospective guilt and shame can prevent adolescents from committing delinquent acts (Matsuda et al., 2013; Melde & Esbensen, 2011; Rebellon et al., 2010; Svensson et al., 2013). It has also been found that levels of prospective guilt and shame are higher among female adolescents than among their male adolescents, and some studies suggest that this may explain a substantial part of the gender gap in delinquency (Rebellon et al., 2015, 2016). These findings raise an important question that has received very little attention in the literature: how to explain individual and gender differences in prospective guilt and shame during adolescence? Answering this question is important, not only for better understanding the link between these emotions and offending in general but also for further clarifying the (gendered) nature of social control.

Following a symbolic interactionist approach to emotions (Shott, 1979) and delinquency (Heimer & Matsueda, 1994), I have argued in the previous chapter that prospective guilt and shame are anticipatory self-evaluative reactions elicited through a process of reflexive role-taking. This process involves seeing oneself and reacting to one's (intended) actions as if from the perspective of others. Hence, to understand differences in prospective guilt and shame for engaging in delinquency, we must look at the different perspectives from which adolescents may see and evaluate themselves when they encounter a delinquent opportunity. In this chapter, I will identify some of these perspectives and discuss how they might influence guilt and shame. The aim is to generate a set of empirically testable hypotheses about the social sources of individual and gender differences in levels of prospective guilt and shame.

As Heimer and Matsueda (1994) argue, role-taking is not a random process but one that is 'conditioned by the broader social organization in which it is embedded' (p. 322). Individuals are likely to assume the perspective of significant others and important reference groups with which they identify. In what follows, I will first look at what are widely considered to be the three most influential reference groups in which adolescents participate and in which they develop and maintain their sense of self: the family, the school and the peer group. In addition, I will look at a group that, despite losing some of its relevance in secularised Western Europe, continues to provide many, mostly ethnic minority adolescents with a powerful perspective for self-monitoring and self-evaluation: the religious group. Finally, I will look at a perspective that is not associated with a concretely identifiable group but rather with a social category: gender. More specifically, I will discuss how societal gender expectations and gender norms may affect prospective guilt and shame among adolescents.

4.1 The family and the school

During adolescence, young people typically spend a major part of their time in two institutions of 'conventional' socialisation: the family and the school. No wonder, then, that these two contexts play such a significant role in the development of their sense of self and identity (Brinthaupt & Lipka, 2002; Crocetti et al., 2017; Verhoeven et al., 2019). Actually, the position of most adolescents in society is such that they cannot escape being a particular kind of 'son' or 'daughter' in relation to their parents and a particular kind of 'student' in relation to their teachers. As they participate in family and school life, adolescents quickly realise that parents and teachers have certain expectations of them and that these must be fulfilled in order for them to maintain a positively valued identity (e.g. as a 'good daughter' in the family or a 'decent student' in the school). Engaging in delinquency, as the social control theorists have unceasingly pointed out, is typically not among these expectations (Heimer & Matsueda, 1994; Hirschi, 1969; Matza, 1964; Sampson & Laub, 1993). Hence, if adolescents evaluate themselves in terms of the anticipated reactions of their parents and teachers at the thought of engaging in delinquency, prospective shame-guilt may follow and signal a threat to the identity that binds them as a self to these others.

In their theory of differential social control, Heimer and Matsueda (1994) argue that the probability that parents and teachers will serve as a 'generalised other' in delinquent situations depends on how *committed* adolescents are to their roles and associated role identities in the family and the school. Following Burke and Reitzes (1991), they distinguish between a cognitive source of commitment, which refers to the anticipated rewards associated with the role-identity (e.g. good job prospects for good students), and a socioemotional source of commitment, which refers to the interpersonal attachments that sustain the role-identity (e.g. good-quality ties with parents and teachers).[10] The socioemotional source of commitment, in the form of interpersonal attachments, should be the most relevant to prospective guilt and shame. So far, only one study by Svensson et al. (2016) has examined how interpersonal attachments may affect moral emotions in relation to offending. They found that changes in adolescents' attachments to parents and teachers indeed predicted changes in their anticipated feelings of guilt and shame for engaging in delinquency.

In light of the above, it is hypothesised here that levels of prospective guilt and shame for engaging in delinquency will be higher among adolescents who are more strongly committed to conventional role identities in the family and the school, as implied by their closer ties with parents and teachers. In addition, it is hypothesised that levels of prospective shame-guilt will be higher among female adolescents than among male adolescents in part because the former maintain closer ties with their parents (e.g. more intense parent-child communication, closer monitoring etc.) (Keijsers & Poulin, 2013; Svensson, 2004; Weerman et al., 2016; Worthen, 2011).

4.2 PEERS AND FRIENDS

Next to the family and the school, the peer group is undoubtedly the third critical context in which young people develop their sense of self and identity. In fact, as they grow into adolescence, young people increasingly spend time with their peers rather than with their parents (Lam et al., 2014; Larson et al., 1996). They also become increasingly sensitive to peer influence (Brown, 2004; Gardner & Steinberg, 2005; Somerville, 2013). In this light, it is perhaps not surprising that criminological research has consistently documented the influence of delinquent peers on adolescents' own delinquent involvement (see Hoeben et al., 2016; McGloin & Thomas, 2019, for recent reviews of the literature).

Heimer and Matsueda's differential social control theory differs from Hirschi's social control theory in acknowledging the causal role of deviant peer influence in offending (Heimer & Matsueda, 1994). According to Hirschi, the association between peer delinquency and individual delinquency is spurious; youngsters who are already delinquent themselves are simply more likely to select similar peers. Differential social control theory, by contrast, while not denying the existence of peer selection effects,

10 In this respect, Heimer and Matsueda's differential social control theory is compatible with Hirschi's (1969) social control theory. Many traditional social bonding variables can be seen as indicators of role commitment.

proposes that peers influence delinquency both *directly*, by pointing out opportunities and providing motives, and *indirectly*, by serving as a generalised other (even if they are not actually present in the situation). In the latter case, the normative perspective that is imputed to the peer group serves as a frame of reference for the evaluation of self and behaviour. Crucially, from an interactionist perspective, normative influence comes from adolescents' *perceptions* of what their friends think and do, even if these perceptions are not always accurate.[11] So far, only one study has examined how (perceived) peer delinquency affects moral emotions in relation to offending. In the earlier-mentioned longitudinal study by Svensson et al. (2016), it was found that perceived peer delinquency predicted lower levels of anticipated guilt and shame during adolescence. Given these findings, it is hypothesised here that adolescents who perceive their friends to be engaged in delinquency will experience lower levels of prospective shame-guilt for offending. In addition, it is hypothesised that levels of prospective shame-guilt will be higher among female adolescents than among male adolescents due to less exposure to delinquent peers (Rebellon et al., 2016; Weerman et al., 2016).

At this point, one may wonder how adolescents manage potential inconsistencies between their conventional role identities, formed and sustained through ties with parents and teachers, and the identity they shape through affiliations with (delinquent) friends. Pathological cases aside, people usually do not possess multiple identities that are characterised by completely opposing values and norms. Do adolescents abandon their conventional roles as their identification with a delinquent peer group increases? As Matza (1964) has sharply observed, this is seldom the case. Although breaches in the relationship with parents and teachers may and do occur, it is rare that adolescents become completely insulated from both the family and the school.[12] Many adolescents are clearly capable of taking up both conventional and delinquent roles intermittently without suffering from dissociative identity disorder. The key to understanding this, according to Matza (1964), is to see that peer groups rarely foster oppositional norms that *require* one's involvement in delinquency. Rather, they introduce and reinforce neutralisations that *justify* or *excuse* the commission of particular delinquent acts under specific circumstances (see Sykes &

---

11 Recent studies using social network data have found that adolescents' perceptions of their peers' delinquency are not always accurate and that especially those who engage in delinquency themselves tend to overestimate how prevalent delinquency is among their peers (e.g. Boman & Ward, 2014; Young et al., 2011). To some, this might suggest that perceptual measures of peer delinquency are inadequate and that researchers should rather use 'direct' measures (i.e. obtained from the peers themselves) to examine normative influence. However, as McGloin and Thomas (2019, p.250) point out, 'by choosing to operationalise peer deviance based on what peers self-report rather than what subjects believe to be their behavior or attitudes, one runs the risk of theoretical misspecification and treating adolescents as objects that are uninvolved in their own social lives.'

12 Recent studies using space-time budget data confirm Matza's observation that most young offenders actively participate in a wide variety of conventional activities most of the time (Wikström et al., 2012).

Matza, 1957). Adolescents may for instance agree that fighting and stealing are generally wrong, while simultaneously condoning such behaviours in specific circumstances (e.g. taking small things from a store once for fun or fighting in response to threats or insults). Through the use of neutralisations or rationalisations, adolescents can reconcile their wrongdoings with their conventional identity and assuage (prospective) feelings of guilt and shame. In addition, Matza (1964) emphasises that the values that are cultivated in the peer group and that motivate much delinquency (e.g. a search for thrills, toughness and status) are not opposite to those of conventional society. Rather, they are 'subterranean values' that are still widely recognised and accepted and that coexist alongside the publicly proclaimed values (Matza & Sykes, 1961).

4.3 Reflected appraisals as a 'troublemaker' by parents, teachers and friends

Symbolic interactionist theories of delinquency are unique in emphasising that informal labelling processes by parents, teachers and peers may negatively influence adolescents' self-identities and thereby facilitate their involvement into delinquent behaviour (Heimer & Matsueda, 1994; Matsueda, 1992). That is, parents, teachers and/or peers may begin to apply labels such as 'troublemaker' or 'rule-violator' to adolescents who do not show the manners and behaviour that are expected of them. Such informal labelling can occur in the absence of formal labelling by the police and the criminal justice system (Matsueda, 1992). In fact, because it typically occurs in the environments where they spend most of their time, informal labelling by significant others may be more consequential for adolescents' self-identities than formal labelling by official authorities.

Following a symbolic interactionist perspective, Matsueda (1992) has argued that informal labelling by significant others may impact an individual's self-identity in the form of reflected appraisals. Reflected appraisals are an individual's perceptions of how the self is appraised or evaluated by others.[13] Consistent with labelling theory, differential social control theory predicts that adolescents who begin to see themselves as troublemakers from the perspective of significant others will become more likely to engage in behaviour consistent with these reflected appraisals (Heimer & Matsueda, 1994). In line with these predictions, longitudinal research has found that reflected appraisals as a troublemaker increase the likelihood of subsequent delinquency, independent of prior delinquency and other risk factors (Bartusch & Matsueda, 1996; De Coster & Lutz, 2018; Heimer & Matsueda, 1994; Lee et al., 2017; Walters, 2016).

13 There need not be a one-to-one correspondence between reflected appraisals and actual appraisals; 'reflected appraisals are a selective perception of others' actual appraisals' (Matsueda, 1992, p. 1586).

Prospective shame-guilt may be one of the mechanisms through which reflected appraisals influence delinquency. Recall that prospective guilt and shame warn people that a given course of action threatens their identity, both in their own eyes and in the eyes of others. However, if adolescents already view themselves as troublemakers from the perspective of others, delinquent behaviour may pose less of a threat. In fact, delinquent behaviour would be consistent with this deviant identity. Hence, it is hypothesised here that reflected appraisals as a troublemaker will be associated with lower levels of prospective guilt and shame for engaging in delinquency. Research suggests that male adolescents are more likely than their female counterparts to be labelled as troublemakers by significant others and more likely to develop reflected appraisals as a troublemaker, even when taking into account gender differences in prior delinquency (De Coster & Lutz, 2018; Zhang, 1997). It is therefore also hypothesised that levels of prospective guilt and shame will be higher among female adolescents than among male adolescents in part because the former are less likely to view themselves as a troublemaker from the perspective of others (i.e. parents, teachers and peers).

The concept of reflected appraisals discussed here has an interesting connection to the concept of shaming as discussed in Braithwaite's reintegrative shaming theory (Braithwaite, 1989). According to Braithwaite (1989, 2018), some degree of social disapproval or shaming is inevitable if societies want to prevent offending, but it has to be of the right kind. Braithwaite famously distinguished between two types of shaming: reintegrative and disintegrative. Reintegrative shaming involves disapproval of the wrongdoing, while still treating the wrongdoer respectfully as a good person. This type of shaming sustains social bonds and builds conscience and should therefore help to prevent subsequent offending. Disintegrative shaming, by contrast, involves stigmatising and labelling the wrongdoer as a 'bad person'. This type of shaming is likely to make things worse because it further alienates the wrongdoer. From the perspective of Braithwaite's theory, reflected appraisals can be conceived of as reflecting the kind of shaming that individuals experience in their immediate environment. More specifically, reflected appraisals as a 'troublemaker' or 'rule-violator' can be conceived of as indicators of (perceived) stigmatic shaming, because such appraisals target the identity of the whole person rather than a specific act.

In a refinement of reintegrative shaming theory, Braithwaite and colleagues have explicated the connection between the two types of shaming and the shame-related emotions (Ahmed et al., 2001). They argue that reintegrative shaming – because it is carried out in a respectful and restorative way – encourages wrongdoers to acknowledge guilt and shame for what they have done. When wrongdoers are shamed in a stigmatising way, by contrast, they will lose their interest in acknowledging guilt and shame, because they have already lost their status in the eyes of others. Evidence consistent with these propositions comes from a study conducted by Harris (2001, 2006). He found that drink-driving offenders who felt stigmatised during court cases and restorative justice conferences were less likely to acknowledge guilt and shame about their actions. Braithwaite and colleagues were mainly interested in understanding the effects of reintegration and stigmatisation on offenders' *retrospective* feelings of guilt and shame (i.e. after the offence). However, when applied to *prospective* feelings of guilt and shame, their hypotheses are similar to those suggested here, namely that perceptions of being stigmatised by significant others (i.e. reflected appraisals as a troublemaker) will be associated with lower levels of guilt and shame for future offending.

4.4 THE RELIGIOUS GROUP OR COMMUNITY

Although not a majority, a significant number of adolescents and young adults in most Western Europe identifies with a religious group, usually some form of Christianity or Islam (Bullivant, 2018). In Belgium, as in other Western European countries, religious affiliation is closely intertwined with ethnicity. Most adolescents who identify as Christian are ethnic majority youth, whereas those who identify as Muslim are usually ethnic minority youth of Turkish or Moroccan descent (Van Droogenbroeck & Spruyt, 2014).

There are good reasons to suggest that religious adolescents may face a higher threat of guilt and shame when considering future delinquent acts than their nonreligious counterparts. Religiosity may affect offence-related guilt and shame indirectly, through some of the other factors already discussed in this chapter. First, as religion is typically transmitted within the family, religious adolescents may have stronger ties with their parents. In other words, one's religious identity could strengthen one's conventional role-identity in the family (and vice versa). Second, religious adolescents may be more likely to affiliate with like-minded friends, while avoiding the company of delinquent peers (who could otherwise serve as a pro-delinquent generalised other). However, religiosity may also have additional effects on prospective guilt and shame that are not captured by these parent- and peer-related factors. Almost all religions provide norms that prescribe and proscribe certain behaviours. As several researchers have pointed out, these religious norms can support and complement secular moral norms against delinquent behaviour (Brauer et al., 2013; Cochran, 1988; Sumter et al., 2018). Particularly important from an interactionist perspective are the intersubjective dynamics through which religiosity might enhance commitment to moral norms (and foster guilt and shame for norm violations). Two such dynamics are identified and discussed here: one is a sense of relationship with a supernatural being and the other is a sense of embeddedness in a larger religious group or community.

Perhaps the thing that makes religion truly unique as a source of identity is that a religious person can adopt the perspective of a supernatural being or 'divine significant other' (e.g. God or Allah or Yahweh). Research indicates that across many religious belief systems these supernatural beings are conceived of as all-knowing, ever-present and especially preoccupied with human behaviour in the moral domain (Bering & Johnson, 2005; Purzycki, 2013). According to McCullough and Willoughby (2009), the perceived presence of, interaction with and inescapable monitoring by supernatural entities should foster self-monitoring. Baumeister et al. (2010, p. 76) add that the 'the assumption of being watched by a divine being also invokes the values and expectations of that being.' This could make religious adolescents more prone to prospective guilt and shame when contemplating behaviour that violates these expectations.

Self-monitoring and self-evaluation from the perspective of a divine being are not the only processes through which religiosity may heighten prospective shame-guilt. Following Durkheim (1951), scholars have emphasised that religiosity is a fundamentally social phenomenon in the sense that religion binds individuals into moral communities (Graham & Haidt, 2010; Stark, 1996). By this view, the normative force of religion does not derive so much from personal beliefs and practices as from the embeddedness of religious individuals in broader communities (that extend beyond the family). As Stark (1996) writes,

> the idea here is that religion is empowered to produce conformity to the norms as it is sustained through interaction and accepted by the majority as a valid basis for action. (p. 164)

In short, the religious group or community with whom adolescents affiliate could serve as a powerful generalised other and source of control in delinquent situations.

If, following the moral community perspective, the effects of religion on people's thoughts, feelings and behaviour depend on the extent to which religiousness is ratified by the social environment, then we might expect to find some differences in levels of prospective shame-guilt between Christian and Muslim adolescents in Western Europe. Compared to the largely secularised Christian majority which treats religion as a private or personal matter, Muslim ethnic minorities are more likely to live in close-knit communities where religion pervades many aspects of daily life (Gungor et al., 2011; Junger & Polder, 1993; Serajzadeh, 2001). It has also been shown that Muslim youth experience higher levels of social pressure for religious conformity than Christian youth (Van Droogenbroeck & Spruyt, 2020). In sum, following the moral community perspective, it can be hypothesised that levels of prospective guilt and shame for engaging in delinquency will be higher among Muslim adolescents than among Christian adolescents, regardless of their individual religious beliefs and practices.

To date, only two quantitative studies provide some empirical evidence regarding the effects of being religious on offence-related feelings of guilt and shame and both were conducted in the United States. Grasmick et al. (1991) found that adults who scored higher on two measures of religiosity – religious service attendance and perceived importance of religion in one's life – perceived a considerably higher threat of guilt and shame when considering future tax evasion. Spivak et al. (2011) observed that university students who endorsed statements such as 'the Bible is the literal word of God' and 'problem drinkers are sinning against god' were more likely to anticipate guilt and shame for violating the campus alcohol policy. No quantitative studies were found that examined whether religiosity influences offence-related guilt and shame among Western European adolescents. Some preliminary qualitative evidence comes from a Dutch study of cultural differences in adolescents' attitudes towards theft and violence. Through individual and group interviews, de Boer (2008) observed that adolescents of Moroccan and Turkish origin, unlike native Dutch adolescents, frequently referred to religious rules when explaining their strong moral disapproval of theft. In explaining their attitudes towards violence, by contrast, they made much less reference to religion. Unlike violence, theft is one of the seven 'Hudud' offences for which punishments are explicitly described in the Quran and the Hadith (al-Thakeb & Scott, 1981).[14]

Summarising the above, it is hypothesised that levels of prospective guilt and shame for engaging in delinquency will be higher among religious than among nonreligious adolescents. In addition, it is hypothesised that levels of prospective shame-guilt will be higher among Muslim adolescents than among Christian and nonreligious adolescents, especially when it comes to theft.

4.5 TRADITIONAL GENDER ROLE NORMS

As Shibutani (1955, p. 565) notes, individuals may not only assume the perspective of the 'membership groups' in which they participate directly (e.g. the family, the school, the peer group and the religious community) but also the perspective attributed to some social category to which they belong, such as social class or gender. Gender is arguably one of the most well-recognised social categories and also one that is particularly salient during adolescence (Galambos et al., 2009). With the onset of puberty, adolescents become increasingly aware of prevailing gender role norms and expectations in society (Chandra-Mouli et al., 2017; Kågesten et al., 2016). Gender role norms describe 'ways in which males and females are expected to appear, believe and act in general, regardless of the specific others with whom they are interacting' (Thoits & Virshup, 1997, p. 124). Societal gender

14 Hudud offences are crimes against the rights of Allah and therefore among the most serious and most severely punished offences in Islamic law. Aside from theft, the other Hudud offences are: sexual intercourse outside marriage, accusing a person of adultery without adequate evidence, apostasy from the Islamic religion, drinking alcohol in public, highway robbery, and defying the Imam or the religious and political authority (see al-Thakeb & Scott, 1981).

expectations may serve as a gendered generalised other (or 'gen(d)eralised other') from which adolescents look at themselves and their behaviour (Lucas & Steimel, 2009). As ideals of manhood and womanhood can differ for men and women of different social classes and ethnic groups, there exist multiple masculinities and femininities (Connell & Messerschmidt, 2005). The focus here is on *traditional* gender role norms and expectations more broadly defined. Whereas traditional masculinity typically emphasises autonomy, assertiveness, competition, status and anti-femininity for men, traditional femininity emphasises being attractive, communally oriented, sensitive, domestic and nurturing for women (Mahalik et al., 2005; Schrock & Schwalbe, 2009).

As delinquency is generally considered to be more inconsistent with traditional femininity than with traditional masculinity, endorsement of traditional gender roles may be a protective factor against delinquency for female adolescents but not for male adolescents (Heimer, 1996; Heimer et al., 2006). In fact, it has been found that traditional masculinity may even serve to encourage and justify certain types of delinquency such as violence (e.g. McCarry, 2010; Messerschmidt, 1993; Sundaram, 2016). Research suggests that anticipated feelings of guilt and shame may be mechanisms through which traditional gender norms regulate delinquent behaviour. Finley and Grasmick (1985), for instance, found that females who endorsed a traditionally feminine gender orientation were more likely to anticipate guilt when contemplating crime than less traditional females. Ford et al. (2002) found that adolescents anticipated experiencing more self-critical affect (such as guilt, shame and regret) for engaging in delinquent acts socially defined as highly inconsistent with the expectations for their gender than for engaging in less gender-inconsistent delinquent acts. An example of a delinquent act that was found to be relatively low in gender inconsistency for males was 'driving faster than the speed limit in a suburban neighbourhood', and an example of a delinquent act that was found to be relatively low in gender inconsistency for females was 'using the dressing room in a department store to steal clothes'.

Based on the above, it can be hypothesised that traditional femininity will be associated with higher levels of prospective guilt and shame for engaging in delinquency among female adolescents. In addition, it can be hypothesised that this association will be stronger for violence than for theft, as the former is generally considered to be more inconsistent with traditional femininity than the latter. As traditional masculinity encourages males to be assertive, tough, dominant and daring, it can be hypothesised that traditional masculinity will be associated with lower levels of prospective guilt and shame among male adolescents. In addition, it can be hypothesised that this association will be stronger for violence than for theft, as the former is generally considered to be more consistent with traditional masculinity than the latter.

4.6 SUMMARY OF THE HYPOTHESES

In summary, based on the theoretical framework outlined above, the following hypotheses are proposed regarding the social factors that may contribute to individual and gender differences in prospective, offence-related guilt and shame:

H1: Levels of prospective guilt and shame for engaging in delinquency will be higher among male adolescents and female adolescents who experience closer relationships with their parents.

H2: Levels of prospective guilt and shame for engaging in delinquency will be higher among male adolescents and female adolescents who have more supportive relationships with their teachers.

H3: Levels of prospective guilt and shame for engaging in delinquency will be lower among male adolescents and female adolescents who perceive their friends to be involved in delinquent activities.

H4: Levels of prospective guilt and shame will be lower among male adolescents and female adolescents who see themselves as a 'troublemaker' or 'rule-violator' from the perspective of parents, teachers and friends.

H5: Gender differences in levels of prospective guilt and shame for engaging in delinquency will be at least partially mediated by gender differences in attachments to parents and teachers, perceived friends' delinquency and reflected appraisals as a 'troublemaker'.

H6: Levels of prospective guilt and shame for engaging in delinquency will be higher among religious adolescents than among nonreligious adolescents.

H7: Levels of prospective guilt and shame for engaging in delinquency will be higher among Muslim adolescents than among Christian adolescents, especially when it comes to theft.

H8: Prospective guilt and shame will be differentially associated with traditional gender role attitudes for male adolescents and female adolescents. More specifically, adherence to traditional masculinity norms will be associated with less prospective shame-guilt among males, whereas adherence to traditional femininity will be associated with more prospective shame-guilt among females. These effects will be stronger for violence than for theft.

The empirical study conducted to test these hypotheses is described in the next three chapters.

5 Data and Methods

> If talking about our mental processes with an interviewer is like describing a criminal suspect to a sketch artist, then answering survey questions is like picking the suspect out of a lineup. The latter is much less cognitively demanding and potentially much more accurate, provided the right choices are in the lineup.
> (Vaisey, 2009, p. 1689)

This chapter provides detailed information on the data and methods used to examine the hypotheses outlined in the previous chapter. I start by describing the research design and the sampling method, followed by the design of the questionnaire and the operationalisation of the dependent and independent variables. I then go on to discuss the statistical techniques that were used to analyse the data: confirmatory factor analysis, multiple regression analysis and path analysis. Finally, I address two methodological concerns: (1) the need to move beyond the dichotomous decision-making of null hypothesis significance testing and (2) causality.

5.1 Research design

Symbolic interactionism is typically described as a theoretical perspective that favours qualitative research methods. Contrary to what is often assumed, however, the pragmatist epistemology that underlies symbolic interactionism does not exclude the use of quantitative research methods (Ulmer & Wilson, 2003). The method should be determined by the purpose of the study. And for some purposes, quantitative methods such as surveys or experiments may be preferable to ethnographic observations or interviews.

Following the work of Matsueda and others (Heimer & Matsueda, 1994; Matsueda, 1992; Matsueda et al., 2020), the symbolic interactionist framework that underpins this study assumes that meanings, selves and emotions are socially patterned in a way that makes them amenable to quantitative analysis. To unearth these patterns – which are reflected in the study's hypotheses – a quantitative survey method was applied. As Ulmer and Wilson point out, survey methods are 'particularly useful for gaining information about things that researchers cannot measure by outside observation' (2003, p. 535). This definitely applies to many of the constructs of interest in this study, which include perceptions and emotions. Furthermore, surveys enable the efficient collection of information from a large and diverse sample of individuals (which was needed for this study in order to examine a wide range of social factors that might affect prospective guilt and shame). Finally, surveys can offer respondents privacy and anonymity, which is an advantage when dealing with sensitive issues such as delinquency (Tourangeau & Yan, 2007).

Ideally, this study's hypotheses should be tested using a longitudinal panel design. This would allow for an assessment of the temporal relationships between the social factors under study and the outcome. Indeed, the theoretical framework assumes that (gender) differences in factors such as the parent-adolescent relationship, associations with delinquent friends, and informal labelling processes precede (gender) differences in prospective guilt and shame. Unfortunately, a longitudinal design was not feasible within the time and budget constraints of this research.

By coincidence, another PhD researcher at the Leuven Institute of Criminology was running a study on youth violence at the same time as the present study. She had already selected a cross-sectional sample of school-going adolescents in the city of Genk for the purpose of administering a self-report survey (Verdonck, 2017). Given that both projects were targeting the same population and that they were sufficiently related in terms of content, we decided to design the survey together and cooperate for the data collection. Unfortunately, because of a difference in timing between the two projects, the design of the survey and the collection of the data had to take place before the theoretical framework of the present study was fully developed. As a consequence, some of the questions included in the survey were not fully tailored to the theoretical constructs of interest.

The content of the survey was partly based on the 'Youth School Monitor 2013', a questionnaire designed by the Flemish Youth Research Platform to collect information about the conditions, attitudes and behaviours of school-going adolescents in Flanders (Bradt et al., 2014).[15] This questionnaire – developed in cooperation with the Research Line on Youth Criminology at the Leuven Institute of Criminology – included several useful and validated measures of sociodemographic characteristics, involvement in delinquency, and established correlates of delinquency (e.g. parenting and peer delinquency). Other measures specific to the theoretical framework of the present study were taken from other sources. A detailed discussion of all relevant measures and their sources can be found below in Section 5.3.

At the time of this study, asking for ethical approval was not yet commonplace for non-interventional observational studies among adolescents. As the study raised no major ethical issues, ethical approval was not sought.

15 The Youth Research Platform is an interdisciplinary centre for research on youth funded by the Flemish Government.

5.2 SAMPLE

Selecting a representative sample of adolescents was not necessary for the purpose of the present study. It was necessary, however, to come up with a sample containing sufficient variation on the variables of interest to allow for the testing of the hypotheses. Cities are typically more diverse in terms of their population composition than are small towns, villages or rural areas. Flanders has two large cities (Antwerp and Ghent) and 11 smaller regional cities. Because schools in Antwerp and Ghent are typically overburdened with requests for involvement in research, the regional city of Genk was chosen as the study site (Verdonck, 2017). Genk is a city of about 66,000 inhabitants located in the east of Flanders (Belgium). Despite being relatively small in size, it is one of the most important industrial cities of Flanders. Because of its rich mining history, Genk is a social and cultural melting pot with more than 100 different nationalities living together. According to the latest figures, about 65% of the city population hails has non-Belgian origins. Italians form the largest foreign community in Genk, followed by the Dutch, the Turks, the Moroccans and the Greeks (Figure 5.1).

Figure 5.1 Location of Genk within Flanders (Belgium)

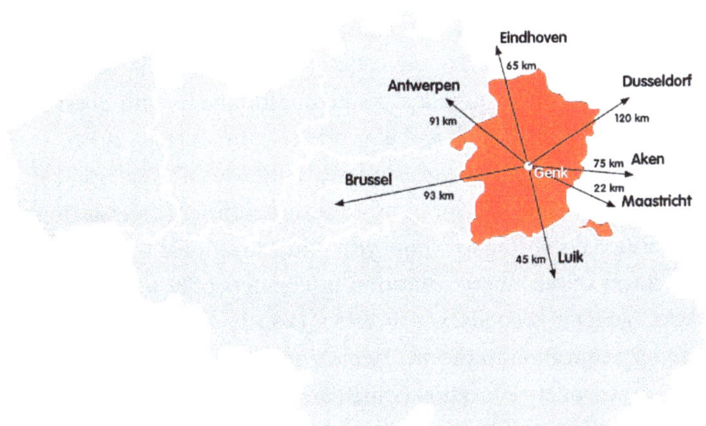

Participants for the study were selected according to a two-stage sampling process. In the first stage, all 11 schools in Genk providing mainstream secondary education were contacted and invited to participate.[16] A total of seven schools agreed to participate, six of which provide full-time secondary education and one that provides alternate learning (combination of learning and working). Three schools explicitly refused to participate, mainly due to time limitations (some of them were already engaged in other research projects). One school ignored all calls and e-mails from the research team. Schools' refusal to participate was not a random process. All four refusing schools were (mainly) offering 'general' secondary education, an educational track that prepares pupils for pursuing higher education. As a consequence, students from this educational track are underrepresented in the sample (see *infra*). However, this is not problematic for the purpose of the present study.

Mainstream secondary education in Flanders is subdivided in three stages. The first stage covers lower secondary education and comprises two years. The second and third stages cover upper secondary education. Whereas the second stage comprises two years, the third stage comprises either two or three years, depending on the educational track.[17] For both substantial and practical reasons, it was decided to only select pupils from the second and third stages (mid-adolescence and late-adolescence/emerging adulthood). First, consistent with the age-crime curve, previous research among adolescents in Flanders has found that the prevalence of delinquency is highest in the second and third stages of secondary education (Cops, 2014). Pupils from these stages are therefore an interesting population to study when it comes to offence-related guilt and shame. Second, pupils in the first stage of secondary education are still in their early adolescence. Examining them would ideally require a separate questionnaire with question wording adapted to their capacities, perspective and lifeworld (e.g. Bradt et al., 2014).

Participating schools provided a list of all classes in the second (year 3 and 4) and third stages (year 5, 6 and 7) of secondary education. To ensure sufficient diversity in the sample, these lists were stratified according to school year and educational track. Specifically, the second and third stages of secondary education in Flanders offer a choice between four educational tracks: general secondary education (which prepares pupils for higher education), secondary education in the arts (which prepares pupils for higher education in the arts), technical secondary education (which prepares students for the labour market and for some types of technical studies in higher education) and vocational secondary

16 Schools offering special secondary education ('BuSO') for pupils with mental, physical or psychological disabilities were not contacted.

17 In general secondary education, the final stage comprises two years. In technical secondary education and in secondary education in the arts, the final stage also comprises two years, but pupils can choose to follow an additional 7th specialisation year ('secondary-after-secondary education'). In vocational secondary education, the final stage always comprises three years.

education (which prepares pupils for the labour market). In line with previous research, the general track and the arts track – which only contains a small proportion of pupils – were grouped together for the purposes of stratification (e.g. Bradt et al., 2014). Taking educational track into account when sampling schools or classes is recommended because Flanders is a region that displays considerable social segregation in education. The educational track is related to factors such as socioeconomic background, ethnicity and school motivation (Van Houtte & Stevens, 2015). From each combination of school year *and* educational track, one class was selected. If the number of pupils in the sampled class was less than 10, a second or third class was sampled to ensure the participation of at least 10 respondents. This was particularly the case in vocational secondary education, where classes tend to be smaller as compared to general and technical secondary education. In this way, a total number of 972 pupils from 107 different classes were selected.

Data collection took place between April and June 2015. The questionnaire was administered in class – during regular school hours – using a traditional paper-and-pencil format. Parental informed consent was not deemed necessary as all students were older than 14 years. A review of the literature indicates that around the age of 14, adolescents are capable of understanding information necessary for consent (Schachter et al., 2005). Two researchers were present to inform all participants about the content and the purpose of the questionnaire. A consent form was not used, but participants were explicitly told that participation in the study was voluntary and that they had the right to withdraw at any moment. Refusal to participate was taken as a lack of consent. Participants were asked not to write their names on the questionnaire to guarantee anonymity. Completed questionnaires were collected in a sealed box in front of the classroom. Teachers, who were sometimes present to ensure discipline, were asked to stay in the back of the classroom in order to protect the privacy of the participants. In total, 867 pupils handed in a questionnaire, which gives a response rate of 89.2%. Non-response was the result of either absenteeism or classes being unable to fill in the questionnaire because of unforeseen circumstances (e.g. school trip). No pupils explicitly refused to fill in the questionnaire.

Questionnaire data were entered into an SPSS file and checked for data entry accuracy, missing data and unreliable response patterns. This led to the removal of seven respondents whose response patterns were completely unreliable. Furthermore, it was decided to remove four respondents who were considered too old to be included in the study, setting the maximum age at 24.[18] None of the variables used in the analysis had more than 5% missing values. The final dataset used in this study contains 856 respondents.

18 After having completed technical secondary education, pupils can choose to follow an additional 7th specialisation year ('secondary-after-secondary education', see footnote 2). Some of them decide to do this at a later age, after having gained some work experience first. In this way, a few markedly older respondents ended up filling in the questionnaire (the oldest one among them was 44).

All pupils in the final sample are between 15 and 24 years of age; 56% are male and 44% are female. Almost half of the pupils come from the vocational track, 34% come from the technical track and 18% from the general track. This affects the age distribution of the sample. Pupils in vocational education tend to be older, on average, than those in general and technical education because vocational education takes one year longer to complete and has higher rates of grade retention. This explains why one-third of the sample is older than 18 years. The sample reflects the population of Genk in being ethnically diverse. More than half of the pupils in the sample have non-Belgian origins (i.e. at least one parent born outside of Belgium). Of these adolescents with a migration background, about half have European origins (mostly Italian or Dutch) and about half have non-European origins. Among those of non-European origin, the majority has a Turkish background. This is not surprising, as people with a Turkish background form the largest non-European community in Genk (Table 5.1).[19]

Table 5.1 Sociodemographic composition of the sample (n = 856)

		%	N
Gender			
	Male	56	477
	Female	44	375
Age			
	15-16	25	208
	17-18	42	350
	18+	34	282
Educational track			
	General	18	147
	Technical	34	286
	Vocational	49	409
Migration background			
	Both parents born in Belgium	43	364
	At least one parent born abroad	57	487

5.3 SURVEY DESIGN AND MEASURES

The survey started with a page containing general information on participation and some basic instructions as to how the questions should be answered. Questions were grouped into five sections. The first section contained questions on the demographic, socioeconomic

19 Demographic data for the city of Genk can be freely consulted at http://limburg.incijfers.be.

and religious characteristics of respondents. The second section focused on respondents' relationships with parents, teachers and fellow students. The third section gathered data about victimisation, own offending and friends' offending. The fourth section sought information about correlates of delinquency such as self-control, attitudes towards violence, gender role attitudes, reflected appraisals and prospective guilt and shame. The fifth and final section contained questions about leisure activities and media use (e.g. videogames). The survey was pre-tested for clarity on a separate sample of 41 adolescents from three classes (one class from technical education and two classes from vocational education). Respondents were told they were participating in a pre-test and invited to comment on the clarity of the questions. This led to several small adaptations in question wording.

In what follows, I discuss how key variables and constructs were measured in the survey. The descriptive statistics, the measurement properties of multi-item scales and the calculation of composite scores are discussed in the next chapter.

5.3.1 *Dependent variable: prospective shame-guilt*

Following previous criminological studies, scenario-based measures were used to assess prospective guilt and shame (e.g. Svensson et al., 2013). In this approach, participants respond to a set of hypothetical situations by indicating the extent to which they would feel a particular emotion if they were in these situations. Two specific delinquent situations were chosen for the purposes of this study: shoplifting and retaliatory violence. In the first situation, participants were asked to imagine they had secretly taken something from a shop without paying for it. In the second situation, they were asked to imagine they had violently hit or kicked someone who had bothered or insulted them.

Why these two specific offences? Obviously, the validity and reliability of answers to hypothetical situations depend upon the ability of respondents to place themselves in those situations. Theft and violence are among the most common forms of youth delinquency. According to the International Self-Report Delinquency Study, the lifetime prevalence of shoplifting reaches up to 20% among (urban) adolescents in Belgium (Vettenburg et al., 2010). Similarly, fighting behaviour is not uncommon during adolescence. A recent large-scale representative survey has found that almost one in three adolescents in Flanders admits to having (violently) hit someone during the previous year (Coenen, 2019). Although retaliatory violence is not representative for all kinds of violence, it is not a rare event. Both qualitative and quantitative studies indicate that youth violence frequently occurs in response to perceived threats, insults and other signs of disrespect (Anderson, 1999; Batchelor, 2005; Kivivuori et al., 2016; Op de Beeck, 2012). In short, it seems reasonable to assume that many adolescents have already had direct or indirect experience with shoplifting and retaliatory violence or, at least, do not find it too far-fetched to imagine themselves engaging in these acts.

Aside from these methodological concerns, the focus on shoplifting and retaliatory violence is also motivated by theoretical considerations. First, some of the hypotheses on the social sources of prospective guilt and shame specified in the previous chapter only apply to specific types of offences. For instance, it was hypothesised that levels of prospective guilt and shame for engaging in theft (but not violence) would be higher among Muslim adolescents than among Christian adolescents. Other hypotheses are assumed to hold across different types of offences. Second, shoplifting and retaliatory violence present an interesting case for examining gender differences in prospective guilt and shame. Although the gender gap in self-reported offending is commonly found to be small (or even nonexistent) for shoplifting, it is usually large for different types of physical violence (Junger-Tas et al., 2010).

As repeatedly discussed throughout this work, (prospective) guilt and shame tend to co-occur in the context of moral transgressions. Hence, this study combines the two emotions into a single scale. Specifically, to measure prospective shame-guilt, respondents were presented with the two hypothetical situations described earlier – shoplifting and retaliatory violence – and asked to rate the following four items (1) 'I would have the feeling that I did something wrong,' (2) 'I would feel guilty,' (3) 'I would feel ashamed of myself' and (4) 'I would feel disappointed with myself' on a 5-point scale ranging from 1 ('not at all') to 5 ('very much'). These items are similar to those used in previous research by Harris (2001) and Ahmed (2001) to measure shame and guilt. Following the advice of Olthof et al. (2000), the prospective shame-guilt scale used in this study combines two measurement approaches. The first approach consists of using items that contain the everyday emotion terms 'guilty' and 'ashamed'. This should make it clear to the participants that they are being asked about an emotionally charged experience. The second approach consists of using items that refer to specific experiential correlates of guilt and shame. Specifically, the first item taps into the perception of being responsible for a harm or wrong (which is typical of guilt), whereas the last item taps into the perception of oneself as inadequate or lacking in some way (which is characteristic of shame). In sum, the scale combines a guilt-related dimension and a shame-related dimension, each represented by two items.

5.3.2 *Independent variables*

a Demographics

Three demographic background variables are included in the analyses: gender, age and immigrant background. Gender was measured by asking the respondents to indicate whether they were male or female (i.e. a measure of biological sex rather than perceived gender identity). Age was measured by self-reported year of birth. Immigrant background was measured by asking respondents to specify in which country their mother and father were born. A fixed list containing the most relevant countries for Belgian adolescents was provided: Morocco, Turkey, Congo, France, The Netherlands, Germany, Italy, Poland and Spain. Additional space was provided for other answers not covered by the given options. Based on this information, a nominal variable with two categories was created: (1) adolescents whose parents were both born in Belgium and (2) adolescents whose mother or father was born abroad.

b Religiosity

Religiosity was assessed with a measure previously used among adolescents in Flanders by Roggemans et al. (2015). More specifically, respondents were asked to pick one of the following answer categories, encompassing both religious affiliation and religious practice: (1) 'I am not religious'; (2) 'I am a religious Christian and I go to church regularly'; (3) 'I am a religious Christian, but I don't go to church often'; (4) 'I'm doubting, but in the end I consider myself sort of Christian'; (5) 'I am a religious Muslim who strictly follows the religious prescriptions'; (6) 'I am a religious Muslim, but I do not strictly follow the religious prescriptions'; or (7) 'I'm doubting, but in the end I consider myself sort of Muslim.' If none of these options was applicable, respondents were invited to describe their religious conviction in a designated space.

c Relationship with parents

As the survey did not include a direct measure of parental attachment or closeness, a set of items on parental knowledge of activities and whereabouts was used to assess the closeness of the parent-adolescent relationship. Mounting evidence suggests that parental knowledge is not so much the result of active parental monitoring and control but rather of a warm and involved family climate in which parents show interest in their children and in which children are willing to voluntarily disclose information because they see their parents as legitimate authorities (Cutrín et al., 2017; Keijsers & Laird, 2014; Soenens et al., 2006; Yun et al., 2016). In light of these findings, parental knowledge can be considered as a reasonably good (albeit not perfect) indicator of the strength of the parent-adolescent bond.

Adolescents responded to a set of three items pertaining to perceptions of the father's (or father figure's) knowledge and three similar items pertaining to perceptions of the mother's (or mother figure's) knowledge: (1) 'My father/mother knows what I do in my spare time'; (2) 'When I go out, my father/mother knows where I am'; and (3) 'My father/mother knows who my friends are.' They provided their answer on a 5-point scale (1 = *never*, 5 = *always*). These items are derived from Stattin and Kerr's (2000) parental knowledge scale and have been previously used in research among adolescents in Flanders (Bradt et al., 2014). Higher scores indicate a closer parent-adolescent relationship.

d Relationship with teachers

Researchers have typically operationalised the quality of the teacher-adolescent relationship through measures of support, respect and fair treatment (Obsuth et al., 2017; Özbay & Özcan, 2006; Seddig, 2014; Theimann, 2016). In this study, respondents were asked to respond to the following three items about the relationship with their teachers: (1) 'The teachers at school respect me'; (2) 'I can openly express my opinion in class, even if it contradicts the opinion of the teachers'; and (3) 'I value my contacts with my teachers.' They provided their answer on a 5-point scale (1 = *completely disagree*, 5 = *completely agree*). These items were taken from the Flemish Youth Monitor 2013 and have been used in previous research to measure the quality of the teacher-adolescent relationship (e.g. Bradt & Bouverne-De Bie, 2014). Higher scores indicate a better teacher-adolescent relationship.

e Perceived delinquency of friends

To measure perceived delinquency of friends, respondents were presented with a list of five offences (truancy, shoplifting, other theft, vandalism and physical assault) and asked to indicate how many of their friends had already committed these offences on a 4-point scale (0 = *none*, 3 = *all of them*). These items were taken from the Flemish Youth Monitor 2013 and have been used in previous research to measure perceived delinquency of friends (e.g. Coenen, 2020; Cops et al., 2014).

f Reflected appraisals as a troublemaker

Following previous research (De Coster & Lutz, 2018; Matsueda, 1992), reflected appraisals as a troublemaker (or perceptions of informal labelling) were captured by three sets of three items asking respondents to indicate whether, respectively, their parents, friends and teachers would agree that they are someone who (1) 'often breaks rules', (2) 'often gets into trouble or causes trouble' and (3) 'often does things that aren't allowed'. They provided their answer on a 5-point scale (1 = *completely disagree*, 5 = *completely agree*). Higher scores indicate stronger perceptions of being judged as a troublemaker.

g Traditional gender role attitudes

Gender role attitudes were measured with two separate scales, one that assessed traditional masculinity and one that assessed traditional femininity. These scales were developed by Vermeersch et al. (2010) to measure adolescents' gender role attitudes in a Flemish context. To measure traditional masculinity in male adolescents, five items were used that represented the following aspects of the construct: autonomy (item= 'a man should avoid being dependent on others'), self-confidence (item = 'a man without self-confidence is a wimp'), risk-taking (item = 'a man likes a bit of danger now and then') and 'anti-femininity' (two items = 'I find it disturbing if a boy behaves like a girl' and 'There is definitely something wrong with a boy practicing ballet as a hobby'). To measure traditional femininity in female adolescents, five items were used that represented the following aspects of the construct: being pretty (item = 'It's only natural that girls pay more attention to their looks than boys'), being domestic (item = 'Women should first consider their children, and only then their career'), being nice (item = 'There is definitely something wrong with girls who use foul language') and anti-masculinity (item = 'I find it disturbing if a girl behaves like a boy' and 'If I heard a woman was a mason or a roofer, I would doubt whether she was feminine'). Respondents were asked to rate these items on a 5-point scale (1 = *completely agree*, 5 = *completely disagree*). All items were reverse-coded so that higher ratings reflected stronger adherence to traditional masculinity and femininity, respectively.

h Prior delinquency

To measure prior involvement in delinquency, respondents were presented with five specific types of delinquent acts: shoplifting, theft from a person (without threat or violence), robbery (using threat or violence), aggravated assault (causing bodily injury) and participating in a gang fight. For each type of act, respondents were asked to write down how many times they had engaged in it during the *past twelve months* (using an open-ended format).

Prior involvement in delinquency is used as a control variable in this study because it is a potential confounder of the relationship between some of the variables of interest and prospective guilt and shame. Research has for instance shown that prior delinquency increases the likelihood of associating with delinquent friends (Matsueda & Anderson, 1998) and of being labelled as a troublemaker (Heimer & Matsueda, 1994). At the same time, prior delinquency may also lead to a decrease in levels of prospective guilt and shame. That is, adolescents who have already committed delinquent acts may be more likely to use neutralisation techniques to excuse or justify such behaviour and, as a consequence, report less prospective guilt and shame for future offences (Maruna & Copes, 2005). Hence, the relationship of both perceived friends' delinquency and reflected appraisals with prospective shame-guilt may be (partly) spurious due to a failure to control for prior involvement in delinquency.

At the same time, however, prior involvement in delinquency may also act as a proxy measure for prior levels of prospective shame-guilt (i.e. the more delinquent acts a person has committed in the past, the less this person has previously been prone to shame-guilt). Controlling for prior delinquency, then, may remove meaningful variance from the dependent variable and lower the variance that remains to be explained by the variables of interest. Since both possibilities are plausible, all analyses will be conducted both with and without controlling for prior delinquency.

5.4 Data analysis

The following three statistical techniques were used in this study to analyse the data: confirmatory factor analysis, multiple regression analysis and path analysis.

5.4.1 *Confirmatory factor analysis*

Confirmatory factor analysis (CFA) was conducted to examine the measurement properties of all scales used in this study. More specifically, the dimensionality of the scale as well as the relationship of each individual scale item to the underlying construct or factor was examined. In addition, multiple-group CFA was conducted to verify whether the measurement properties of the scales were equivalent across gender groups. In other words, it was tested whether constructs were measured in the same way for male adolescents and female adolescents. To be able to meaningfully compare observed scale scores across gender groups, scalar invariance is needed (De Boeck et al., 2014; van de Schoot et al., 2012). Scalar invariance holds when the factor structure, the factor loadings and the intercepts of the scale items are equivalent across groups. A top-down approach was followed to test for measurement invariance, starting with the full scalar invariant model. The results of all CFAs will be presented in the next chapter.

Estimating CFA models with ordinal Likert-type items can be done in either one of two ways. The first option is to treat these items as approximately continuous instead of categorical and to use robust maximum likelihood (ML) estimation to adjust test statistics and standard errors for the violation of the normality assumption. The second option is to use diagonally weighted least squares (DWLS) estimation, which is specifically designed for categorical items. Simulation studies suggest that both methods give acceptable estimates if the sample size is sufficiently large and the ordinal items have five or more response categories (see Li, 2016; Rhemtulla et al., 2012). Nevertheless, as an extra check on the reliability of the results, all models in this study were estimated using both the robust ML and the DWLS estimation method. This was done with the software program Mplus 6.11, in which robust ML estimator is denoted 'MLR' and DWLS estimator is denoted 'WLSMV' (Muthén & Muthen, 1998). As both methods generated results that led to similar substantive conclusions, only the robust ML results are reported because they are easier to interpret.[20]

To test the 'exact' fit of each model to the observed data, the Satorra-Bentler scaled model chi-square (χ^2) with its associated degrees of freedom (df) and p-value was used. A nonsignificant χ^2 value indicates that the model fits the data (i.e. that there is no significant difference between the model-implied data and the observed data). In addition, the following three indices of 'approximate' model fit were used: the Root Mean Square Error of Approximation (RMSEA), the Comparative Fit Index (CFI) and the Standardised Root Mean Square Residual (SRMR) (Kline, 2016). These approximate fit indices each have their own cutoffs to evaluate the acceptability of the model. For the RMSEA, values below 0.08 are generally considered to suggest acceptable model fit and values below 0.05 suggest a close fit. For the CFI, values greater than 0.95 are considered to reflect an acceptable fit. For the SRMR, finally, values lower than 0.08 are considered to indicate acceptable fit (Hu & Bentler, 1999).

Although the χ^2 test is the only real test of model fit (P. Barrett, 2007), researchers frequently ignore its results. The χ^2 test is so sensitive to sample size, so the argument goes, that even theoretically trivial discrepancies between the model and the data will result in a statistically significant misfit if the sample size is sufficiently large. Though this is true, a significant χ^2 test can be caused by either trivial or serious misspecifications, *regardless of sample size* (Hayduk, 2014). Therefore, even if approximate fit indices such as the RMSEA suggest that the overall fit of a model is 'acceptable', a significant χ^2 test should never be simply ignored. Specifically, one should always carefully examine the model for local misspecifications and their substantive implications (Barrett, 2007; Ropovik, 2015).

In this study, potential misspecifications were evaluated using a procedure developed by Saris et al. (2009) and implemented into the software program Jrule by Oberski (2010). To decide whether a parameter in the model is misspecified, this procedure takes into account the expected parameter change (EPC), which indicates the size of the misspecification; the modification index (MI), which indicates whether the EPC is statistically significant; and the statistical power of the MI test to detect misspecifications of a given size. Following recommendations by Saris et al. (2009), the power to detect potential misspecifications was set at 0.75 and the type I error at 0.05. The threshold used to define a substantive misspecification was set at a minimum of 0.20 for omitted residual correlations and 0.40 for omitted factor loadings or cross-loadings. Although all cut-off criteria are to a certain extent arbitrary, this strategy uses widely accepted critical values in

20 The results generated by the DWLS estimator are somewhat more difficult to interpret, because the observed responses are linked to an underlying latent response variable through a threshold structure, and the factor loadings come in the form of probit regression coefficients (see Brown, 2015).

social science research and ensures that the most substantive misspecifications are taken into consideration. The software program Jrule reads the Mplus output of a given model and uses the EPC, the MI and the power of the MI test to detect potential parameter misspecification.

5.4.2 *Multiple regression analyses*

Multiple regression analysis was used to assess the relative effect of each independent variable on levels of prospective shame-guilt. The results of these analyses will be presented in Chapter 7. The linear regression model makes the following four assumptions: (1) linearity in the parameters, (2) independence of the residuals, (3) equal variance of the residuals and (4) normality of the residuals (Williams et al., 2013). The linearity assumption was checked by inspecting a plot of the residuals versus the predicted values. If necessary, polynomial terms were added to the model to allow for nonlinearity. The second assumption, independence of the residuals, was violated from the outset in this study because a clustered sample was selected (i.e. students were clustered in schools). This clustering may bias the standard errors. Unfortunately, the number of clusters was too low (only 7 schools) to apply multilevel modelling or to calculate cluster-robust standard errors. Fortunately, additional analyses using fixed-effects models (models including a dummy variable for each except one school) indicated that the effect of clustering on the standard errors was negligible (McNeish & Stapleton, 2016). The third assumption, equal variance of the residuals or 'homoscedasticity', was checked by inspecting a plot of the square root of the standardised residuals versus the predicted values. Ideally, the residuals should not grow smaller or larger as a function of the predicted values. Because heteroscedasticity was present in some of the models, heteroscedasticity-robust standard errors were used throughout the analysis.[21] The assumption of normality, finally, is the least important assumption in this study because of the relatively large sample size. That is, in sufficiently large samples, the central limit theorem ensures that the sampling distribution of the coefficients will approximate normality, regardless of the distribution of the residuals in the sample. Simulation studies have shown that even with extremely non-normal data, least-squares regression performs well with 500 or more observations (Lumley et al., 2002).

Aside from these four assumptions, two other potential problems threaten the validity of the regression results: the presence of outliers and multicollinearity (M. N. Williams et al., 2013). Cook's distance was used to check for influential outliers that might unduly affect the regression coefficients, but no problems were detected in this regard. Following

21 This is done using the jtools package in R (see https://jtools.jacob-long.com/).

the advice of Johnston et al. (2018), multicollinearity was assessed not only by looking at the Variance Inflation Factor (VIF) statistic but also by running separate regressions including only subsets of the independent variables (to explore confounding effects created by the interrelationships among the independent variables).

5.4.3 *Multiple mediator path analysis*

Finally, multiple mediator path models were estimated in Mplus version 6.11 (Muthén & Muthen, 1998) to identify potential mediators of the relationship between gender and prospective shame-guilt. The results of these analyses will also be presented in Chapter 7. With a path analysis, it is possible to examine all hypothesised pathways through which gender may affect shame-guilt in a single model. Because some of the mediator variables were binary, the diagonally weighted least squares estimator (WLSMV) was used to estimate all parameters.[22] Following best practices in mediation research, bias-corrected bootstrapped confidence intervals were estimated to evaluate the size and significance of the indirect effects (using 1,000 bootstrap samples) (Preacher & Hayes, 2008).

5.5 METHODOLOGICAL NOTES

5.5.1 *Beyond null hypothesis significance testing*

Null hypothesis significance testing (NHST) is still the dominant paradigm in quantitative criminology. In this approach, two competing hypotheses are considered: the null hypothesis and the research hypothesis. The null hypothesis is the logical contradictory of the hypothesis the researcher wants to examine. For instance, one of the research hypotheses advanced in this study is that religious adolescents will anticipate higher levels of guilt and shame for engaging in delinquency than nonreligious adolescents. The corresponding null hypothesis, then, is that religiosity is unrelated to prospective shame-guilt. If the null hypothesis can be proved false, its logical contradictory, the research hypothesis, is thereby proved true. Researchers typically rely on the p-value to decide if the data provide enough evidence against the null hypothesis. The p-value gives the probability of observing the current data (or data that are more extreme) if the null hypothesis is true.[23] Put differently, the p-value is a continuous measure of the compatibility between the observed data and the null hypothesis. It takes a value between 0 (= complete

22 The distribution of the variable measuring perceived delinquency of friends was highly skewed and therefore recoded into a binary variable (see next chapter).

23 And if the underlying assumptions used to calculate the p-value are valid.

incompatibility) and 1 (= complete compatibility). It is common practice to reject the null hypothesis and accept the research hypothesis if the p-value falls below a predefined significance threshold (usually $p < 0.05$).

Despite being widely used, NHST suffers from a number of important drawbacks (Bernardi et al., 2017; Greenland et al., 2016; Hoekstra et al., 2006). First, the p-value is a *continuous* measure of the strength of the evidence against the null hypothesis. In NHST, however, the p-value is used to support a *binary* accept-reject decision based on an arbitrary threshold. All too often, results are considered important and worth discussing if the associated p-value falls below the 0.05 threshold and ignored or even not reported otherwise. Yet, the difference between, say, $p = 0.04$ and $p = 0.06$, is obviously minimal. In general, NHST encourages dichotomous thinking and ignores the uncertainty that is inherent in statistical inference. Second, and even more worrisome, rejecting or failing to reject a null hypothesis is actually not as informative as it may seem. If the sample size is sufficiently large, any nonzero effect, no matter how tiny, can produce a small p-value. A difference of 1 millimetre in the average height of baby boys and girls may be 'statistically significant', but not necessarily clinically relevant. By itself, the p-value tells us nothing about the size or substantial relevance of an effect. Furthermore, and contrary to what is sometimes believed, the p-value also tells us nothing about the truth of the null hypothesis; it *assumes* that the null hypothesis is true. Thus, researchers sometimes mistakenly conclude that there is 'no difference', 'no association' or 'no effect' solely because the p-value is statistically insignificant. However, absence of evidence is not evidence of absence. Substantial effects may produce large p-values if the sample size is too small or the measurements are too imprecise. The right conclusion in such cases is that the data are statistically inconclusive, not that 'there is no effect.'

To overcome the drawbacks of NHST, this study will not simply consider whether the coefficients of interest have corresponding p-values that fall below a certain threshold or not (their 'statistical significance'); it will also consider the size of these coefficients and their substantive relevance. In other words, the aim is not to make binary accept/reject decisions based solely on levels of statistical significance but to provide a more nuanced evaluation of the potential importance of the factors hypothesised to affect shame-guilt. In addition, this study will always report the confidence intervals associated with the coefficients of interest. The confidence intervals give a range of values for these coefficients that are consistent with the observed data. As Bernardi et al. (2017) write, 'confidence intervals make transparent the degree of precision of our estimations and shift our attention towards their size' (p. 6).

5.5.2 *Causality*

The theoretical framework used in this study assumes that at least some of the variation between adolescents in levels of prospective shame-guilt is related in a causal manner (through the mechanism of role-taking) to social factors such as social bonds to parents or exposure to delinquent friends. However, it can reasonably be assumed that the causal relationship is bidirectional for some of the identified factors. Guilt and shame are as much products of one's engagements with others as emotions that prevent one from doing things that could threaten these engagements. More specifically in the context of this study, close relationships with parents and teachers may stimulate prospective shame-guilt at the thought of offending, but also, vice versa, prospective shame-guilt may serve a relationship-enhancing function. Likewise, spending time in the company of delinquent friends may decrease levels of prospective shame-guilt for engaging in delinquency, but also, vice versa, adolescents with lower levels of prospective shame-guilt may be more likely to experience rejection by conventional peers and seek the company of delinquent friends. Unfortunately, the cross-sectional nature of the data does not allow the inference of causal processes that occur within individuals (whether unidirectional or bidirectional). This requires longitudinal panel data and the use of appropriate controls for possible confounders. Therefore, associational language will be used in the description of the results. The word 'effect' is used as a statistical term referring to the coefficients in a regression analysis; it implies predictability but not necessarily causality.

6 Descriptive Findings and Measurement Aspects

> Reporting only coefficient alpha is not sufficient evidence to make valid interpretations of the scores from an instrument or to prove that a set of items measure only one underlying construct.
> (Knekta et al., 2019, p. 6)

In this chapter, I present descriptive statistics for all key variables used in the empirical analysis. I also examine the measurement properties of all multi-item scales using confirmatory factor analysis (CFA). Particular attention is given to two questions regarding the dimensionality of the items measuring prospective guilt and shame. First, are the guilt- and shame-related items sufficiently interrelated to warrant combining them into a single construct, or should they rather be treated as separate dimensions? Second, do prospective feelings of guilt and shame generalise across different types of offences, or are they organised in a crime-specific way? I also conduct multiple-group CFA to assess the degree to which scale items function equivalently across gender groups. Measurement equivalence is necessary to be able to compare scale scores between male adolescents and female adolescents. Finally, I perform a series of t-tests and chi-square tests to assess gender differences in prospective shame-guilt and all independent variables of interest. Given the results of previous studies, meaningful gender differences in prospective guilt and shame are anticipated. Independent variables that differ significantly by gender in the theoretically expected direction are potential mediators of the association between gender and prospective shame-guilt.

6.1 Prospective guilt and shame

6.1.1 Descriptive results

Eight Likert-type items are used to measure prospective guilt and shame in this study: two guilt-related items ('I would feel guilty' and 'I would have the feeling that I did something wrong') and two shame-related items ('I would feel ashamed of myself' and 'I would feel disappointed with myself'), one pertaining to a hypothetical shoplifting offence and one pertaining to a hypothetical violent offence. Figures 6.1 and 6.2 give an overview of the levels of prospective guilt and shame reported by male adolescents and female adolescents in relation to shoplifting and retaliatory violence, respectively.

Figure 6.1 Prospective guilt and shame for shoplifting

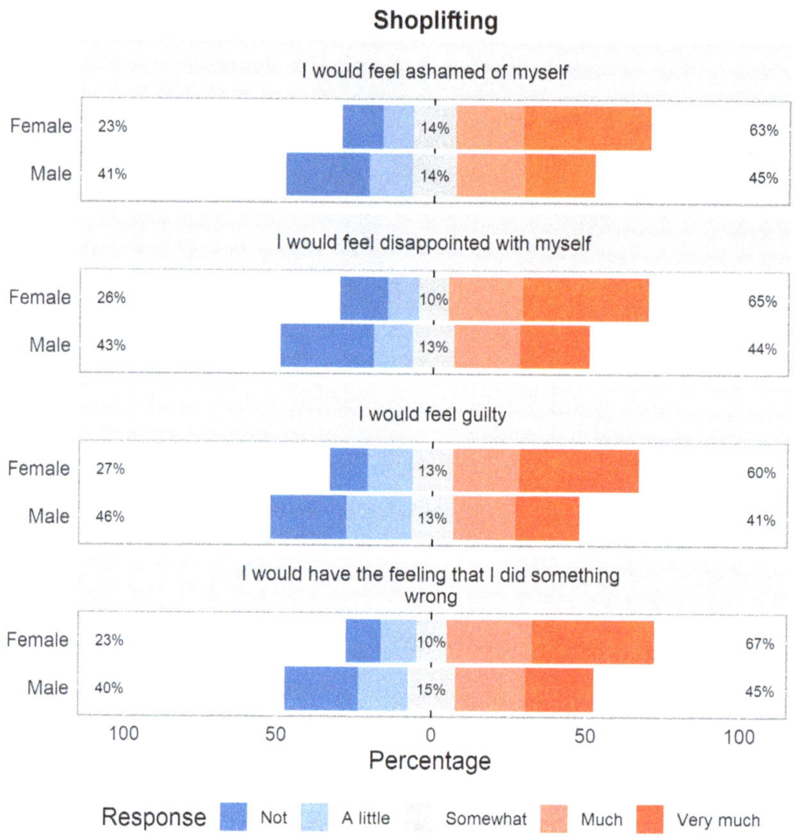

Figure 6.2 Prospective guilt and shame for retaliatory violence

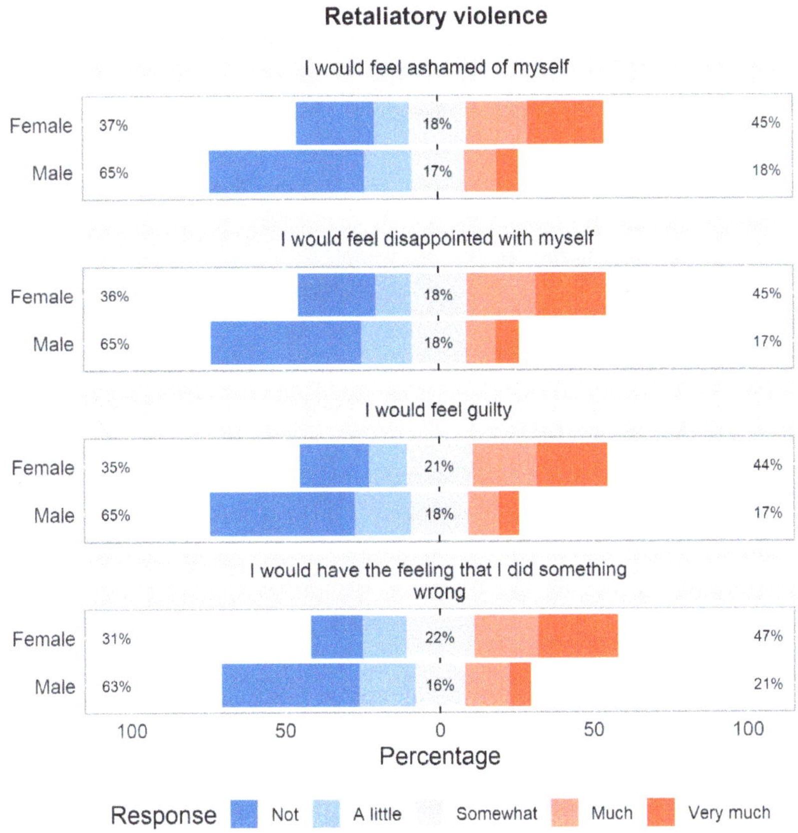

Three general observations can be made on the basis of these figures. First, there is meaningful variation in the levels of prospective guilt and shame reported by the adolescents in the sample. In the case of shoplifting, the responses given by male adolescents are more or less evenly distributed between low and high levels of guilt and shame. The responses given by female adolescents, by comparison, are skewed to higher levels of guilt and shame, with roughly three in five reporting that they would feel 'much' or 'very much' guilt and shame if they stole something from a shop. The reverse is true for retaliatory violence, with responses given by female adolescents more evenly distributed and responses given by male adolescents skewed to lower levels of guilt and shame. More specifically, only about one in five boys report that they would feel 'much' or 'very much' guilt and shame if they hit someone who annoyed or insulted them.

Second, across both offences, female adolescents anticipate considerably higher levels of guilt and shame than male adolescents. This is in line with previous studies showing that the threat of guilt and shame is unevenly distributed across gender (Pauwels & Svensson, 2015; Rebellon et al., 2015, 2016; Svensson, 2004).

Third, both male adolescents and female adolescents anticipate higher levels of guilt and shame for engaging in shoplifting than for engaging in retaliatory violence. These findings may seem somewhat surprising, given that violence is generally perceived by the public as more serious and morally wrong than theft (Adriaenssen et al., 2018). However, as research by Thomas (2018) has shown, many adolescents disapprove of violence in an abstract sense, but simultaneously approve of such behaviour under certain circumstances (e.g. when one is being insulted or threatened). This discrepancy between global and situation-specific attitudes in Thomas's study was more strongly pronounced for violence than for theft. Thomas discusses possible explanations for his findings, which are also relevant to the present study:

> One explanation may be that society has made it easier to justify violence over the taking of property – most justifications in the legal code relate to the use of physical violence (e.g., self-defense). It is also possible that the capitalistic culture of the U.S. leads individuals to place greater import on material property than personal safety (Messner & Rosenfeld, 1994). Another explanation is that not using violence can have negative consequences (loss of social status), whereas choosing not to commit theft is unlikely to adversely affect individuals (i.e. there is something to gain but little to lose). As a result, individuals view violence as a necessary, and therefore more acceptable, behavioral response. (Thomas, 2018, p. 335)

6.1.2 Dimensionality

Is there evidence that items measuring prospective guilt and shame in relation to delinquency form a unidimensional construct? Looking in particular at the eight items used in this study, two potential sources of multidimensionality warrant further investigation.

First, one may wonder whether the guilt- and shame-related items are sufficiently interrelated to warrant combining them into a single construct or whether they should be studied as separate dimensions. As discussed previously, several researchers have argued that feelings of guilt are frequently accompanied by or intertwined with some form of shame, especially when it comes to moral transgressions such as delinquency (Ferguson et al., 2007; Karlsson & Sjöberg, 2009; Olthof et al., 2004; Schmader & Lickel, 2006).

Unfortunately, most criminological studies have focused on either one or the other emotion and therefore provide little information as to how strongly they might be intertwined. One exception is Harris' study of the emotions experienced by drink-driving offenders in court and restorative justice conferences (Harris, 2001). He found that items measuring guilt and shame loaded on one and the same underlying factor, suggesting that the two emotions are indeed strongly related. Harris' study, however, was carried out in a specific context and focused on people's emotional responses to current events rather than on their prospective emotions with respect to future or hypothetical events. Another exception is a study by Svensson et al. (2013) that included measures of both anticipated guilt and shame. They found a strong correlation ($r = 0.72$) between guilt items and shame items, but they did not use factor analysis to determine whether these items could be merged into a single construct.

Second, one may wonder whether prospective guilt and shame for shoplifting can be meaningfully distinguished from prospective guilt and shame for retaliatory violence. Put differently, are prospective feelings of guilt and shame organised in a crime-specific way or do they generalise across different types of offences? Again, previous studies provide little guidance on this issue. Those working from a rational choice/deterrence perspective have typically measured prospective guilt and shame in an offence-specific way, so as to be able to examine their offence-specific effects (e.g. Grasmick & Bursik, 1990). Other criminologists have summed responses across multiple guilt items or shame items involving different types of offences, thereby assuming that prospective feelings of guilt and shame are organised in a crime-general way (e.g. Svensson et al., 2013).[24] The latter approach has typically been justified by reference to the finding that guilt and shame items have a high Cronbach's alpha. As is well known, however, high alphas do not guarantee that items form a unidimensional construct (Sijtsma, 2009).

The most appropriate way to examine the dimensionality of a set of items is through exploratory or confirmatory factor analysis. A major disadvantage of the former, however, is that it does not provide any inferential test statistics or information about the extent to which the obtained factor structure fits the observed data. Confirmatory factor analysis (CFA) is superior in allowing the researcher to statistically test and compare the fit of different possible models that are prespecified based on substantive considerations. Specifically, based on the theoretical reasoning mentioned above, the following four CFA models are proposed and examined:

24 Actually, this is similar to the assumption made by control theorists that moral beliefs are unidimensional, so that people with a strong belief in the moral validity of the law do not discriminate between different types of infractions.

1. A model with all items loading on a single factor. This model assumes that all items used in this study reflect a unidimensional construct, namely, an adolescent's general propensity towards prospective guilt and shame across different kinds of offences.
2. A two-factor model with all guilt-related items (both in relation to shoplifting and in relation to violence) loading on one factor and all shame-related items (again, both with respect to shoplifting and violence) loading on a second factor. This model assumes that prospective guilt can be meaningfully distinguished from prospective shame.
3. A two-factor model with all shame- and guilt-related items pertaining to shoplifting loading on one factor and all shame- and guilt-related items pertaining to violence loading on a second factor. This model assumes that prospective guilt and shame feelings are strongly interrelated but organised in an offence-specific way. In other words, prospective shame-guilt for shoplifting can be meaningfully distinguished from prospective shame-guilt for engaging in retaliatory violence.
4. A four-factor model, with two guilt-related items for shoplifting loading on a first factor, two shame-related items for shoplifting loading on a second factor, two guilt-related items for violence loading on a third factor and two shame-related items for violence loading on a fourth factor. This model assumes the presence of both emotion-specific and offence-specific subdimensions among the items.

Looking at the fit of the CFA models in Table 6.1; it is clear that Model 1 (the one-factor model) and Model 2 (the two-factor model with separate guilt and shame factors) do not fit the data. The χ^2 values are very large for models with so few degrees of freedom. Additionally, the values for the approximate fit indices are nowhere near their commonly accepted thresholds. The fit of Model 3 (the two-factor model with separate shame-guilt factors for each offence) is acceptable according to the RMSEA (≈ 0.08) and good according to the CFI (>0.95) and SRMR (<0.08) indices. However, the best fit is obtained with Model 4 (the four-factor model with both emotion-specific and offence-specific factors). Although this model fails the χ^2 test of exact fit, the output of the Jrule software program indicates that it contains no substantive misspecifications.

Table 6.1 Goodness-of-fit statistics for the alternative 'shame-guilt' models

	χ^2 (df)	*P*	RMSEA	CFI	SRMR
Model 1 (one factor)	1598.059 (20)	<0.001	0.304	0.594	0.224
Model 2 (two factors)	1567.026 (19)	<0.001	0.309	0.601	0.229
Model 3 (two factors)	132.256 (19)	<0.001	0.084	0.971	0.014
Model 4 (four factors)	**31.587 (14)**	**=0.005**	**0.038**	**0.995**	**0.009**

Figure 6.3 provides a visualisation of the results of Model 4. This model indicates the presence of four subdimensions in the data: prospective guilt for shoplifting, prospective shame for shoplifting, prospective guilt for using violence and prospective shame for using violence. All items have high loadings on their respective factors, implying excellent convergent validity. However, the correlations between the shame- and guilt-related factors pertaining to the same offence are so strong (r = 0.96) that these factors lack discriminant validity. That is, they are so strongly correlated that they are unlikely to have any predictive or explanatory utility beyond that of a common shame-guilt factor. To foster parsimony and interpretability, it is better to collapse the highly overlapping guilt and shame factors so as to retain two unified shame-guilt factors – one pertaining to shoplifting and one pertaining to violence. In fact, this reconfiguration turns the four-factor Model 4 into the earlier-discussed two-factor Model 3.

Figure 6.3 Prospective shame-guilt – Model 4 (fully standardised solution)

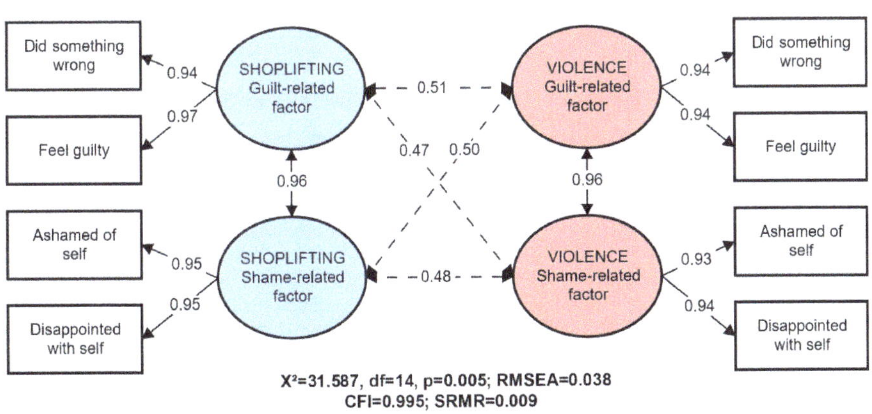

Figure 6.4 Prospective shame-guilt – Model 3 (fully standardised solution)

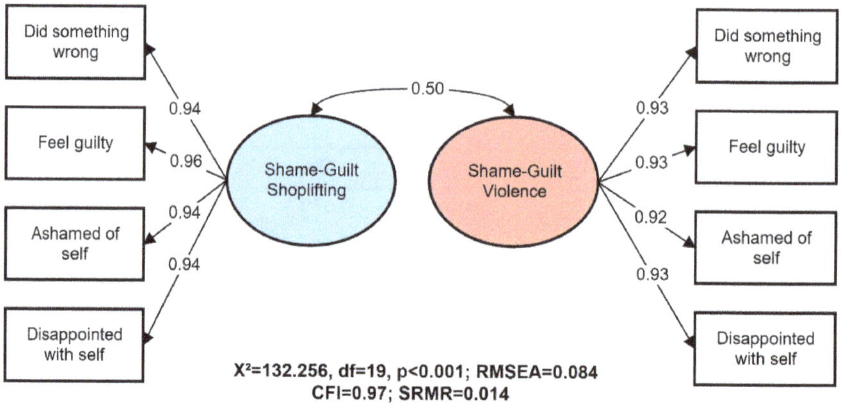

Figure 6.4 illustrates the results of Model 3. The fit of this more parsimonious two-factor model is less good than the four-factor model but still acceptable.[25] Guilt- and shame-related items pertaining to the same offence load highly and positively on a common factor, indicating that they are sufficiently interrelated to warrant combining them into a single 'shame-guilt' construct. Furthermore, the model suggests that shame-guilt for shoplifting can be meaningfully distinguished from shame-guilt for using violence. Nevertheless, the two factors are moderately strongly correlated ($r = 0.50$), indicating that higher levels of shame-guilt for shoplifting go hand in hand with higher levels of shame-guilt for engaging in retaliatory violence. According to the output of Jrule, the fit of the model can be improved by adding residual correlations *either* between the pairs of guilt-related items *or* between the pairs of shame-related items, indicating that the former share some unique variance that is not shared with the latter and vice versa. This is not surprising; both residual correlations are simply the by-product of collapsing the highly overlapping, but not fully equivalent, guilt and shame factors into a single 'shame-guilt' factor. Adding these residual correlations does not substantially affect the factor loadings.[26]

25 This is a good example of a situation in which a complex initial solution fits better than a reconfigured solution that fosters parsimony and interpretability (see Brown, 2015). In this case, the better-fitting but more complex Model 4 indicates some multidimensionality in the items that, in reality, offers no real practical or substantive benefits.

26 Adding residual correlations between the pairs of guilt-related items slightly attenuates the magnitude of their loadings on the common factor and slightly increases the loadings of the shame-related items. In other words, in this reconfiguration, the common factor is slightly more dominated by the shame-related items. Vice versa, adding residual correlations between the pairs of shame-related items slightly attenuates the magnitudes of their loadings on the common factor and slightly increases the factor loadings of the guilt-related items. In other words, in this reconfiguration, the common factor is slightly more dominated

Next, a multiple-group CFA is carried out in which the factor loadings and item intercept values of Model 3 are constrained to be equal across gender groups. This scalar-invariant model shows an acceptable fit to the data (χ^2 = 183.033, df = 50, p < 0.001; RMSEA = 0.079, CFI = 0.97, SRMR = 0.027). According to the output of the Jrule, there are no substantial misspecifications with respect to the invariant intercepts and factor loadings. However, in both gender groups, the fit of the model can be improved by adding residual correlations between pairs of guilt- or shame-related items. Again, this is simply the by-product of collapsing the overlapping, but still not fully equivalent, guilt and shame factors into a single 'shame-guilt' factor. Adding these residual correlations did not substantially affect the structural model parameters. In both gender groups, guilt- and shame-related items pertaining to the same offence load highly and positively on a single factor (standardised factor loadings are all higher than 0.88). In sum, the results suggest that prospective shame-guilt is measured in a sufficiently similar way across gender groups.

Table 6.2 Prospective shame-guilt by gender: descriptive statistics and t-test

			Males	Females	
Variable	Range	Omega reliability	M (SD)	M (SD)	t
Shame-guilt – shoplifting	1-5	0.97	2.97 (1.45)	3.67 (1.37)	−7.19***
Shame-guilt – violence	1-5	0.96	2.14 (1.20)	3.11 (1.42)	−10.69***

*p < 0.05, **p < 0.01, ***p < 0.001.

In light of these CFA results, two composite scores are created by averaging respondents' scores across the four guilt- and shame-related items pertaining to shoplifting and retaliatory violence, respectively. The internal consistency reliability of these composite scores is ω = 0.97 for shoplifting and ω = 0.96 for retaliatory violence.[27] Mean composite scores are presented by gender in Table 6.2. Again, one can see that levels of prospective shame-guilt are considerably lower among male adolescents than among female adolescents. In addition, we can see that the gender gap in shame-guilt is somewhat more pronounced with retaliatory violence than with shoplifting. In the former case, there is on

by the guilt-related items. However, the differences between these two solutions are substantively insignificant. In either case, all items load highly on their respective common shame-guilt factors.

27 Reliability of the composite scores was assessed using hierarchical omega (ω_h), estimated with the MBESS package in R (Kelley & Pornprasertmanit, 2016). This reliability coefficient gives the proportion of variance in the total score that is accounted for by a general underlying factor. It makes less unrealistic assumptions than Cronbach's alpha. More specifically, unlike Cronbach's alpha, hierarchical omega does not assume tau-equivalence (equal factor loadings) or uncorrelated residuals.

average almost an entire point difference (on a 5-point scale) between male adolescents and female adolescents. According to Cohen's d-statistic, this is a large effect (d = 0.75). It implies that up to 77% of female adolescents report levels of shame-guilt that are higher than the average level of shame-guilt among male adolescents.

6.2 INDEPENDENT VARIABLES

6.2.1 *Religiosity*

To measure religiosity, respondents were asked to pick one of eight possible answer categories, encompassing both religious group affiliation and religious practice (see supra, Section 5.2.2.). Table 6.3 displays their answers. Only one in five adolescents reports to be nonreligious. About 38% identify as Christian, but the vast majority of them are non-practising or even in doubt about their religious affiliation. Only about 1% of the Christians in the sample regularly go to church. The situation is completely different among those who identify as Muslim, and who make up approximately 38% of the sample. Specifically, more than half of them report to strictly follow Islamic rules and practices. There are only very few Muslims in the sample who are in doubt about their religious faith and identity (2%). The category 'other', finally, contains adolescents who identify with other denominations such as Jehovah's witnesses or Alevism.

Table 6.3 Religious affiliation and religious practice among adolescents in Genk

Affiliation	Practice	%	(n)
Not religious	Not applicable	20	(168)
Christian	Churchgoing	1	(11)
	Non-churchgoing	23	(197)
	In doubt	14	(117)
Muslim	Strict	21	(182)
	Non-strict	15	(127)
	In doubt	2	(16)
Other	Unknown	4	(32)

For analytic purposes, the religiosity variable is recoded into five categories, the first of which is considered the reference category, containing the nonreligious respondents as well as the (many) Christian and (few) Muslim adolescents who are in doubt about their religious faith and identity. The 'doubters' are put together with the nonreligious rather than with the religious respondents to keep the latter group as 'religious' as possible. The second category contains all adolescents who self-identify as 'religious Christian', both those who regularly go to church and those who do not. However, as only 11 Christians in the sample regularly go to church, this category really is a category of religious but non-practising Christians. The third category contains adolescents who identify as 'religious Muslim' and who report to strictly follow Islamic rules and practices. The fourth category contains adolescents who identify as 'religious Muslim' but who report *not* to strictly follow Islamic rules and practices. The fifth category is a 'rest' category, comprising the few respondents who identify with other denominations. This category is too small and heterogeneous to draw any meaningful conclusions from, but it is included in the analyses nonetheless to avoid having to remove these respondents from the sample. Table 6.4 presents the distribution of the respondents over the different categories by gender. One can see that the gender differences are too small to be of significance ($\chi^2 = 2.02$, df = 3, $p = 0.57$).

Table 6.4 Religiosity (recoded variable) by gender: descriptive statistics

	Male adolescents		Female adolescents	
	%	(n)	%	(n)
Not religious/hesitant	37	(174)	34	(127)
Christian	24	(112)	25	(95)
Muslim, strict	21	(97)	22	(84)
Muslim, non-strict	15	(69)	15	(57)
Other	3	(21)	3	(11)

6.2.2 *Relationship with parents*

To evaluate the dimensionality and factor structure of the items tapping into the closeness of the parent-adolescent relationship, a model with two correlated factors is specified in which the items pertaining to fathers' knowledge of their children's activities, whereabouts and friends load on the first factor and the items pertaining to mothers' knowledge of their children's activities, whereabouts and friends load on the second factor. Overall, this model has a poor fit to the data ($\chi^2 = 212.457$, df = 8, $p < 0.001$, RMSEA = 0.17, CFI = 0.88, SRMR = 0.037). The output of Jrule indicates that the fit can be improved by allowing residual correlations between identical items that differ only with respect to the referent parent (e.g. 'my *father* knows who my friends are' and 'my *mother* knows who my friends are'). This implies that adolescents' perceptions of their mothers' and fathers' knowledge are correlated not only in general, but also, over and above that, with respect to specific issues. A reconfigured model including these residual correlations has a very good fit to the data ($\chi^2 = 3.44$, df = 5, $p = 0.63$, RMSEA = 0.00, CFI = 1.00, SRMR = 0.01).

Figure 6.5 displays the results of the final model. All items load highly on their respective factors, with standardised loadings ranging from 0.76 to 0.90 for the adolescents' relationship with the fathers and 0.77 to 0.95 for the adolescents' relationship with the mothers. Adolescents' perceptions of their mothers' and fathers' knowledge are moderately correlated. A multiple-group model in which the factor loadings and intercepts of the final model are constrained to be equal for male adolescents and female adolescents (scalar invariance) has a good fit to the data ($\chi^2 = 31.286$, df = 18, p = 0.03, RMSEA = 0.04, CFI = 0.99, SRMR = 0.04). This implies that the meaning of the constructs and the levels of the underlying items are similar across gender groups and, consequently, that observed composite scores can be meaningfully compared between male adolescents and female adolescents.

Figure 6.5 Relationship with parents, final CFA model (fully standardised solution)

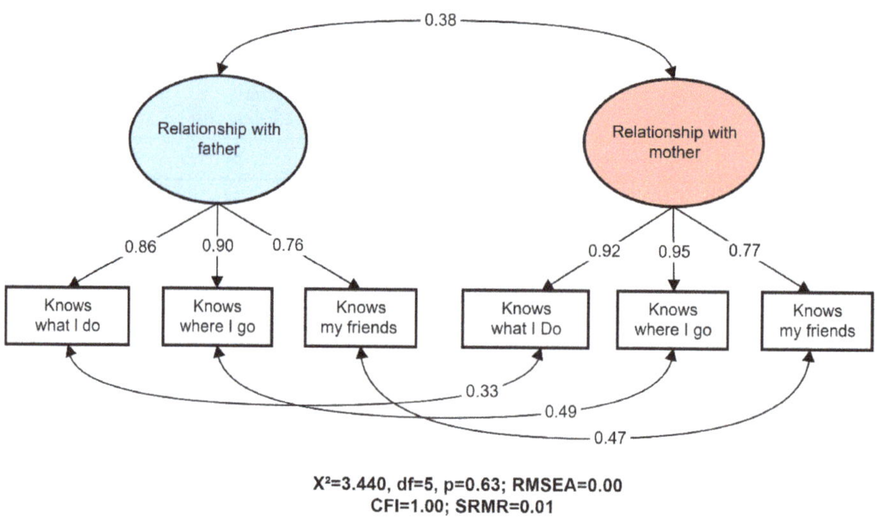

Ideally, based on these CFA results, two separate composite scores should be created to represent the two factors: closeness of the father-adolescent relationship and closeness of the mother-adolescent relationship. However, the theoretical framework that guides this study offers little in the way of predictions about the relative or unique importance of the relationship with the father versus the mother for prospective shame-guilt. Therefore, a single composite score is calculated by averaging respondents' scores across all six items. This gives us a global view of the quality of the relationship with the parents. Averaging (rather than summing) the responses across all items mitigates against artificially low composite scores resulting from missing responses (i.e. from respondents with only one parent).[28] Furthermore, by averaging, the original scale range is retained. Mean composite scores are presented by gender in Table 6.5. One can see that female adolescents report a closer relationship to their parents than male adolescents. Although statistically significant, however, the magnitude of this difference is small.

Table 6.5 Strength of the relationship with parents by gender: descriptive statistics and t-test

			Males	Females	
Variable	Range	Omega reliability	M (SD)	M (SD)	t
Relationship parents (combined)	1-5	/	3.84 (0.91)	4.02 (0.86)	−3.20**

*p < 0.05, **p < 0.01, ***p < 0.001.

6.2.3 *Relationship with teachers*

The CFA results displayed in Figure 6.6 suggest that a single factor structure is a good fit to the three items measuring the quality of the teacher-adolescent relationship ($\chi^2 = 2.407$, df = 1, p = 0.12, RMSEA = 0.041, CFI = 0.99, SRMR = 0.032).[29] All items have relatively high standardised loadings on the underlying factor, ranging from 0.65 to 0.78. According to the output of Jrule, the model contains no substantive misspecifications. The results of a multiple-group model in which the loadings and intercepts are constrained to be equal for male adolescents and female adolescents shows a good fit to the data ($\chi^2 = 31.286$, df = 18, p = 0.03, RMSEA = 0.04, CFI = 0.99, SRMR = 0.04). In other words, scalar invariance is supported, and observed composite scores can be meaningfully compared between male adolescents and female adolescents.

28 Only a very small portion of the respondents filled in the mother-related but not the father-related items or vice versa (<5%).

29 A single-factor model with three indicator variables is just-identified (zero degrees of freedom) and is thus not testable. To free up degrees of freedom and arrive at a testable model, the unstandardised factor loadings (not shown in the figure) were restricted to be equal (tau-equivalence).

Figure 6.6 Relationship with teachers, final CFA model (fully standardised solution)

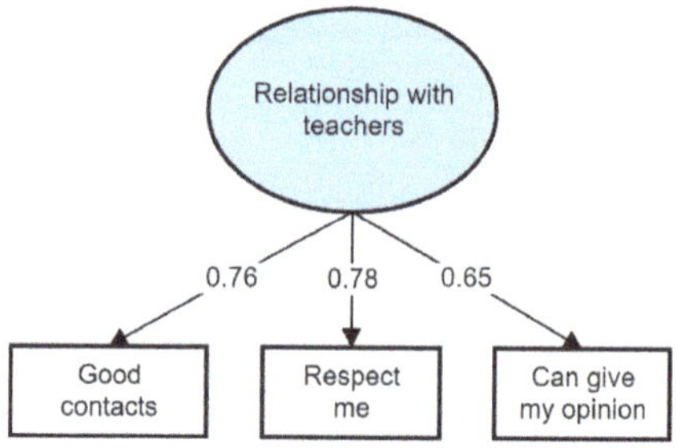

Composite scores are obtained by averaging respondents' scores across the three items. The internal consistency reliability of these composite scores is good ($\omega = 0.77$). Mean composite scores are presented by gender in Table 6.6. Perhaps somewhat surprisingly, there is no gender difference in the quality of the teacher-student relationship in our sample.

Table 6.6 Strength of the relationship with teachers by gender: descriptive statistics and t-test

			Males	Females	
Variable	Range	Omega reliability	M (SD)	M (SD)	t
Relationship teachers	1-5	0.77	3.55 (0.81)	3.58 (0.78)	−0.66

$^{*}p < 0.05$, $^{**}p < 0.01$, $^{***}p < 0.001$.

6.2.4 *Perceived delinquency of friends*

Respondents were asked to indicate how many of their friends engaged in various forms of delinquency, including shoplifting and violence (i.e. physical assault). In accordance with the measurement of prospective guilt and shame in relation to shoplifting and violence, only the items measuring perceptions of friends' involvement in shoplifting and violence will be used in this study. The distribution of the responses is presented by offence type and by gender in Table 6.7.

Table 6.7 Peer delinquency by offence type and by gender

		Males		Females	
	How many friends?	%	(n)	%	(n)
Shoplifting					
	None	64	(302)	73	(273)
	A few of them	30	(141)	23	(86)
	Most of them	5	(25)	4	(13)
	All of them	2	(7)	1	(2)
Violence					
	None	58	(277)	83	(309)
	A few of them	30	(144)	15	(57)
	Most of them	8	(40)	1	(5)
	All of them	3	(13)	1	(3)

About 37% of the male adolescents report having at least a few friends who shoplifted, compared to only 28% of the female adolescents ($\chi^2 = 8.06$, df = 1, $p < 0.01$). The gender difference is more strongly pronounced in the case of violence. Up to 41% of the male adolescents report having at least a few friends who violently hit someone, compared to only 17% of the female adolescents ($\chi^2 = 56.13$, df = 1, $p < 0.001$). For both male adolescents and female adolescents, delinquent friends are usually a minority among friends. Indeed, regardless of gender, few respondents report that 'most' or 'all' of their friends shoplifted or hit someone. Because of these low numbers, the two variables are dichotomised into two categories for further analyses: 'not having shoplifting/violent friends' versus 'having shoplifting/violent friends'.

6.2.5 *Reflected appraisals as a troublemaker*

To evaluate the dimensionality and factor structure of the items measuring reflected appraisals of the self as a troublemaker, a model with three correlated factors is specified. All items pertaining to parent-reflected appraisals load on the first factor, all items pertaining to teacher-reflected appraisals load on the second factor and all items pertaining to peer-reflected appraisals load on the third factor. Following De Coster and Lutz (2018) and Matsueda (1992), the measurement model contains residual correlations between identical items that differ only with respect to the referent significant other (e.g. 'causes troubles' from the standpoint of parents, teachers and friends). The CFA results suggest that the model has a good fit to the data ($\chi^2 = 26.615$, df = 18, p = 0.09, RMSEA = 0.024, CFI = 0.99, SRMR = 0.018). According to the output of Jrule, the model contains no substantive misspecifications.

Figure 6.7 Reflected appraisals as a troublemaker, final CFA model (fully standardised solution)

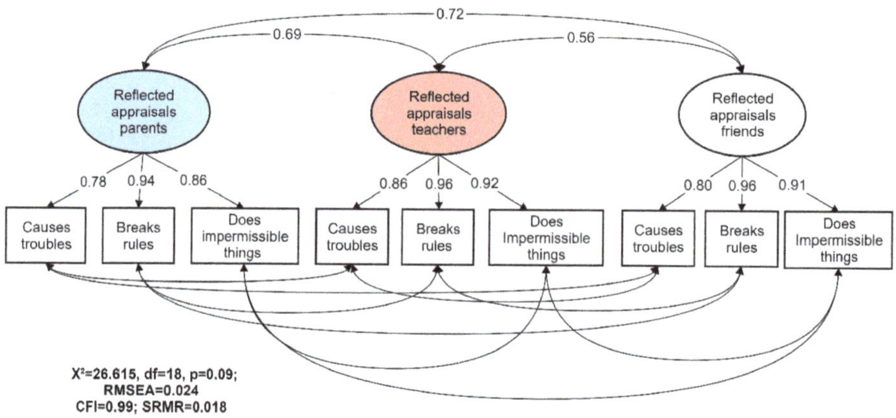

Figure 6.7 displays the results of the final model.[30] All items load highly on their respective factors, with standardised loadings ranging from 0.78 to 0.94 for parent-reflected appraisals, from 0.86 to 0.96 for teacher-reflected appraisals and from 0.80 to 0.91 for peer-reflected appraisals. Parent-, teacher- and peer-reflected appraisals of the self as a troublemaker are highly correlated, ranging from 0.56 (between teacher- and peer-reflected appraisals) to 0.72 (between parent- and peer-reflected appraisals). A multiple-group model in which the factor loadings and intercepts of the final model are constrained to be equal for male adolescents and female adolescents (scalar invariance) has an excellent fit to the data ($\chi^2 = 41.719$, df = 48, p = 0.73, RMSEA = 0.00, CFI = 1.00, SRMR = 0.023). This implies that the meaning of the constructs and the levels of the underlying items are similar across gender groups and, consequently, that observed composite scores can be meaningfully compared between male adolescents and female adolescents.

Three composite scores – for each of the three factors – are created by averaging the respondents' scores across items. The internal consistency reliability of these composite scores is high, ranging from $\omega = 0.90$ for parental appraisals to $\omega = 0.94$ for teacher appraisals. Higher scores indicate stronger perceptions of being seen as a troublemaker. Table 6.8 presents mean composite scores by subscale and gender. Mean scores are low, indicating that most adolescents in the sample do not view themselves as troublemakers from the perspective of others. Nevertheless, male adolescents have significantly stronger perceptions of themselves as troublemakers from the perspective of others than are female

30 The correlated errors are omitted from the figure to simplify the presentation.

adolescents. This gender difference is larger for teacher- and peer-reflected appraisals (on average, almost half a point on a 1-5 scale) than for parent-reflected appraisals.

Table 6.8 Reflected appraisals as a troublemaker by gender: descriptive statistics and t-test

			Males	Females	
Variable	Range	Omega reliability	M (SD)	M (SD)	t
Reflected appraisals by parents	1-5	0.90	1.84 (0.96)	1.64 (0.92)	3.14**
Reflected appraisals by teachers	1-5	0.94	1.99 (1.09)	1.61 (0.89)	5.63***
Reflected appraisals by friends	1-5	0.92	2.2 (1.1)	1.81 (1.02)	4.95**

*p < 0.05, **p < 0.01, ***p < 0.001.

6.2.6 *Traditional gender role attitudes*

The scale that is used in this study to measure traditional gender role attitudes, developed by Vermeersch et al. (2010), encompasses two subscales: a traditional masculinity subscale for male adolescents and a traditional femininity subscale for female adolescents. Accordingly, the factor structure and dimensionality of the traditional masculinity items is tested in the male subsample and the factor structure and dimensionality of the traditional femininity items is tested in the female subsample.[31]

A single-factor model for the masculinity items has a poor fit to the data ($\chi^2 = 63.313$, df = 5, $p < 0.001$, RMSEA = 0.16, CFI = 0.87, SRMR = 0.052). The output of Jrule indicates that the model fit can be improved by adding a residual correlation between the items 'I find it disturbing if a boy behaves like a girl' and 'There is definitely something wrong with a boy practicing ballet as a hobby.' These residuals are allowed to correlate because the items share considerable conceptual overlap (the latter item can be seen as a specific instance of the former, more general item). A reconfigured model including this residual correlation has a good fit to the data ($\chi^2 = 7.845$, df = 4, p = 0.10, RMSEA = 0.045, CFI = 0.99, SRMR = 0.017). Figure 6.8 displays the results of this model. Notwithstanding the residual correlation, all items load sufficiently high on a single underlying factor, with standardised loadings ranging from 0.50 to 0.76. Composite scores are obtained by averaging adolescents' scores across the five items. The reliability of the composite score is good ($\omega = 0.78$).

31 Also in subsequent analyses, the relationship between traditional masculinity and prospective shame-guilt will be tested in the male subsample, whereas the relationship between traditional femininity and prospective shame-guilt will be tested in the female subsample.

Figure 6.8 Traditional masculinity, final CFA model (fully standardised solution, male subsample)

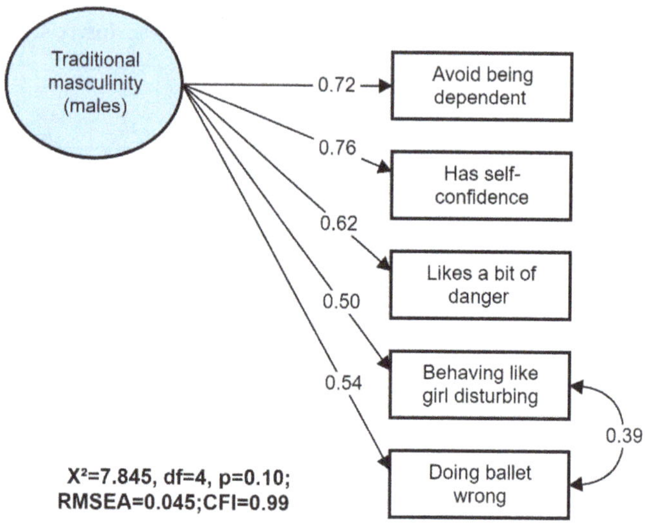

Figure 6.9 Traditional femininity, final CFA model (fully standardised solution, female subsample)

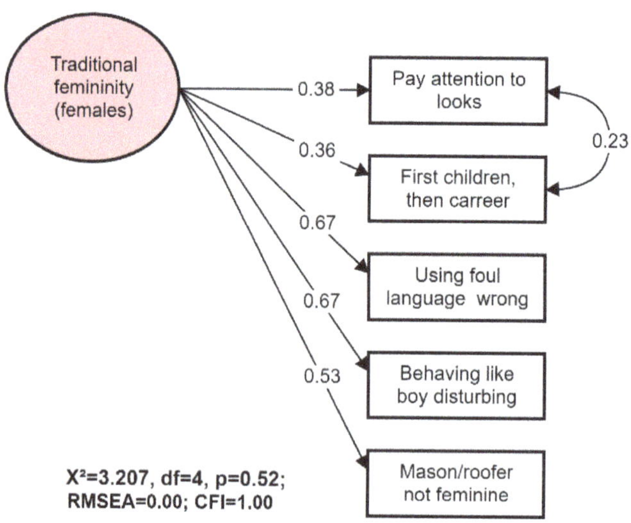

Next, a single-factor model is specified for the femininity items. This model demonstrated a mediocre but acceptable fit to the data (χ^2 = 15.781, df = 5, p = 0.008, RMSEA = 0.076, CFI = 0.94, SRMR = 0.041). According to the output of Jrule, the fit can be improved by adding a residual correlation between the items 'It's only natural that girls pay more attention to their looks than boys' and 'Women should first consider their children, and only then their career.' Both items refer to prescriptive gender norms (what women should do), whereas the three others items refer to proscriptive gender norms (what women should not do): 'There is definitely something wrong with girls who use foul language'; 'If I heard a woman was a mason or a roofer, I would doubt whether she was 'feminine'; and 'I find it disturbing if a girl behaves like a boy.' Including this residual correlation results in a good-fitting model (χ^2 = 3.207, df = 4, p = 0.52, RMSEA = 0.00, CFI = 1.00, SRMR = 0.016). However, as can be seen in Figure 6.9, the two items have relatively low standardised factor loadings (0.38 and 0.36, respectively) on the underlying factor, indicating that they may represent a different dimension of traditional femininity. One possibility to deal with this issue is to remove these two items from the scale.[32] However, this would lead to a loss of generality of the factor (i.e. a decrease in content validity). As an alternative solution, two composite scores are created for further analyses: a total score (respondents' average score across all five items) and a reduced score (respondents' average score across the three items that load sufficiently high on the underlying factor). The reduced score can be used for sensitivity checks. The reliability of both scores can be considered mediocre but acceptable (ω = 0.66 for the total score and ω = 0.67 for the reduced score).

Table 6.9 presents mean composite scores by subscale and gender. Higher scores indicate higher adherence to traditional masculinity/femininity norms. In line with previous studies (e.g. Halimi et al., 2018), we find that male adolescents hold more traditional gender role attitudes than female adolescents in the sense that the formers' scores on traditional masculinity are higher than the latters' scores on traditional femininity.

Table 6.9 Traditional masculinity and femininity: descriptive statistics

			Males	Females
Variable	Range	Omega reliability	M (SD)	M (SD)
Traditional masculinity	1-5	0.78	3.04 (0.91)	/
Traditional femininity (total score)	1-5	0.66	/	2.78 (0.83)
Traditional femininity (reduced score)	1-5	0.67	/	2.39 (0.95)

32 Another possibility is to create a second factor. However, with only two items and little theoretical guidance, this factor would be difficult to interpret.

6.2.7 *Prior delinquency*

To measure prior involvement in delinquency, using an open-ended format, the respondents were asked how many times they had engaged in various delinquent acts in the past 12 months. Responses to the two items concerning theft ('shoplifting' and 'theft from a person') were summed and censored at 6 to create a 7-point index of self-reported theft (with '0' indicating no delinquent activity and '6' indicating six or more acts of theft). A similar procedure was used to create a 7-point index of self-reported violence (based on the items 'robbery', 'aggravated assault' and 'group fight'). Mean delinquency scores are presented by gender in Table 6.10. As with most delinquency research in nonforensic samples, these score are low, indicating that most respondents did not commit any delinquent offences during the reference period. In line with the criminological literature, there are significant differences between male adolescents and female adolescents in their delinquent behaviour. In general, male adolescents commit more offences than female adolescents, and the gender gap is considerably larger for violent offences than for theft.

Table 6.10 Prior delinquency: descriptive statistics and t-test

			Males	Females	
Variable	Range	Omega reliability	M (SD)	M (SD)	t
Prior Theft	0-6	/	0.49 (1.30)	0.31 (1.06)	2.21*
Prior Violence	0-6	/	0.91 (1.76)	0.34 (0.97)	6.01***

*p < 0.05, **p < 0.01, ***p < 0.001.

6.3 CONCLUSION

This chapter has presented descriptive statistics for all variables used in this study. In addition, the dimensionality and validity of all multi-item scales were assessed using CFA, with specific attention for the items measuring prospective guilt and shame. Multiple-group CFA was used to test for measurement invariance across gender groups. Finally, a series of t-tests and chi-square tests were performed to assess gender differences in prospective shame-guilt and all independent variables of interest.

The descriptive analysis showed that there was considerable variation in the degree to which adolescents in the sample anticipated feeling guilty and ashamed for engaging in delinquency. According to a CFA of the responses, guilt- and shame-related items pertaining to the same offence loaded highly and positively on a single common factor, suggesting that prospective guilt and shame are closely intertwined rather than separate processes when adolescents consider offending. The CFA results also revealed that prospective shame-guilt for shoplifting could be meaningfully distinguished from prospective shame-guilt for retaliatory violence, although the two factors were moderately correlated. This suggests that explanations of differences between adolescents in prospective shame-guilt should consider not only factors that may affect the general propensity for shame-guilt across different types of offences but also factors that may increase or decreases levels of shame-guilt in relation to particular offences. A multiple-group CFA further indicated that the factor structure, factor loadings and intercepts of the guilt and shame items were invariant across gender, enabling a meaningful comparison of the scale scores between male adolescents and female adolescents. In line with previous research, it was found that levels of prospective shame-guilt were considerably higher for female adolescents than for male adolescents.

With one exception, all independent variables measured through multi-item scales had good measurement properties, with items loading highly on their hypothesised and theoretically meaningful factors. Two items of the 'traditional femininity' subscale of the traditional gender role attitudes scale had relatively low factor loadings and correlated errors of measurement, suggesting that content revision may be required for these items. In addition, the internal consistency reliability of the composite score was mediocre. To deal with this problem, two separate composite scores were computed: one that took into account these two items and one that did not. Several independent variables differed significantly by gender: the closeness of the relationship with parents, perceived delinquency of friends, and reflected appraisals as a troublemaker. These variables are potential mediators of the association between gender and prospective shame-guilt.

7 MAIN FINDINGS

> Sociology might move forward more rapidly if we gave much more attention to applying substantive standards to see if a variable has a big or small effect rather than worrying about whether a coefficient should receive two or one stars in reporting statistical significance.
> (Bollen, 1995, p. 468)

In the fourth chapter, I formulated a set of hypotheses about the social factors that might contribute to individual and gender differences in prospective guilt and shame. This chapter presents the analyses conducted to test these hypotheses. I start by describing the analytical strategy, the statistical models and the benchmarking of the estimates. I then report the results of a series of multivariate regression and path analyses, both in tables and in graphs. I conclude this chapter with a discussion of these results in light of the research hypotheses and previously published studies on the topic. The general conclusion, the main limitations and directions for future research will be presented in the next and final chapter.

7.1 ANALYTIC STRATEGY

The analyses will proceed in three steps. In a first step, a series of multivariate regression models is estimated for the whole sample, once with prospective shame-guilt for shoplifting and once with prospective shame-guilt for retaliatory violence as the dependent variable. The baseline model (Model 1) includes the sociodemographic variables gender, age and migration background. The key variables of interest are added separately to this baseline model. More specifically, Model 2 adds the religiosity variable, comparing adolescents who are not religious (or hesitant about their faith) to Christian adolescents, Muslim adolescents who are strict in following religious rules, Muslim adolescents who are not strict in following religious rules and a rest category.[33] Model 3 adds the variables measuring the closeness of the parent-adolescent relationship and the quality of the teacher-adolescent relationship. Model 4 adds the variable measuring perceptions of friends' delinquency, comparing adolescents who report having delinquent friends to those who do not. Model 5 adds the informal labelling processes, in the form of three

33 This rest category will not be discussed because it is too small and heterogeneous to draw any meaningful conclusions from. It is included in the model nonetheless to avoid reducing the sample size.

variables measuring reflected appraisals of the self as a 'troublemaker' from the perspective of parents, teachers and friends, respectively. The purpose of these five models is: (1) to examine the extent to which each of these variables is associated with prospective shame-guilt and (2) to examine the extent to which adding each variable separately to the baseline model reduces the magnitude of the gender coefficient (and thus possibly accounts for gender difference in prospective shame-guilt). Finally, two full models are estimated to isolate the effect of each variable on shame-guilt while adjusting for the effects of all other variables, once without (Model 6) and once with (Model 7) controlling for prior involvement in theft/violence.

Recall that prior delinquency may be a potential confounder of the relationship between some of the independent variables in this study and prospective shame-guilt (see Chapter 5, Section 5.3.2.*h*). Alternatively, prior involvement in delinquency may also act as a proxy measure for prior levels of prospective shame-guilt (i.e. the more delinquency one committed in the past, the less one may have previously been prone to shame-guilt). Adjusting for prior delinquency, then, removes meaningful variance from the dependent variable and lowers the variance that remains to be explained by the variables of interest. Since both possibilities are plausible, the full models are estimated both with and without controlling for this variable. The results from the full model adjusting for prior delinquency (Model 7) may be considered conservative or lower-bound estimates.

In a second step, the full model (Model 7) is disaggregated by gender to examine whether the proposed social factors affect prospective shame-guilt differently for male adolescents and female adolescents. These subgroup analyses are particularly important to test the hypothesis proposing that traditional gender attitudes (traditional masculinity and traditional femininity) have different effects on shame-guilt across gender. The formula provided in Paternoster et al. (1998) is used to test for gender differences in the coefficients.

In a third and final step, a multiple mediation path analysis is conducted to more robustly evaluate potential mediators of the relationship between gender and prospective shame-guilt. A variable's viability as a mediator of the relationship between gender and shame-guilt is evaluated on the basis of the following criteria: (a) the variable differs significantly by gender (see previous chapter); (b) the variable is a significant predictor of shame-guilt in the multiple regression analysis; and (c) adding the variable to the baseline model reduces the magnitude of the gender coefficient (see Rebellon et al., 2016, for a similar strategy).

7.2 BENCHMARKING OF THE COEFFICIENT ESTIMATES

The results of the multivariate regression analyses are presented in tables and figures. The tables present unstandardised regression coefficients. Unlike their standardised counterparts, unstandardised coefficients are not scaled in terms of the variability of the sample or subsample. Therefore, they are more robust and comparable between different studies and between different subgroups within the same study (Baguley, 2009). When comparing the magnitude of regression coefficients across gender, for instance, it is important to use unstandardised coefficients.

However, a disadvantage of using unstandardised coefficients is that it becomes difficult to compare the effect sizes of variables with different metrics within the same model. To facilitate the interpretation and comparison of the effect sizes of different variables, the coefficients are also standardised and graphically represented in figures using an approach by Gelman (2008). In this approach, regression coefficients of binary variables such as gender (or dummy variables) are left unstandardised. In this way, they are easily interpretable as the change in levels of shame-guilt when moving from the reference category (coded as '0') to the category of interest (coded as '1'). Regression coefficients of continuous variables, on the other hand, are standardised by subtracting the mean and dividing by 2 standard deviations. In this way, they are easily interpretable as the change in levels of shame-guilt when moving from low (mean – 1 SD) to high (mean + 1 SD) values on the variable in question. This standardisation makes the regression coefficients of continuous variables comparable with each other and puts them on roughly the same scale as the coefficients of the untransformed binary variables (see Gelman, 2008, for a detailed explanation).

Evaluating whether the effect of a given independent variable on prospective shame-guilt is not only statistically significant but also substantively relevant is not an easy task. It requires an informed benchmarking of effect sizes (Bernardi et al., 2017). One way to do this is by comparing the effect sizes of the variables of interest with those of other, more established variables. In this study, the effect size of gender is used as a benchmark. Gender is a good benchmark because it is a consistent correlate of both guilt and shame (Else-Quest et al., 2012). Furthermore, research suggests that gender differences in guilt and shame may have important real-life consequences, leading to lower levels of delinquency among girls and young women (Rebellon et al., 2015, 2016). As discussed in the previous chapter, the largest gender difference observed in this study is in levels of prospective shame-guilt for engaging in retaliatory violence. More specifically, there was a full point difference in the mean shame-guilt scores between male adolescents and female adolescents (on a scale ranging from 1 to 5). In light of this, it seems reasonable to consider effect sizes around 1.0 or higher to be 'large', effect sizes between 0.5 and 1.0 to be 'moderate', and effect sizes lower than 0.5 to be 'small'. This means that for an effect to be considered 'moderate', moving from the reference category to the category of interest, for binary variables, and moving from low to high values, for continuous variables, should be associated with at least a 0.5-point increase in levels of shame-guilt (on a scale ranging from 1 to 5). Ultimately, of course, benchmarking remains a subjective exercise, but making the process explicit increases transparency and allows other researchers to scrutinise and challenge the choices that have been made.

7.3 Prospective shame-guilt for shoplifting

Table 7.1 presents the unstandardised coefficients of seven multivariate regression models with prospective shame-guilt for shoplifting as the dependent variable. Figure 7.1 graphically represents all coefficients of interest and their associated 95% confidence intervals from the full models, estimated without adjustment (Model 6) as well as with adjustment for prior involvement in theft (Model 7). Recall that for the purposes of this figure, the continuous variables are rescaled by subtracting the mean and dividing by two times the standard deviation (whereas the binary variables are left unstandardised).[34] The confidence intervals give us a range of values for the coefficients of interest that are consistent with the data. This allows for a discussion of effect sizes and for conveying uncertainty in inference. The dotted lines in the figure at −0.5/+0.5 and at −1.0/+1.0 indicate the minimum threshold for, respectively, a moderate and a large effect. The results warrant six conclusions.

First, Model 1 reveals a positive effect of age on shame-guilt for shoplifting. Though statistically significant, the effect is very small, indicating that the average level of shame-guilt increases only marginally during middle to late adolescence. Model 1 further reveals that levels of shame-guilt for shoplifting are considerably higher among adolescents with an immigrant background than among adolescents with Belgian-born parents. Net of these associations, levels of shame-guilt for shoplifting remain considerably higher among female adolescents than among male adolescents. For exploratory purposes, it was also examined whether the magnitude of the gender gap varied by migration background, but this was not the case.

34 In this way, the regression coefficients are interpretable as the change in levels of shame-guilt when moving from low (mean − 1 SD) to high (mean + 1 SD) values, for continuous variables, and from the reference category (coded as '0') to the category of interest (coded as '1'), for binary variables.

Table 7.1 Multiple regression models with shame-guilt for shoplifting as dependent variable

	Model 1	Model 2	Model 3	Model 4	Model 5	Model 6	Model 7
Female	0.73***	0.69***	0.64***	0.61***	0.60***	0.50***	0.48***
Age	0.07**	0.07**	0.06*	0.03	0.06*	0.03	0.01
Immigrant background	0.49***	−0.08	0.51***	0.45***	0.59***	0.06	0.10
Religiosity (0: not/hesitant)							
Christian		0.45***				0.35**	0.37***
Muslim strict		1.39***				1.08***	0.96***
Muslim non-strict		0.91***				0.89***	0.79***
Relationship with parents			0.37***			0.23***	0.23***
Relationship with teachers			0.28***			0.27***	0.25***
Shoplifting friends (0: no)				−0.97***		−0.62***	−0.42***
Troublemaker (by parents)					−0.07	0.00	0.02
Troublemaker (by teachers)					0.10	0.12*	0.11*
Troublemaker (by friends)					−0.42***	−0.32***	−0.26***
Prior theft							−0.65***
(Prior theft)^2							0.08***
N	829	824	824	828	820	810	810
Adjusted R^2	0.09	0.19	0.18	0.19	0.18	0.36	0.40

*p < 0.05, **p < 0.01, ****p < 0.001.
Note: All variables are unstandardised.

Figure 7.1 Shame-guilt for shoplifting: plot of coefficients and 95% CIs

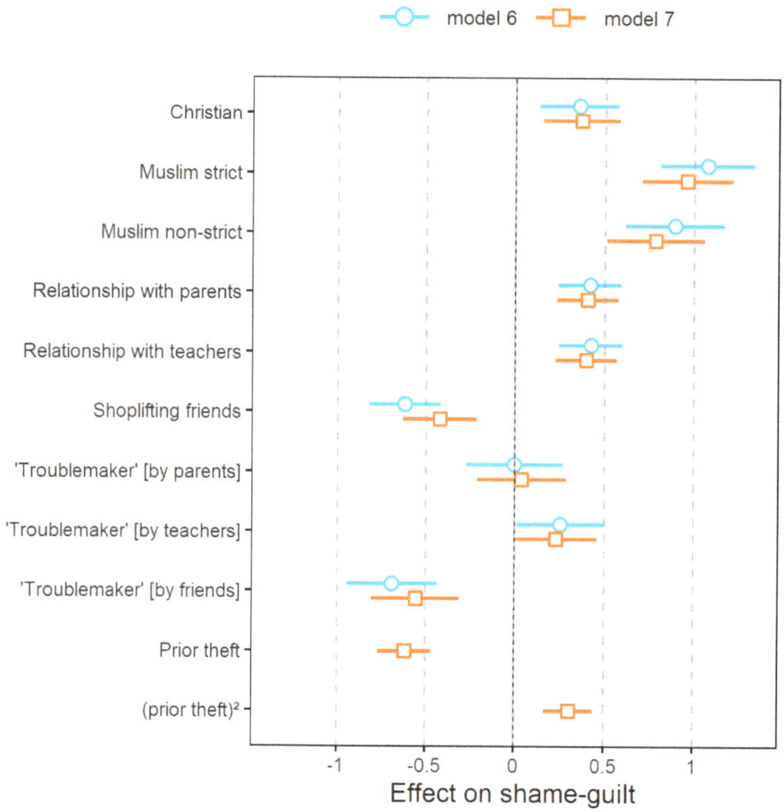

Note: Binary variables are unstandardised. Continuous variables are mean-centred and scaled by 2 SDs.

Second, there is a clear effect of religiosity on shame-guilt for shoplifting throughout the analysis (see Models 2, 6 and 7). Both Christian and Muslim adolescents anticipate higher levels of shame-guilt than adolescents who are not religious or hesitant about their faith. As hypothesised, the magnitude of the effect differs by religious affiliation, with Muslims anticipating considerably higher levels of shame-guilt for shoplifting than Christians. The confidence intervals for the effects of being a strict or a non-strict Muslim contain moderate and large effects. The confidence interval for the effect of being Christian is more compatible with a small effect. Recall that almost all Christian adolescents in the sample are non-practising Catholics. Model 2 further reveals that levels of shame-guilt are higher among strict than among non-strict Muslims (approximately half-a-point difference). When taking into account the effects of other factors, however, the difference between the two groups reduces considerably and becomes statistically indistinguishable from 0 (see Models 6 and 7). Finally, though religiosity does little to mediate the effects of gender, it does seem to fully mediate the effect of immigration background on shame-guilt. As we have seen, levels of shame-guilt for shoplifting are considerably higher among adolescents with an immigrant background than among adolescents with two native Belgian parents. These differences disappear when the effects of religiosity and religious affiliation are taken into account.

Third, as hypothesised, adolescents who experience closer relationships with parents and more supportive relationships with teachers anticipate higher levels of shame-guilt for shoplifting (see Model 3). This holds true even when controlling for the effects of other social factors and prior involvement in theft (see Models 6 and 7). Though statistically significant, the confidence intervals for these two variables mostly contain small effects. Furthermore, we can see that the gender coefficient of Model 3 is slightly lower than the corresponding coefficient of Model 1 (a decrease by about 12%), suggesting that the closeness of the parent-adolescent relationship – a variable that differs significantly by gender – may account for a (small) part of the gender gap in shame-guilt for shoplifting.

Fourth, as hypothesised, adolescents who report having friends who engage in theft anticipate considerably lower levels of shame-guilt than those who do not (see Model 4). Although the effect decreases somewhat in size when adjusting for the effects of other social factors and prior involvement in theft (see Models 6 and 7), the confidence interval is still consistent with a moderate effect. Furthermore, we can see that the gender coefficient of Model 4 is lower than the corresponding coefficient of Model 1 (a decrease by 16%), suggesting that perceived friends' delinquency – a variable that differs significantly by gender – may account for a (small) part of the gender gap in shame-guilt for shoplifting.

Fifth, the effects of reflected appraisals as a troublemaker on shame-guilt depend on who is holding up the mirror. As hypothesised, reflected appraisals as a troublemaker *by friends* have a negative effect on levels of shame-guilt (see Model 5). Although the effect decreases somewhat when adjusting for the effects of other social factors and prior involvement in theft (see Models 6 and 7), the confidence interval is still consistent with a moderate effect. Although there is little evidence to support the hypothesis that reflected appraisals as a troublemaker *by parents* affect shame-guilt, reflected appraisals as a troublemaker *by teachers* appear to have a small but unexpectedly positive effect. However, additional analyses indicate that the latter finding may be a consequence of collinearity and should therefore be interpreted with caution.[35] Furthermore, we can see that the

35 Specifically, to investigate this issue, Models 5, 6 and 7 are re-estimated three times, each time including only one of the three variables measuring reflected appraisals. When included separately in the reduced model (Model 5), reflected appraisals as a troublemaker by parents, by teachers and by friends, all have the hypothesised negative effect on shame-guilt. In the full models (Models 6 and 7), however, the effect of reflected appraisals by friends on shame-guilt remains both statistically and substantively significant,

gender coefficient of Model 5 is lower than the corresponding coefficient of Model 1 (a decrease by 18%), suggesting that reflected appraisals as a troublemaker by friends – a variable that differs significantly by gender – may explain some of the gender gap in shame-guilt for shoplifting.

Sixth and finally, prior involvement in theft has a moderate negative effect on prospective shame-guilt for shoplifting (see Model 7). As shown in Figure 7.2, this effect is nonlinear.[36] That is, levels of prospective shame-guilt decrease rapidly with each successive act of theft, but only up to a certain point. After approximately three or four self-reported prior offences, average levels of prospective shame-guilt are low to absent.

Figure 7.2 Effect of prior involvement in theft on shame-guilt for shoplifting

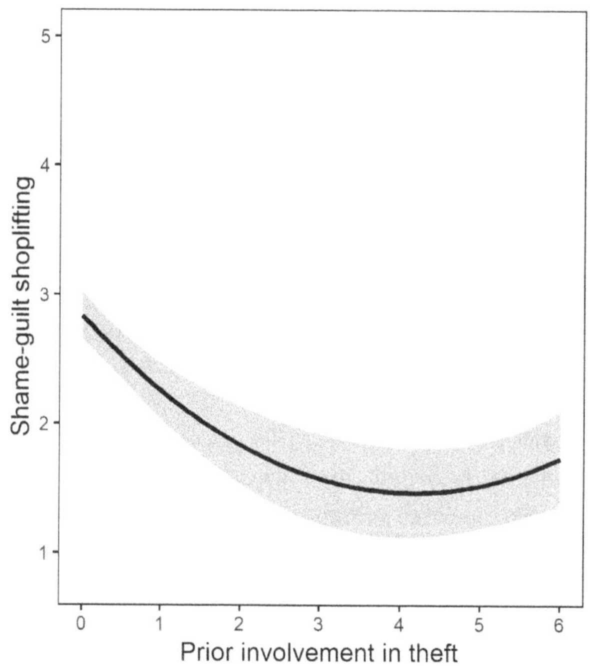

whereas the effects of reflected appraisals by parents and teachers become small and statistically indistinguishable from zero.

36 Hence, the inclusion of a quadratic term in Model 7.

Given the strong positive effect of religious affiliation on levels of shame-guilt, it makes sense to explore whether this variable moderates or buffers the (negative) effects of other independent variables in the model (e.g. having shoplifting friends). However, additional exploratory analyses using interaction terms found no evidence to support such moderation effects.

The models discussed thus far assume that all variables have similar effects on shame-guilt across gender groups. However, one variable in this study is hypothesised to affect shame-guilt differently across gender: traditional gender role attitudes. More specifically, it is expected that adherence to traditional masculinity will be associated with *lower* levels of shame-guilt among male adolescents and that adherence to traditional femininity will be associated with *higher* levels of shame-guilt among female adolescents. To examine this hypothesis, the full regression model (Model 7) is disaggregated by gender. Traditional masculinity is added to the model for male adolescents, and traditional femininity is added to the model for female adolescents. The results are presented in Table 7.2.

As can be seen in Table 7.2, prospective shame-guilt for shoplifting is affected by the same factors in the same way across gender. None of the differences between the coefficients for male adolescents and female adolescents is significant, either statistically or substantially. Also, contrary to expectations, there is no evidence in the data to support the hypothesis that traditional gender role attitudes affect shame-guilt for shoplifting differentially across gender. In fact, neither among male adolescents nor among female adolescents are traditional gender role attitudes associated with shame-guilt; the effects are trivial and not statistically significant.

Table 7.2 Multiple regression model with shame-guilt for shoplifting as dependent variable, estimated separately for male adolescents and female adolescents

	Male adolescents		Female adolescents		Gender difference
	B	(95% CI)	b	(95% CI)	Z
Religiosity (0: not/hesitant)					
Christian	0.45**	(0.16, 0.74)	0.29	(−0.04, 0.63)	0,71
Muslim strict	0.97***	(0.50, 1.45)	0.88**	(0.35, 1.40)	0,25
Muslim non-strict	0.65**	(0.19, 1.11)	0.88**	(0.36, 1.41)	−0.65
Relationship with parents	0.27***	(0.14, 0.40)	0.17*	(0.02, 0.33)	0.94
Relationship with teachers	0.22**	(0.07, 0.37)	0.26**	(0.08, 0.43)	−0.33
Shoplifting friends (0: no)	−0.46***	(−0.72, −0.19)	−0.39*	(−0.74, −0.05)	−0.30
Troublemaker (by parents)	0.05	(−0.11, 0.21)	−0.04	(−0.31, 0.22)	0.59
Troublemaker (by teachers)	0.13	(−0.01, 0.26)	0.10	(−0.12, 0.32)	0.23
Troublemaker (by friends)	−0.23***	(−0.37, −0.10)	−0.26*	(−0.49, −0.03)	0.22
Traditional masculinity	−0.08	(−0.22, 0.06)			
Traditional femininity			−0.11	(−0.28, 0.06)	
N	453		357		
Adjusted R²	0.39		0.35		

*p < 0.05, **p < 0.01, ***p < 0.001.

Note: All variables are unstandardised. Demographic variables 'age' and 'migration background' and control variable 'prior involvement in theft' are not shown.

Given its remarkably strong positive effect on shame-guilt for shoplifting among both male adolescents and female adolescents in the study sample, it makes sense to explore whether religiosity moderates the effects of other variables in the model. Additional analyses using interaction terms show that religiosity strongly moderates the effect of traditional gender role attitudes on shame-guilt, both for male adolescents and female adolescents. Figure 7.3 presents the coefficients for the main and interaction terms. Table 7.3 depicts the interaction effect for ease of interpretation. As the pattern of effects is similar among both strict Muslims and non-strict Muslims, both groups are collapsed into a single category to increase statistical power and precision.

Figure 7.3 Interaction effects of religiosity and traditional gender role attitudes on shame-guilt for shoplifting

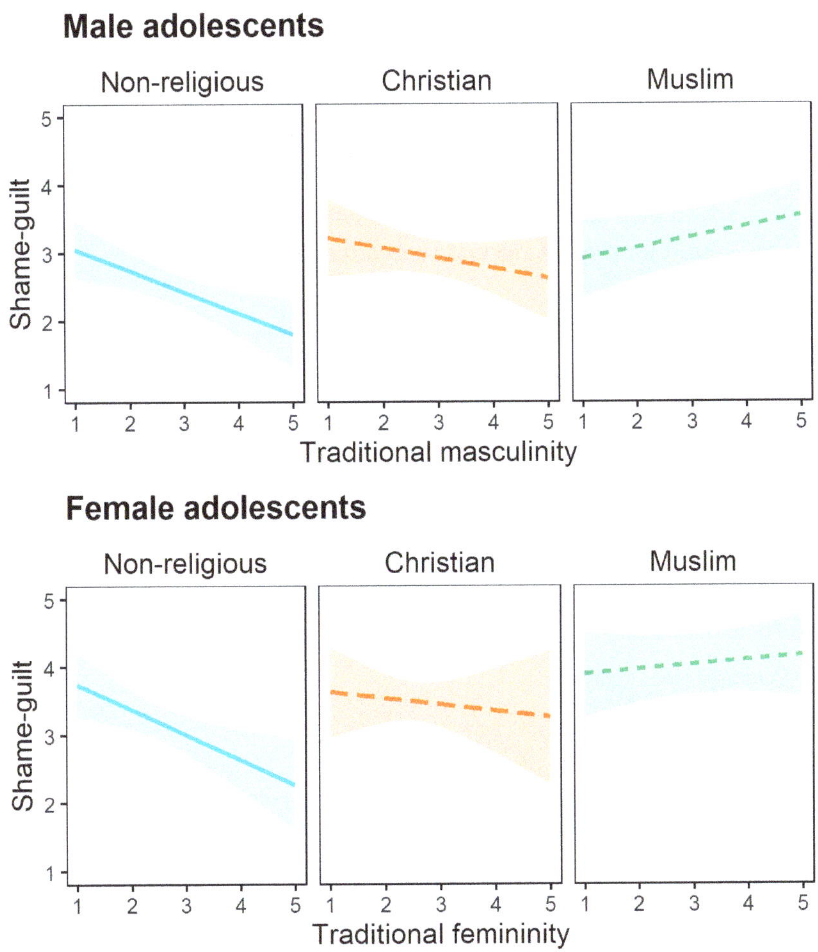

For nonreligious young men, adherence to traditional masculinity has the hypothesised negative effect on prospective shame-guilt. That is, levels of shame-guilt for shoplifting are *lower* among male adolescents who hold more traditional gender role attitudes. As can be seen in Figure 7.3, this effect is both statistically and substantially significant.[37] For Christians, the negative effect of traditional masculinity on shame-guilt is attenuated, and

37 Going from low (mean – 1 SD) to high values (mean + 1SD) on traditional masculinity is associated with a decrease of 0.57 points on the shame-guilt scale (95% CI = –0.97, –0.17).

for Muslims, it completely disappears.[38] A remarkably similar pattern is found among female adolescents. Contrary to expectations, adherence to traditional femininity has a negative effect on prospective shame-guilt for shoplifting among nonreligious female adolescents. That is, levels of shame-guilt are *lower* among those who hold more traditional gender role attitudes. As can be seen in Figure 7.3, this effect is both statistically and substantially significant.[39] For Christians, the negative effect of traditional femininity on shame-guilt is attenuated, and for Muslims, it completely disappears.

Table 7.3 Interaction effects of religiosity and traditional gender role attitudes on shame-guilt for shoplifting: main and interaction terms

	Male adolescents	Female adolescents
	b	B
Religiosity (0: not/hesitant)		
Christian	0.50**	0.38*
Muslim	0.82***	0.93***
Other	1.69***	0.73
Traditional masculinity	−0.31***	
Traditional femininity		−0.37***
Christian * Traditional masculinity	0.16	
Muslim * Traditional masculinity	0.47**	
Other * Traditional masculinity	0.05	
Christian * Traditional femininity		0.28
Muslim * Traditional femininity		0.44**
Other * Traditional femininity		0.04

*p < 0.05, **p < 0.01, *p < 0.001.
Note: All variables are unstandardised. Traditional masculinity and traditional femininity are mean-centred.

7.4 PROSPECTIVE SHAME-GUILT FOR RETALIATORY VIOLENCE

Table 7.4 presents the results of a sequence of seven multivariate regression models with prospective shame-guilt for retaliatory violence as the dependent variable. Figure 7.4 graphically represents all coefficients of interest and their associated 95% confidence intervals from the full models, estimated without adjustment (Model 6) and with adjustment for prior involvement in violence (Model 7). Recall that for the purposes of this figure, the continuous variables are rescaled by subtracting the mean and dividing by

38 Actually, the effect is even positive, but small and not statistically distinguishable from zero.

39 Going from low (mean − 1 SD) to high values (mean + 1SD) on traditional femininity is associated with a decrease of 0.61 points on the shame-guilt scale (95% CI = −1.04, −0.18).

two times the standard deviation (whereas the binary variables are left unstandardised). Again, the results warrant six conclusions.

First, Model 1 reveals a positive association between age and shame-guilt for retaliatory violence. Though statistically significant, the effect is very small, indicating that the average level of shame-guilt increases only marginally during middle to late adolescence. There is little evidence to suggest that levels of shame-guilt for retaliatory violence differ by migration background. Net of these associations, and consistent with the descriptive results discussed in the previous chapter, levels of shame-guilt for retaliatory violence are considerably higher among female adolescents than among male adolescents (approximately a full point difference on a 5-point scale). For exploratory purposes, it was also examined whether this gender difference varied by migration background, but this was not the case.

Table 7.4 Multiple regression models with shame-guilt for retaliatory violence as dependent variable

	Model 1	Model 2	Model 3	Model 4	Model 5	Model 6	Model 7
Female	1.03***	1.02***	0.98***	0.87***	0.94***	0.83***	0.80***
Age	0.08**	0.08**	0.06**	0.07**	0.07**	0.06*	0.05*
Immigrant background	0.00	−0.09	0.01	0.04			
Religiosity (0: not/hesitant)							
Christian		0.21				0.15	0.14
Muslim strict		0.30				0.15	0.14
Muslim non-strict		0.18				0.27	0.29
Relationship with parents			0.17***			0.08	0.09
Relationship with teachers			0.22***			0.20**	0.20**
Violent friends (0: none)				−0.64***	−0.47***		−0.32**
Troublemaker (by parents)					−0.09	−0.06	−0.05
Troublemaker (by teachers)					−0.01	0.04	0.05
Troublemaker (by friends)					−0.17**	−0.13*	−0.09
Prior violence							−0.31**
(Prior violence)^2							0.03*
N	829	824	824	827	820	809	809
Adjusted R^2	0.13	0.14	0.17	0.18	0.17	0.21	0.23

*p < 0.05, **p < 0.01, ***p < 0.001.
Note: All variables are unstandardised.

Second, religiosity is only weakly associated with shame-guilt for retaliatory violence (see Model 2). Although both Christians and Muslims anticipate higher levels of shame-guilt for retaliatory violence than adolescents who are not religious or hesitant about their faith, the differences are small and statistically indistinguishable from zero. At the same time, it should be noted that the confidence intervals around the coefficients associated with the effect of being Muslim (strict or non-strict) are relatively wide, reflecting substantial within-group variance.

Third, as hypothesised, adolescents reporting a closer relationship with their parents and a more supportive relationship with their teachers anticipate higher levels of shame-guilt for retaliatory violence (Model 3). Upon adjusting for the effects of other factors in a full model (see Models 6 and 7), however, the effect of the parent-adolescent relationship weakens considerably and becomes statistically indistinguishable from zero. The confidence interval for the effect of the teacher-adolescent relationship continues to indicate a small but statistically significant effect. The gender coefficient of Model 3 is barely lower than the corresponding coefficient of Model 1 (a decrease by less than 5%), indicating that these two variables do little to mediate gender differences in shame-guilt for retaliatory violence.

Fourth, as hypothesised, adolescents who report having friends who engage in violent behaviour anticipate considerably lower levels of shame-guilt than those who do not (see Model 4). Upon adjusting for the effects of other social factors and prior involvement in violence, however, the effect of friends' violent behaviour decreases somewhat and the confidence interval is more compatible with a small effect (see Models 6 and 7). We can see that the gender coefficient of Model 4 is lower than the corresponding coefficient of Model 1 (a decrease by 15%), indicating that exposure to violent friends – a variable that differs significantly by gender – may account for a small part of the gender gap in shame-guilt for retaliatory violence.

Figure 7.4 Shame-guilt for retaliatory violence: plot of coefficients and 95% CIs

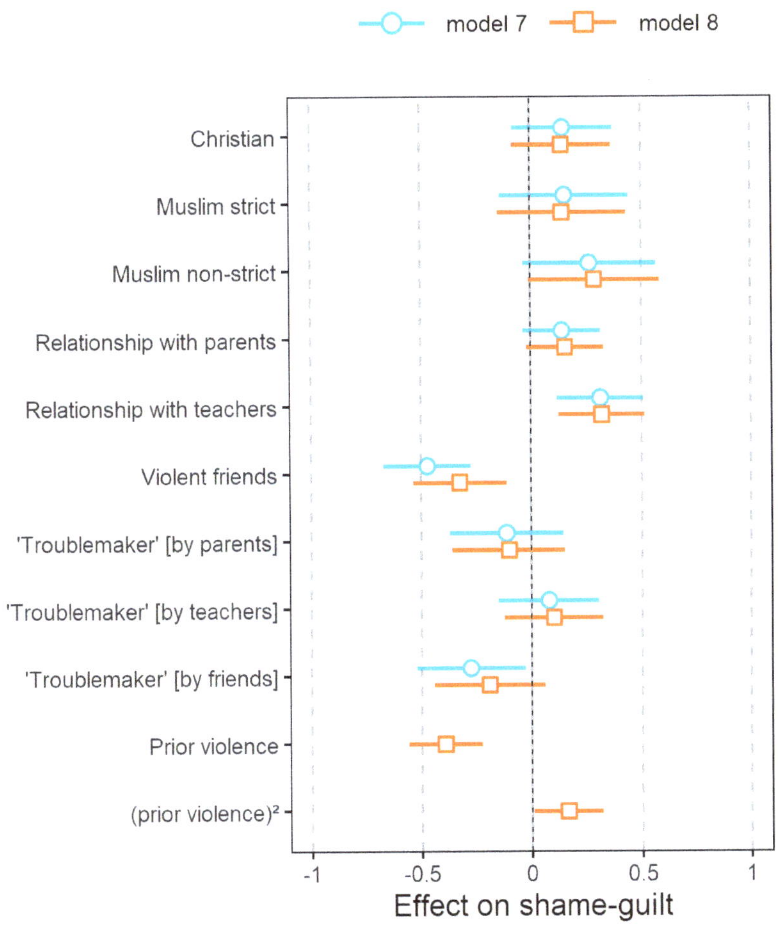

Note: Binary variables are unstandardised. Continuous variables are mean-centred and scaled by 2 SDs.

Fifth, as hypothesised, reflected appraisals as a troublemaker by friends have a negative effect on levels of shame-guilt for retaliatory violence (see Model 5). Upon adjusting for prior involvement in violence (see Model 7), however, the confidence interval indicates that the effect is small or even absent. There is little evidence to support the hypothesis that reflected appraisals by parents and teachers affect levels of shame-guilt for retaliatory violence.[40] We can see that the gender coefficient of Model 4 is only slightly lower than the corresponding coefficient of Model 1 (a decrease by 9%), indicating that reflected appraisals as a troublemaker by friends may account for only a minor part of the gender gap in shame-guilt for retaliatory violence.

Sixth and finally, prior involvement in violence is associated with lower levels of shame-guilt for future retaliatory violence (see Model 7). As Figure 7.5 shows, however, the effect is small. The average level of shame-guilt - relatively low even among those without prior involvement in violence - decreases only slightly with each successive act of violence.

Figure 7.5 Effect of prior involvement in violence on shame-guilt for retaliatory violence

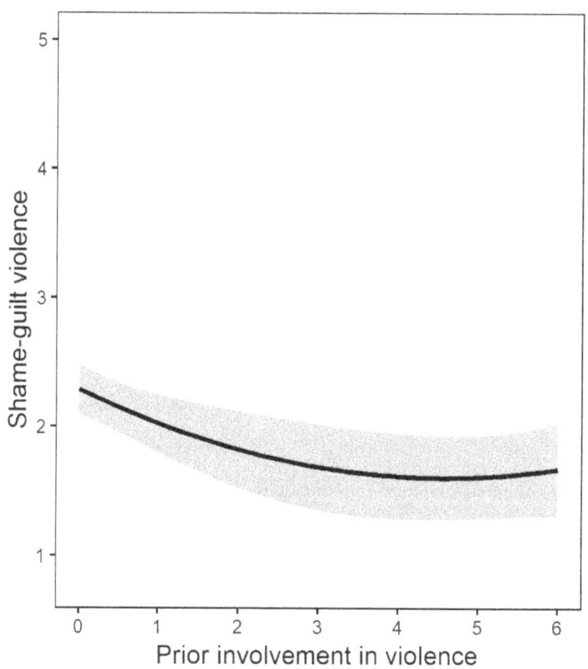

40 To investigate possible collinearity issues, Model 4 and Model 7 are again re-estimated three times, each time including only one of the three variables measuring reflected appraisals. When included separately in a reduced model, reflected appraisals as a troublemaker by parents, by teachers and by friends, all have the hypothesised negative effect on shame-guilt. In the full model, however, the effects of reflected appraisals by parents and teachers become small and statistically indistinguishable from zero. The effect of reflected appraisals by friends remains statistically significant but small nevertheless.

Is shame-guilt for retaliatory violence affected by the same factors in the same way for male adolescents and female adolescents? Again, the full model (Model 7) is disaggregated by gender to answer this question. Traditional masculinity is added to the model for male adolescents and traditional femininity is added to the model for female adolescents to examine whether traditional gender roles attitudes affect shame-guilt differently across gender. Table 7.5 presents the results of these gender-specific regression models. The results warrant four comments.

Table 7.5 Multiple regression model with shame-guilt for retaliatory violence as dependent variable, estimated separately for male adolescents and female adolescents

	Male adolescents		Female adolescents		Gender difference
	b	(95% CI)	b	(95% CI)	Z
Religiosity (0: not/hesitant)					
Christian	0.06	(−0.21, 0.33)	0.26	(−0.13, 0.64)	−0.85
Muslim strict	0.36	(−0.12, 0.84)	−0.08	(−0.70, 0.55)	1.1
Muslim non-strict	0.29	(−0.12, 0.71)	0.28	(−0.35, 0.91)	0.03
Relationship with parents	0.12	(−0.01, 0.24)	0.08	(−0.09, 0.25)	0.37
Relationship with teachers	0.27***	(0.12, 0.42)	0.08	(−0.12, 0.29)	1.56
Violent friends (0: no)	−0.22	(−0.47, 0.03)	−0.47*	(−0.87, −0.07)	1.05
Troublemaker (by parents)	0.00	(−0.15, 0.15)	−0.09	(−0.36, 0.17)	0.59
Troublemaker (by teachers)	0.06	(−0.06, 0.18)	0.03	(−0.20, 0.26)	0.22
Troublemaker (by friends)	−0.05	(−0.18, 0.08)	−0.12	(−0.35, 0.11)	0.50
Traditional masculinity	−0.16*	(−0.29, −0.03)			
Traditional femininity			−0.06	(−0.26, 0.14)	
N	452		357		
Adjusted R^2	0.16		0.15		

*p < 0.05, **p < 0.01, ***p < 0.001.
Note: All variables are unstandardised. Demographic variables 'age' and 'migration background' and control variable 'prior involvement in violence' are not shown.

First, as with the total sample, the average effects of being Christian or Muslim on shame-guilt for retaliatory violence are statistically indistinguishable from zero for both gender groups. At the same time, the confidence intervals around the coefficients are wide, indicating a large within-group variance.

Second, and again as with the total sample, the gender-specific analyses suggest that the closeness of the parent-adolescent relationship has either very little or no effect on shame-guilt for retaliatory violence. A positive relationship with teachers, by contrast, has a small-to-moderate positive effect on shame-guilt among male adolescents but not among female adolescents.[41] Although this might be interpreted as preliminary evidence that the teacher-adolescent relationship affects shame-guilt differently across gender, the z-score indicates that the difference between the coefficients derived for male adolescents and female adolescents is not statistically significant. Furthermore, there is no prior evidence or theoretical rationale to expect a differential effect of this variable. Nevertheless, the observed differences may be worthy of further investigation in a larger sample.

Third, perceptions of friends acting violent have a negative effect on prospective shame-guilt for both gender groups, but the effect is clearly larger for female adolescents than for male adolescents. Although this may be taken as preliminary evidence that the former are more susceptible to the influence of perceived peer violence than the latter, the z-scores indicate that the difference between the coefficients derived for male adolescents and female coefficients is not statistically significant. Also, there is no prior evidence or theoretical rationale to expect a differential effect of this variable. At the same time, however, the confidence interval around the effect size for female adolescents is relatively large,[42] implying that the difference with the effect size for male adolescents could be large and substantially relevant. Therefore, the observed differences are worthy of further investigation in a larger sample.

Fourth and finally, as hypothesised, levels of shame-guilt for retaliatory violence are lower among male adolescents who adhere more strongly to traditional masculinity, but the effect is relatively small (see Figure 7.6). Contrary to expectations, there is no evidence in the data for an association between traditional femininity and shame-guilt for retaliatory violence.[43] In other words, regardless of whether they endorse traditional gender role norms, female adolescents anticipate higher levels of shame-guilt than male adolescents do in regards to engaging in retaliatory violence.

---

41 Going from low (mean – 1 SD) to high values (mean + 1SD) on the scale measuring the quality of the relationship with teachers is associated with an average increase of 0.44 points on the shame-guilt scale for male adolescents (95% CI = 0.20, 0.68).

42 This is due to the low number of female respondents who report having friends who use violence.

43 The model for female adolescents was re-estimated using the reduced traditional femininity score (see previous chapter). This led to similar results.

Figure 7.6 Effect of traditional gender role attitudes on shame-guilt for retaliatory violence

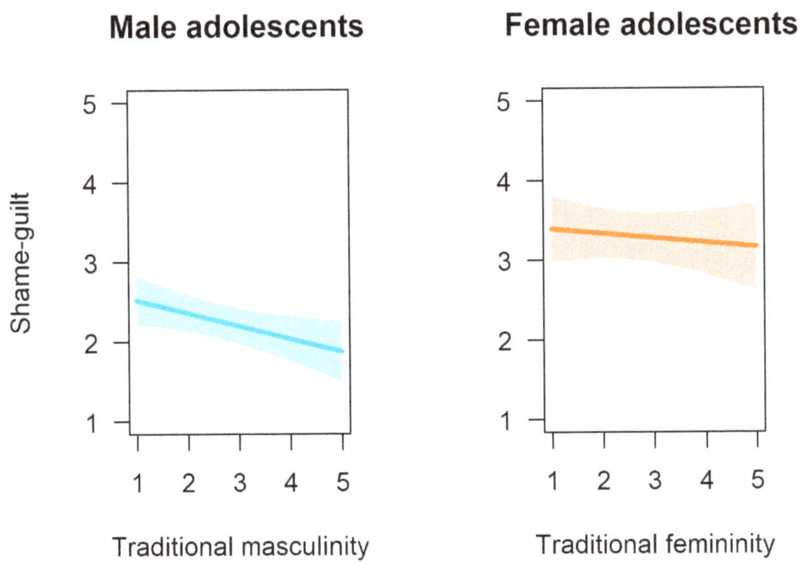

7.5 DIFFERENTIAL EFFECTS FOR SHOPLIFTING VERSUS RETALIATORY VIOLENCE?

By way of an interim summary of the results reported thus far, Figure 7.7 brings together and compares the effects of key independent variables on prospective shame-guilt for shoplifting versus retaliatory violence. The coefficients are taken from the final models (controlling for prior involvement in theft and violence). The figure suggests that several social factors are differentially associated with our two outcomes of interest. More specifically, most variables seem to have stronger effects on shame-guilt for shoplifting than they have on shame-guilt for retaliatory violence. These stronger associations are also reflected in the explained variance, which is higher in the regression model for shoplifting (40%) than in the regression model for retaliatory violence (23%).

Figure 7.7 Differential effects on shame-guilt for shoplifting versus retaliatory violence

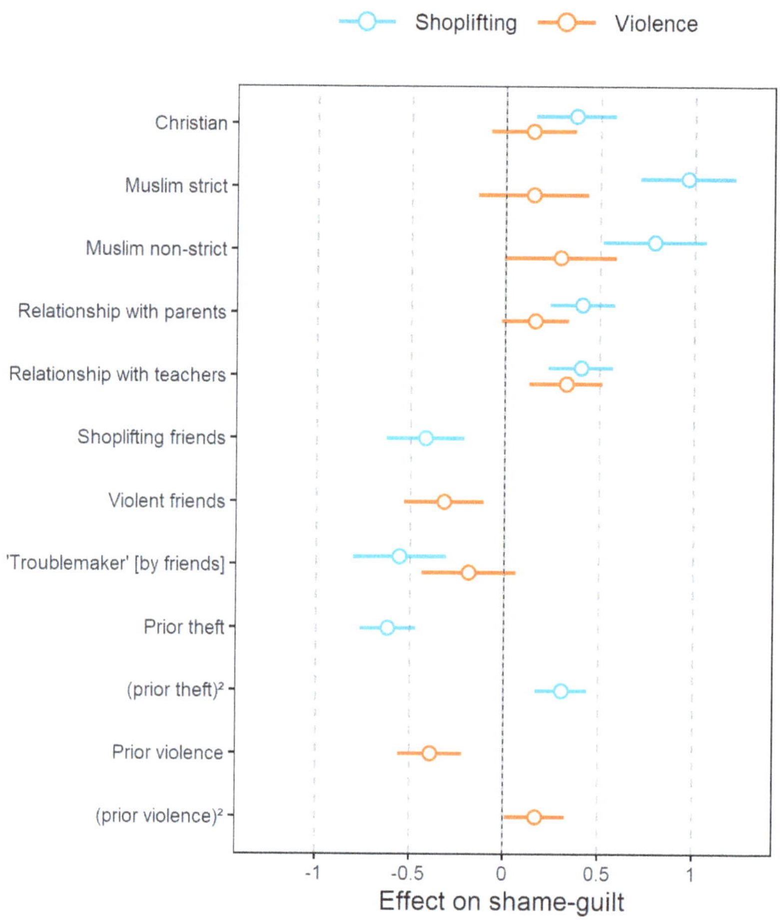

To be able to formally compare the coefficients across the two outcomes, the two multiple regression equations are estimated simultaneously in a multivariate regression analysis.[44] A Wald chi-square test is used to test the null hypothesis that two corresponding coefficients are equal.[45] In line with our expectations, Muslims anticipate significantly higher levels of shame-guilt for engaging in shoplifting than for engaging in retaliatory violence (for strict Muslims: Wald chi-square = 28.442, df = 1, $p < 0.001$; for non-strict Muslims: Wald chi-square = 9.033, df = 1, $p < 0.01$). By contrast, there is only weak

44 The model is estimated in Mplus version 6.11 (Muthén & Muthen, 1998) and contains a residual covariance between the two dependent variables (as these are not independent of each other).

45 Using the MODEL TEST option in Mplus.

evidence that levels of prospective shame-guilt reported by Christian adolescents differ across the two offence types (Wald chi-square = 3.017, df = 1, $p = 0.08$). There are also some unexpected findings. First, experiencing a closer relationship with one's parents has a significantly stronger *positive* effect on shame-guilt for shoplifting than it has on shame-guilt for retaliatory violence (Wald chi-square = 5.58, df = 1, $p = 0.02$). Second, perceived labelling as a troublemaker (by friends) has a significantly stronger *negative* effect on shame-guilt for shoplifting than it has on shame-guilt for retaliatory violence (Wald chi-square = 7.508, df = 1, $p < 0.01$). The effects of the other independent variables do not differ significantly across offence type.

7.6 A CLOSER EXAMINATION OF GENDER DIFFERENCES IN PROSPECTIVE SHAME-GUILT

To more precisely assess the relative mediating (or indirect) effects of different social factors on the relationship between gender and prospective shame-guilt, the regression analyses presented above are supplemented by a multiple mediation path analysis. This type of analysis allows one to examine, in a single model, both the direct and indirect paths through which gender may operate to influence prospective shame-guilt. Recall that for a variable to be considered as a possible mediator of the relationship between gender and shame-guilt, three criteria have to be met: (a) the variable differs significantly by gender, (b) the variable is a significant predictor of prospective shame-guilt and (c) adding the variable to a multivariate analysis reduces the magnitude of the gender coefficient. Whereas the first criterion was addressed in the previous chapter, the latter two criteria can be evaluated based on the results of the regression analyses presented earlier in this chapter. Following these criteria, the indirect effects of gender on shame-guilt through the following variables should be taken into consideration: the relationship with parents, perceptions of friends' involvement in shoplifting/violence, and perceived labelling as a troublemaker by friends. Traditional gender role attitudes cannot be included in the path models as these are measured by different variables for male adolescents (masculinity subscale) and female adolescents (femininity subscale).

Two path models are hypothesised and tested: (1) a model with shame-guilt for shoplifting as the dependent variable and (2) a model with shame-guilt for retaliatory violence as the dependent variable. Again, the models are estimated controlling for as well as without controlling for previous involvement in theft/violence. Because the variables measuring friends' involvement in shoplifting/violence are binary, all models are estimated using the weighted least squares mean-and variance-adjusted (WLSMV) estimator available in

Mplus.[46] Following best practices in mediation research, bias-corrected bootstrapped confidence intervals were estimated to evaluate the size and significance of the indirect effects (Preacher & Hayes, 2008).

Figure 7.8 Multiple mediator path model explaining the gender difference in shame-guilt for shoplifting

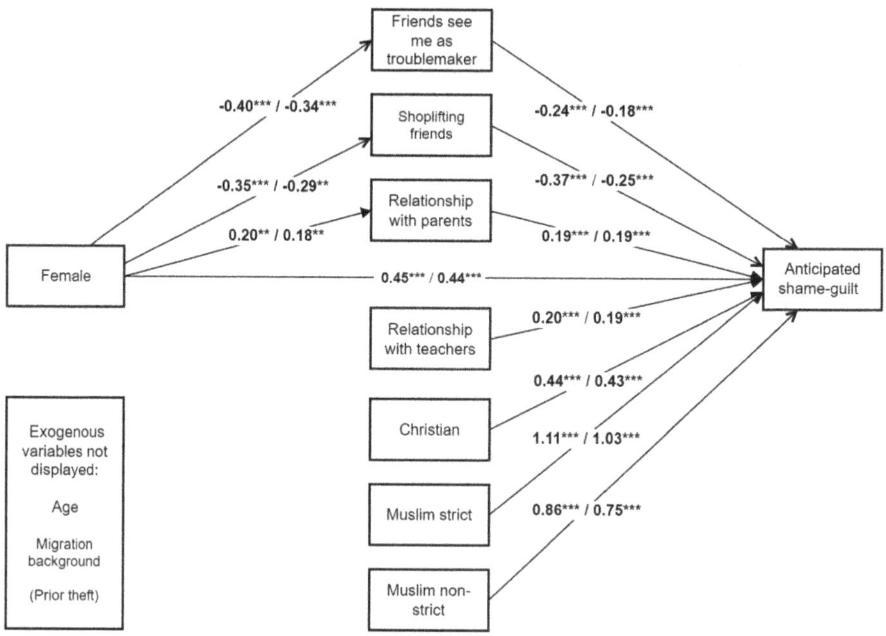

*p < 0.05, **p < 0.01, ***p < 0.001.
Note: All variables are unstandardised. Coefficients for the model without prior involvement in theft are to the left of the slash, and coefficients for the model including prior involvement in theft are to the right of the slash.

Figure 7.8 presents the direct effects of gender, religiosity, relationships with parents and teachers, having shoplifting friends, and being seen as a troublemaker (by friends) on shame-guilt for shoplifting.[47] The model also accounts for the effects of the

46 When using the WLSMV estimator, binary mediators are treated as continuous latent response variables rather than as observed variables. As a consequence, the coefficients for the direct effects might differ somewhat from those obtained through the multiple regression analyses discussed earlier (using ordinary least squares). However, the substantial implications should be the same.

47 Only reflected appraisals by friends are included in the model (this has been done to avoid loss of power and precision due to collinearity with the other variables measuring reflected appraisals by parents and teachers).

sociodemographic variables age and migration background. Coefficients for the model unadjusted for prior theft are presented to the left of the slash, whereas coefficients for the model adjusted for this variable are presented to the right of the slash.[48] The indirect effects of gender on shame-guilt through the mediating variables in the model (parent-adolescent relationship, having friends who are perceived to shoplift, and reflected appraisals as a troublemaker by friends) are presented in Table 7.6.

Table 7.6 Direct and indirect effects of gender on shame-guilt for shoplifting

	(a) Unadjusted for prior involvement in theft		(b) Adjusted for prior involvement in theft	
	Point Estimate	95% CI	Point Estimate	95% CI
Total effect of gender on shame-guilt	0.71**	(0.53-0.89)	0.61**	(0.43-0.78)
Direct effect	0.45**	(0.27-0.63)	0.44**	(0.27-0.63)
Indirect effect through:				
Relationship with parents	0.04*	(0.01-0.08)	0.03*	(0.01-0.07)
Shoplifting friends	0.13**	(0.06-0.22)	0.07*	(0.02-0.14)
Troublemaker (by friends)	0.10**	(0.06-0.15)	0.06*	(0.03-0.11)

*p < 0.05, **p < 0.01.

As can be seen in Table 7.6, the path model shows that gender differences in shame-guilt for shoplifting are partly mediated by differences in the parent-adolescent relationship, differences in exposure to shoplifting friends and differences in reflected appraisals (i.e. being seen as a troublemaker by one's friends). The model also suggests that peer-related factors have the strongest mediating effects. Judging by the proportion of the total effect that is mediated, however, the magnitude of the indirect effects is modest (Preacher & Kelley, 2011). More specifically, together the three explanatory variables mediate only slightly over one-third of the association between gender and shame-guilt in the model that does not control for prior involvement in theft ($P_m = 0.37$). When adjusting for the effects of prior theft, the mediated proportion is only 28% ($P_m = 0.28$). As discussed earlier, the latter should be seen as the most conservative estimate (see Section 7.1). Because the direct effect of gender on shame-guilt remains both substantially and statistically significant, these findings suggest that our model can only partially explain gender differences in shame-guilt for shoplifting.

48 Both models have a good fit to the data ($\chi^2 = 28.741$, df = 17, p = 0.04, RMSEA = 0.029, CFI = 0.97, for the unadjusted model; $\chi^2 = 25.828$, df = 17, p = 0.08, RMSEA = 0.025, CFI = 0.98, for the adjusted model).

Figure 7.9 presents the multiple mediator path model for shame-guilt in relation to retaliatory violence. Again, coefficients for the model that is unadjusted for prior involvement in violence are presented to the left of the slash, whereas coefficients for the model adjusted for this variable are presented to the right of the slash.[49] The indirect effects and their 95% confidence intervals are presented in Table 7.7.

Figure 7.9 Multiple mediator path model explaining the gender difference in shame-guilt for using retaliatory violence

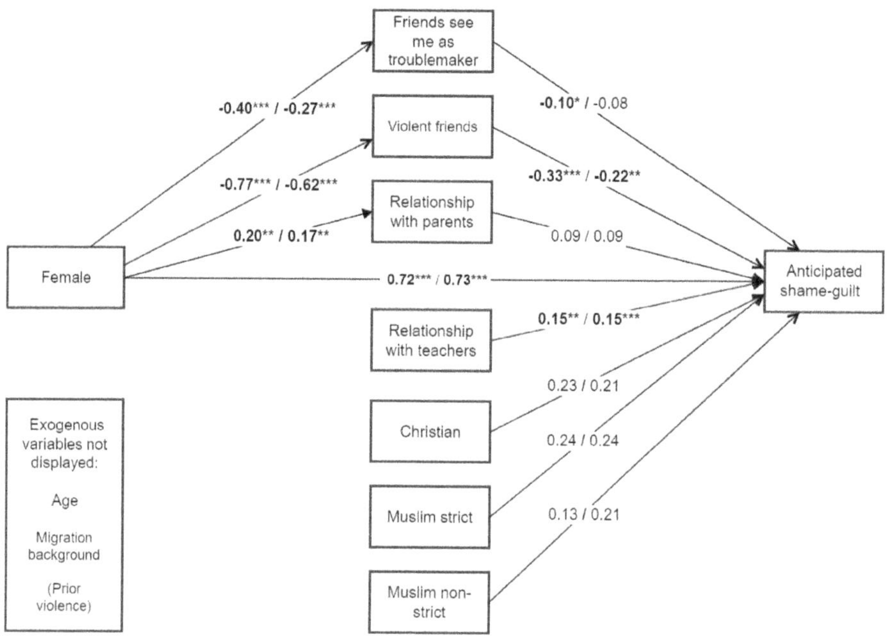

*p < 0.05, **p < 0.01, ***p < 0.001.
Note: All variables are unstandardised. Coefficients for the model without prior involvement in violence are to the left of the slash, and coefficients for the model including prior involvement in violence are to the right of the slash.

As can be seen in Table 7.7, the results of the mediation analysis show that gender differences in shame-guilt for engaging in retaliatory violence are partly mediated by differences in exposure to friends who (are perceived to) engage in violent behaviour. The mediating effects of the parent-adolescent relationship and reflected appraisals are

49 Both models have a good fit to the data ($\chi^2 = 35.424$, df = 17, p = 0.01, RMSEA = 0.036, CFI = 0.95, for the unadjusted model; $\chi^2 = 32.378$, df = 17, p = 0.01, RMSEA = 0.033, CFI = 0.97, for the adjusted model).

negligible and statistically insignificant. Judging by the proportion of the total effect that is mediated, however, the magnitude of the indirect effect is modest. More specifically, perceived peer violence mediates only one-fourth of the association between gender and shame-guilt for engaging in retaliatory violence ($P_m = 0.25$). When adjusting for the effects of respondents' prior involvement in violence, the mediated proportion is only 16% ($P_m = 0.16$). Again, the direct effect of gender on shame-guilt remains both substantially and statistically significant, indicating that our model can only account for a small part of the gender gap in shame-guilt for retaliatory violence.

Table 7.7 Direct and indirect effects of gender on shame-guilt for retaliatory violence

	(a) Unadjusted for prior involvement in violence		(b) Adjusted for prior involvement in violence	
	Point Estimate	95% CI	Point Estimate	95% CI
Total effect of gender on shame-guilt	1.02**	(0.83-1.19)	0.90**	(0.43-0.78)
Direct effect	0.72**	(0.51-0.92)	0.73**	(0.52-0.92)
Indirect effect through:				
Relationship with parents	0.01	(0.00-0.05)	0.01	(0.00-0.04)
Violent friends	0.25**	(0.14-0.38)	0.14*	(0.06-0.24)
Troublemaker (by friends)	0.04	(0.00-0.08)	0.02	(0.00-0.05)

*p < 0.05, **p < 0.01.

7.7 DISCUSSION

The aims of the analyses presented in this chapter were twofold. The first aim was to examine the hypothesised relationships between different social factors and prospective shame-guilt for engaging in two types of delinquency: shoplifting and retaliatory violence. The second aim was to examine the extent to which these factors could account for the observed differences in prospective shame-guilt between male adolescents and female adolescents.

7.7.1 *Social factors and prospective shame-guilt*

Families, educational institutions and peer groups are key social contexts in which adolescents develop their self-identity and evaluate themselves in relation to, and from the perspective of, others. It was hypothesised that adolescents who have closer ties to their parents and teachers would be more likely to adopt the perspective of these 'conventional' others when contemplating delinquency and therefore anticipate higher levels of guilt and shame. It was also hypothesised that adolescents with delinquent friends whose perspective they can adopt would anticipate lower levels of guilt and shame. The results mostly supported these hypotheses; the observed effect sizes were small (for the relationship with parents and teachers) to moderate (for perceived delinquency of friends). More supportive relationships with teachers were associated with higher levels of prospective shame-guilt for both shoplifting and retaliatory violence, whereas the opposite association was found for perceptions of friends' involvement in theft and violence. Contrary to expectations, closer relationships with parents were only associated with higher levels of shame-guilt for shoplifting. No evidence was found that the closeness of the parent-adolescent relationship was associated with prospective shame-guilt for retaliatory violence. This finding may reflect the moral ambiguity surrounding the use of violence in response to provocations (Herman & Pogarsky, 2020; Thomas, 2018). Indeed, several studies have documented a significant degree of heterogeneity in parental attitudes towards violence, with some parents condemning and others condoning defensive or retaliatory forms of violence (Copeland-Linder et al., 2007; Esala, 2013; Solomon et al., 2008). This could have attenuated the effect of the parent-adolescent relationship on prospective shame-guilt. Schools, by contrast, may provide a moral context in which violence is more categorically condemned. This would explain why the teacher-adolescent relationship had a stronger effect on prospective shame-guilt in relation to retaliatory violence than the parent-adolescent relationship.

The results presented here are mostly in line with those of a previous study among Dutch adolescents by Svensson et al. (2016). Using a longitudinal design, these authors observed that improvements in parental attachment and school commitment were associated with increases in levels of prospective guilt and shame for offending, whereas increases in perceived peer delinquency had the opposite association. Unlike the present study, however, Svensson et al. (2016) did not distinguish between different types of offences. Their study assumes that adolescents are socialised into a single unified and unambiguous moral order, so that those who are 'successfully' socialised do not discriminate across offence types. Put differently, their study assumes that socialisation processes that serve to increase prospective guilt and shame for one type of offence will automatically increase prospective guilt and shame for all other offences in lock-step. But the findings presented here suggest that social bonds may have offence-specific effects on prospective guilt and shame. This resonates with the results of an interesting Taiwanese study by Jou (1995, cited in Braithwaite & Braithwaite, 2001), who found that shame had an inhibitory effect on delinquency except for those offences condoned by Taiwanese families (e.g. cheating at school, driving a motorcycle without a licence, and illegal gambling).

Some level of moralisation and disapproval of delinquency in one's social environment is necessary for prospective guilt and shame to arise and inhibit delinquent involvement. At the same time, however, both labelling and reintegrative shaming theory predict that persistent disapproval in the form of stigmatisation may set off a criminogenic transformation of a person's identity and increase the risk of (subsequent) offending (Braithwaite, 1989; Matsueda, 1992). Against this background, the present study examined whether adolescents' reflected appraisals of what significant others think about them affect their levels of prospective shame-guilt for engaging in delinquency. More specifically, it was hypothesised that adolescents who believe that parents, teachers and friends see them as troublemakers would anticipate lower levels of guilt and shame. In support of this hypothesis, levels of prospective shame-guilt for shoplifting were found to be considerably lower among adolescents who report that friends see them as a troublemaker (even when controlling for prior involvement in theft). Perceptions of being seen as a troublemaker by friends were also negatively associated with prospective shame-guilt for retaliatory violence, but this association was much weaker. Additional bivariate models also showed support for the hypothesised negative associations between, respectively, reflected appraisals by parents and teachers, and prospective shame-guilt, but these associations disappeared when controlling for the effects of peer-reflected appraisals. In sum, whereas perceptions of being seen as a troublemaker by parents, teachers and friends are substantially correlated, perceived labelling by friends seems to carry the most weight.

Although the study is cross-sectional, the findings are nonetheless congruent with a growing body of evidence documenting the potential criminogenic effects of (perceived) labelling by significant others in general and peers in particular (Brownfield & Thompson, 2005; De Coster & Lutz, 2018; Lee et al., 2017; Walters, 2016). More specifically, they suggest that reduced levels of prospective guilt and shame may be among the criminogenic processes triggered by informal labelling. In addition, the results complement those of Harris (2001) who found that offenders who experienced stigmatisation during court cases or restorative justice conferences reported lower feelings of shame-guilt over their offence. In line with reintegrative shaming theory, Harris argued that 'individuals who are rejected and disrespected by the social group are less likely to be concerned with maintaining respectability in the eyes of those people who have stigmatised them' (Harris, 2001, p. 162). At the same time, one may wonder whether the labelled adolescents in our sample really felt rejected and disrespected. Alternatively, they might just as well (mistakenly) perceive that they are seen as 'cool' and 'daring' by their peers and wear the 'troublemaker' label as a badge of honour. They may cherish this label or identity and, as a consequence, anticipate less guilt and shame for engaging in behaviour consistent with their assigned deviant status. This point illustrates the difference between labelling, on the one hand, and stigmatisation and rejection, on the other; the former does not necessarily imply the latter.

Next to the family, school and peer group, religious groups can be another significant source of self-identity during adolescence, especially for ethnic minority youth (Verkuyten, 2007). Of course, religious groups rarely exist in complete isolation from these other groups. Quite the contrary, parents and friends are usually part of the religious group and play an important role in the transmission and reinforcement of religious identities (Phalet et al., 2018). But religious identities also connect individuals to a larger community that extends beyond the immediate circle of intimates (Ysseldyk et al., 2010). Crucially, religious groups may impose norms for moral conduct that are clearer and stricter than those of secular groups (Cochran, 1988). In this way, they can provide adolescents with a powerful perspective for self-monitoring and self-evaluation. Against this background, it was hypothesised that adolescents who identify with a religious group would anticipate higher levels of guilt and shame for engaging in delinquency. However, this main hypothesis was further qualified in two important ways. First, following the moral community hypothesis, it was hypothesised that levels of prospective shame-guilt would be higher among Muslim adolescents than among Christian adolescents as the former are more likely than the latter to grow up in an environment that validates and reinforces their religious identity (Van Droogenbroeck & Spruyt, 2020; Voas & Fleischmann, 2012). Second, given the severe disapproval of theft in Islam, it was expected that this differential effect would manifest itself particularly in the case of shoplifting. The results partially supported these hypotheses. As predicted, levels of prospective shame-guilt for shoplifting were considerably higher for Muslims than for their Christian and religiously unaffiliated counterparts. Christians, too, anticipated higher levels of shame-guilt for shoplifting than religiously affiliated adolescents, but the difference was much smaller than for Muslims. Contrary to expectations, little evidence was found that either Christians or Muslims anticipated higher levels of shame-guilt for retaliatory violence.

At least two explanations can account for the weak or absent effects of being Christian on prospective shame-guilt. One explanation is that the vast majority of Christians in the sample are non-practising and, therefore, presumably, highly secularised. Their religious beliefs may be too weak to be influential in guiding their self-evaluations. Alternatively, following the moral community hypothesis, religion's influence on people's thoughts, feelings and actions depends on the extent to which religiousness is ratified by the social environment, much more than it depends on the intensity of personal religious beliefs or commitments (Stark, 1996). That is, religion can have a strong influence only 'if religious influences permeate the culture and the social interactions of the individuals in question' (Stark & Bainbridge, 1996, p. 72). This is unlikely to be the case for many, if not most, of the Christians in our sample. Muslim adolescents of Turkish and Moroccan origin, by contrast, are likely to grow up in ethnic communities and neighbourhoods where religion still pervades many aspects of daily life (Gungor et al., 2011). Indeed, according to a recent Belgian study, Muslims experience higher levels of pressure for religious conformity than their Christian peers (Van Droogenbroeck & Spruyt, 2020. Consistent with the moral community hypothesis, it was found that Muslims anticipated considerably higher levels of shame-guilt than other adolescents, irrespective of their personal religious commitment. Yet, this effect was only found in the case of shoplifting and not in the case of retaliatory violence. This was not unexpected given the particular moral significance of theft in the Muslim community. Indeed, unlike violence, theft is one of the seven 'Hudud' offences against god for which mandatory punishments are described in the Quran or the Sunna (al-Thakeb & Scott, 1981). The results presented here resonate with those of a study by de Boer (2008) in The Netherlands. She observed that adolescents of Moroccan and Turkish origin strongly disapproved of theft on the basis of religious considerations, whereas their attitudes towards violence were more complex and less influenced by religious considerations.

7.7.2 *Gender differences in prospective shame-guilt*

A second major objective of this study was to examine gender differences in prospective guilt and shame. In line with previous research (Rebellon et al., 2015, 2016; Svensson, 2004; Svensson et al., 2013), the 'gender gap' in prospective shame-guilt was also observed in this study with female adolescents anticipating considerably higher levels of shame-guilt for both shoplifting and retaliatory violence (see previous chapter). These gender differences may occur because young men and women are *differentially exposed* to social factors that tend to increase or decrease shame-guilt and/or because they are *differentially affected* by these factors. To examine the latter possibility, all models were estimated separately by gender.

Consistent with the findings of a previous longitudinal study by Svensson et al. (2016), associations between social factors and prospective shame-guilt were found to be similar across gender. Also consistent with previous work (Mears et al., 1998; Svensson, 2003; Weerman et al., 2016; Zhang, 1997), it was found that female adolescents report closer relationships to their parents, less exposure to shoplifting friends, and lower perceptions of being labelled as a troublemaker by their friends (see previous chapter). Results from a multiple mediator path analysis suggest that together these factors may account for a small-to-moderate portion of the gender gap in shame-guilt for shoplifting. It was also found that female adolescents report less exposure to violent friends. A multiple mediator path analysis supports the hypothesis that this factor accounts for a small part of the gender gap in prospective shame-guilt for engaging in retaliatory violence. Findings from these analyses also suggest that peer effects are more important than parent effects in mediating gender differences. In fact, the mediating effect of the parent-adolescent relationship was weak in the case of shoplifting and absent in the case of retaliatory violence.

One factor in this study was explicitly hypothesised to affect prospective shame-guilt differently for male adolescents and female adolescents: endorsement of traditional gender role norms. The latter are societal expectations of how one is supposed to be, or act, based one's sex category. Whereas traditional femininity norms encourage females to be attractive, gentle, nurturing, submissive and domestic, traditional masculinity norms encourage males to be autonomous, assertive, tough, dominant and daring (Halimi et al., 2018; Vermeersch et al., 2010). Through social interactions and relationships, traditional gender norms may become part of one's 'generalised other' and then serve as a source of self-evaluation (Lucas & Steimel, 2009). As delinquency is generally considered to be inconsistent with traditional femininity, but not with traditional masculinity, it was hypothesised that adherence to traditional femininity would be associated with higher levels of prospective shame-guilt and that adherence to traditional masculinity would be associated with lower levels of prospective shame-guilt. Furthermore, it was hypothesised that this differential effect would be more pronounced for violence than for theft. The results support the hypothesis about the effects of traditional masculinity but not the hypothesis about the effects of traditional femininity.

In line with our expectations, levels of prospective shame-guilt for shoplifting were lower among male adolescents who strongly endorsed traditional masculinity. Indeed, shoplifting can be seen as consistent with traditional masculinity, which encourages risk-taking and thrill-seeking. Contrary to expectations, however, female adolescents who strongly endorsed traditional femininity *also* reported lower levels of shame-guilt for shoplifting. Upon further reflection, however, this finding does not necessarily contradict the theoretical framework that guided this study. Rather, it casts doubt on our initial assumption that shoplifting is inconsistent with traditional femininity. Others have argued that shoplifting is 'consistent with a normatively feminine activity (i.e. shopping)' (Curry, 2014, p. 553). It has also been observed that the items frequently stolen by females (e.g. makeup, clothes and jewellery) are consistent with traditional feminine roles in society (Steffensmeier & Allan, 1996). This may explain why levels of shame-guilt were *lower* rather than higher among female adolescents who more strongly endorsed traditional gender roles. Finally, it was interesting to observe that adherence to traditional gender role attitudes did not affect prospective shame-guilt for shoplifting among male and female Muslim adolescents. In line with the prohibition and strong disapproval of theft in Islam, Muslims anticipated feeling very guilty and ashamed about shoplifting, irrespective of their adherence to traditional gender roles and expectations.

As hypothesised, young men who strongly endorsed traditional masculinity also anticipated lower levels of shame-guilt for retaliatory violence. These results shed light on the mechanisms that may underlie the frequently observed masculinity-violence association (Archer, 2004; Newburn & Stanko, 1994; Santana et al., 2006; Tharp et al., 2013). The observed effect was small, however, and levels of prospective shame-guilt were relatively low even among male adolescents with less traditional gender views. This may indicate that moral ambiguity about retaliatory violence is widespread and not limited to those with strong masculine ideals. Contrary to expectations, no evidence was found that female adolescents who adhered more strongly to traditional femininity anticipated higher levels of prospective shame-guilt for retaliatory violence. A possible explanation for this finding could be that retaliatory violence is actually perceived as less gender-inconsistent than is sometimes assumed. Whether or not this is due to changing gender norms in society is difficult to tell. Unfortunately, little research is available on the association between adherence to traditional femininity and attitudes towards violence (in contrast to the abundance of research on the association between traditional masculinity and violence). All in all, the results are consistent with past research (Ford et al., 2002) in suggesting that traditional gender role expectations can influence self-regulation in delinquency situations through their impact on anticipated self-directed emotions. However, they also suggest that, to fully understand this impact, one has to examine the degree to which specific delinquent acts are socially perceived as gender-consistent or gender-inconsistent for men and women.

8 General Conclusion

In this final chapter, I summarise the key pillars of this study, review key findings from the previous chapters and discuss their broader significance. I also identify some of the key limitations of the data and methods that were used, and I make suggestions for future avenues of research. I conclude the chapter with some implications for theory and policy/practice.

8.1 Summary of the main results

Both guilt and shame are negative self-evaluative emotions felt in response to moral and non-moral failures and transgressions. As I have argued in the first chapter, the main difference between them lies in the nature and content of their evaluative focus on the self (Ferguson et al., 2007; Katz, 1999; Lindsay-Hartz, 1984; Miceli & Castelfranchi, 2018). In guilt, the self is negatively evaluated as responsible for some harmful event or state of affairs (e.g. a wrongdoing), whereas in shame the self is negatively evaluated as inadequate or unwanted. Put differently, guilt highlights one's *ability* to bring about negative outcomes, whereas shame highlights one's *inability* to be the right kind of person. Accordingly, shame has a more profound and transformative impact on our view of ourselves than guilt does. Notwithstanding these differences, guilt and shame are complementary rather than mutually exclusive emotions. Indeed, several studies have shown that guilt and shame typically co-occur in situations of moral wrongdoing (Ferguson et al., 2007; Harris, 2003; Olthof et al., 2004; Schmader & Lickel, 2006). In such cases, there exists a natural connection between the two emotions. That is, self-appraisals of responsibility for a wrongdoing (i.e. self-appraisal associated with guilt) can easily lead to self-appraisals of moral inadequacy (i.e. self-appraisal associated with shame).

Without the capacity to experience guilt and shame, people's ability to function adaptively in society would be seriously hampered. This is not to say that people should regularly feel guilty or ashamed. In fact, both emotions can become problematic if they are experienced too frequently and too intensely or if they persist for too long (Cibich et al., 2016; Dempsey, 2017; Nelissen et al., 2013; Quiles & Bybee, 1997). But to have a sense of guilt and shame, and to experience episodes of guilt and shame when the circumstances call for it, is generally adaptive (Ahmed et al., 2001; de Hooge et al., 2010, 2011; Deonna et al., 2012; Ferguson et al., 2007; Lickel et al., 2014; Quiles & Bybee, 1997). Feelings of guilt lead us to acknowledge our transgressions and can motivate reparative behaviour. Feelings of shame lead us to acknowledge the deficiencies in ourselves that may predispose us to act in (morally) inappropriate ways and can motivate self-reform.

Being disposed to experience guilt and shame *after* having committed a transgression is only one manifestation of a healthy sense of guilt and shame. Equally valuable is the capacity for *prospective* guilt and shame, that is, the capacity to imagine and pre-emptively feel guilt and shame when considering *future* transgressions. In the second chapter, I have presented a review of criminological research demonstrating the relevance of prospective guilt and shame for understanding why people do or do not commit crime. More specifically, the findings summarised in this review clearly showed that individuals who anticipate guilt and shame reactions following moral transgressions are considerably less likely to be involved in crime and delinquency (Grasmick & Bursik, 1990; Matsuda et al., 2013; Melde & Esbensen, 2011; Svensson, 2004; Svensson et al., 2013; Tibbetts, 1997b, 2003). Interestingly, the reviewed studies also found that the threat of guilt and shame is unevenly distributed across gender. Women anticipate higher levels of guilt and shame than men, and these differences may explain a substantial part of the gender gap in delinquency (Rebellon et al., 2015, 2016).

Against the background of these findings, the aim of this work was to get a better understanding of the role of prospective guilt and shame in the explanation of delinquency and to identify social factors that may explain individual and gender differences in prospective guilt and shame. In the third chapter, I proposed an interactionist theoretical framework to address these issues. This framework has two theoretical foundations: the symbolic interactionist analysis of the self-conscious emotions by Shott (1979) and the symbolic interactionist theory of delinquency developed by Heimer and Matsueda (1994), both of which draw upon Mead's social psychology of the self and role-taking.

Following Shott (1979), I conceptualised prospective guilt and shame as anticipatory self-evaluative reactions elicited through a process of role-taking. That is, prospective guilt and shame occur when individuals imaginatively adopt towards themselves what they anticipate would be the negative or disapproving attitudes of others if they followed through on a certain course of action. The result of this simulation is an affectively laden image of the (future) self as a wrongdoer and a morally inadequate person. This emotional self-conception then acts as a warning signal and motivates individuals to align their behaviour with social and moral norms (Giner-Sorolla, 2001; Kotabe et al., 2019; Shott, 1979).

Next, I showed how prospective guilt and shame can be incorporated in differential social control theory, a symbolic interactionist theory of delinquency developed by Heimer and Matsueda (1994). Drawing on Mead (1934), differential social control theory argues that role-taking processes affect the likelihood of delinquency. These processes are at work in 'problematic action situations', when individuals are confronted with the choice of 'selecting a delinquent or non-delinquent solution to the problem' (Matsueda, 2001,

p. 129). Role-taking can lead either to delinquency or conformity depending on the normative orientations of the significant others and reference groups whose perspective the individual adopts. Thus, when individuals look at themselves from the perspective of conventional reference groups, and adopt their (unfavourable) attitudes to delinquency, the likelihood of delinquency should decrease. Like Mead, however, Heimer and Matsueda emphasised the cognitive dimension of role-taking. They did not pay attention to emotions that may arise in connection with role-taking experiences and how these may facilitate social control by encouraging self-control. I have argued in the third chapter that prospective guilt and shame are pivotal in this respect (Abell & Gecas, 1997; Shott, 1979). Unlike other emotions that facilitate social control such as fear or embarrassment, prospective guilt and shame can inhibit delinquent behaviour even when there is no threat of detection. These emotions do not simply reflect fear of losing the approval of others. In guilt and shame, the actual or anticipated responses of others infiltrate one's own evaluation of self (Harris et al., 2004; Miceli & Castelfranchi, 2018). Put differently, these emotions signal a threat to one's ethical identity, both in one's own eyes and in the eyes of others (Harris, 2011).

Role-taking is not a random process but one that is conditioned by the social context in which it is embedded (Heimer & Matsueda, 1994). Hence, to understand role-taking emotions in relation to delinquency, we must look at the significant others and reference groups whose perspectives adolescents are likely to adopt. Drawing on the criminological literature in general, and differential social control theory in particular, I identified and discussed several social factors that might explain individual and gender differences in prospective guilt and shame (Chapter 4). More specifically, the following factors were hypothesised to affect prospective guilt and shame for engaging in delinquency: relationships with parents and teachers, associations with delinquent friends, reflected appraisals of the self as a troublemaker (from the standpoint of parents/teachers/friends), religiosity, and societal gender role expectations. To examine the hypotheses, I used survey data collected from a sample of 856 secondary school adolescents in Genk, a city in the northeast of Belgium.

Before examining the hypotheses, confirmatory factor analyses (CFAs) were conducted to evaluate the dimensionality of prospective guilt and shame. Items measuring anticipated guilt and shame reactions to delinquency either formed a unidimensional construct or two factors so highly correlated that any differentiation between them was not practically useful. This finding is consistent with those of other studies showing that guilt and shame tend to co-occur in response to wrongdoing (Harris, 2003; Schmader & Lickel, 2006). According to some scholars, this co-occurrence is actually desirable since guilt would lack inhibiting power without the bite of shame (Sabini & Silver, 1997). The results further indicate that high levels of anticipated shame-guilt for one type of offence may not necessarily go hand in hand with high levels of anticipated shame-guilt for other types of offences. Shame-guilt for engaging in shoplifting and shame-guilt for engaging in retaliatory violence were only moderately correlated in this study and formed distinct factors. Nevertheless, it is difficult to draw firm conclusions about the generalisability of anticipated guilt and shame reactions across different forms of delinquency based on this study because only two rather specific acts were examined.

Despite growing evidence for their delinquency-inhibiting effects, few studies have directly examined factors that may affect prospective guilt and shame. The present study identified several factors associated with adolescents' anticipated guilt and shame reactions to shoplifting and retaliatory violence. Religious affiliation, closer relationships with parents, and more supportive relationships with teachers were associated with higher levels of anticipated shame-guilt for shoplifting, whereas friends' involvement in theft and reflected appraisals of self as a troublemaker were associated with lower levels of anticipated shame-guilt. Effect sizes ranged from large (religious affiliation) to moderate (friends' involvement in theft and reflected appraisals of self as a troublemaker) to small (relationships with parents and teachers). More supportive relationships with teachers were also associated with higher levels of anticipated shame-guilt for engaging in retaliatory violence, whereas friends' involvement in violence and reflected appraisals of self as a troublemaker were associated with lower levels of anticipated shame-guilt for engaging in this kind of behaviour. Effect sizes ranged from moderate (friends' involvement in violence) to small (relationships with teachers and reflected appraisals of self as a troublemaker). All in all, these findings are consistent with a symbolic interactionist view of guilt and shame that emphasises the social embeddedness of these emotions. More specifically, they suggest that looking at the variety of reference groups with whom adolescents interact can increase our understanding of their anticipated guilt and shame reactions to delinquent behaviour.

The results also contribute to a better understanding of the aetiology of youth crime. Previous research has consistently shown that strong bonding with parents and teachers can decrease the likelihood of delinquency (Costello & Laub, 2020; Hoeve et al., 2009; Sabatine et al., 2017) and that associating with delinquent friends can increase its likelihood (Hoeben et al., 2016; McGloin & Thomas, 2019). The present study identifies prospective shame-guilt as a potential explanatory mechanism for these effects (see also Svensson et al., 2013). The more adolescents are committed to conventional roles in the family and the school, the more likely they will adopt the perspective of their parents and teachers in 'problematic' situations, and the more likely they will anticipate guilt and shame for violating the norms attached to the conventional role-identities they hold. At the same time, individuals begin to spend more time with their friends during adolescence and this adds another perspective to their developing understanding of self. Delinquent friends can serve as a 'pro-delinquent generalised other' and facilitate the neutralisation of guilt and shame by providing 'delinquent conceptions of self, pro-delinquent attitudes, justifications, and motives, and potential positive reactions to delinquent behaviour' (Heimer & Matsueda, 1994, p. 368).

Symbolic interactionist theories of delinquency are unique in emphasising how informal labelling processes by parents, teachers and peers can negatively influence adolescents' self-identities and thereby facilitate their involvement into delinquent behaviour (Heimer & Matsueda, 1994; Matsueda, 1992). That is, parents, teachers and/or peers may begin to apply labels such as 'troublemaker' or 'rule-violator' to adolescents who do not exhibit the behaviour, manners and attitudes that are expected of them. The present study found that adolescents who held reflected appraisals as a troublemaker anticipated less shame-guilt for engaging in delinquent activities. Although perceptions of being seen as a troublemaker by parents, teachers and friends were highly correlated, perceived appraisals from friends had the strongest negative effect on prospective shame-guilt. This finding contributes to a growing body of evidence documenting the potential criminogenic effects of (perceived) informal labelling by significant others in general and peers in particular (Brownfield & Thompson, 2005; De Coster & Lutz, 2018; Lee et al., 2017; Walters, 2016). More specifically, the results presented here suggest that informal labelling processes may increase the likelihood of (subsequent) involvement in delinquency by reducing offence-related guilt and shame.

In addition to parents, teachers and friends, the present study also observed the potential importance of the religious reference group, especially for ethnic minority youth. Muslims anticipated considerably higher levels of shame-guilt for shoplifting than nonreligiously affiliated adolescents. Christians also anticipated higher levels of shame-guilt than nonreligiously affiliated adolescents, but the difference was much smaller. This may be explained by the fact that our sample mostly included non-practising 'secular' Christians. In addition, it has been found that young Belgian Muslims experience considerably higher levels of social pressure for religious conformity than their Christian peers (Van Droogenbroeck & Spruyt, 2020, which might explain their higher levels of prospective shame-guilt for an act that violates religious norms. In a recent study of delinquency among both the ethnic majority youth and the ethnic minority youth in Belgium and Germany, Carol et al. (2020) found that religious adolescents, and Muslims in particular, were less likely to be involved in shoplifting. The present study extends this prior work by identifying prospective shame-guilt as a process through which religion may inhibit certain types of delinquency.

At the same time, the findings regarding retaliatory violence suggest that reference groups may not necessarily influence prospective shame-guilt across all delinquent acts. No evidence was found for an association between religious affiliation and prospective shame-guilt for engaging in retaliatory violence. This finding is consistent with those of other studies that have found relatively weak or mixed associations between religiosity and violence among Christian and Muslim adolescents in Western Europe (Baier, 2014;

Carol et al., 2020). Together, these findings speak to the complexity of the relationship between religion and violence. Indeed, as Cottee (2017) rightly argues, religion can be used to morally condemn certain acts of violence but also to legitimatise others (e.g. those committed against the out-group). This ambivalent stance towards violence is not unique to religion. Though most people disapprove of violence in general, justifications for violence used in self-defence or in response to threats or insults are relatively widely accepted (Agnew, 1994; Esala, 2013; Thomas, 2018). Esala (2013) observed how parents often condone and sometimes even justify certain forms of violence in their children (e.g. self-defence or retaliation), especially in their sons. The (perceived) ambivalence of parental attitudes towards violence might explain why the present study also failed to find an association between the strength of the parent-adolescent relationship and prospective shame-guilt for engaging in retaliatory violence.

Replicating the results of previous research (Rebellon et al., 2015, 2016; Svensson, 2004; Svensson et al., 2013), substantial gender differences were found in levels of prospective guilt and shame. More specifically, female adolescents anticipated considerably higher levels of guilt and shame than their male peers, in relation to both shoplifting and retaliatory violence. They also reported less exposure to friends who steal or fight and were less likely to believe that their friends see them as 'troublemakers'. Results from a multiple mediation analysis suggest that these two factors may explain part of the gender difference observed in this study. Thus, whereas previous research has demonstrated that peer influence contributes to gender differences in delinquent behaviour (Mears et al., 1998; Weerman & Hoeve, 2012), the present study extends these findings by suggesting that this influence occurs at least partly through the role-taking emotions of guilt and shame.

The present study tried to further clarify the observed gender differences in prospective shame-guilt by examining the role of societal gender role expectations. Based on the assumption that delinquency is generally inconsistent with traditional gender norms for female adolescents but not for male adolescents (Heimer, 1996; Steffensmeier & Allan, 1996), it was expected that female adolescents who endorse traditional femininity would anticipate *more* shame-guilt for engaging in delinquency and that male adolescents who endorse traditional masculinity would anticipate *less* shame-guilt for engaging in such behaviour. However, the findings suggest that adherence to traditional gender role expectations does not necessarily lead young women to experience a higher threat of guilt and shame. Contrary to expectations, not only traditional masculinity (for males) but also traditional femininity (for females) was associated with *less* shame-guilt for shoplifting. Furthermore, no evidence was found for an association between traditional femininity and shame-guilt for retaliatory violence, whereas traditional masculinity was weakly associated with lower levels of shame-guilt for this kind of behaviour. The findings regarding shoplifting call into question our initial assumption that delinquency is generally inconsistent with traditional femininity. In fact, some scholars have argued that minor offences such as petty theft and shoplifting are more consistent than inconsistent with traditional female roles in society (Steffensmeier & Allan, 1996). The findings regarding retaliatory violence are more surprising given the incompatibility of violence with traditional feminine ideals such as submissiveness and kindliness. One may wonder whether retaliatory violence is a special case, less influenced by traditional gender norms than other types of violence (e.g. instrumental or proactive violence). All in all, the findings presented here suggest that traditional gender norms do little to explain the observed gender difference in prospective shame-guilt. In fact, an important final conclusion is that the various social factors examined in this study could only account for a small part of the gender gap in prospective guilt and shame, suggesting that other more important factors are likely to be in play. In Section 8.3 below I will suggest other potential explanatory factors which should be examined in future work.

8.2 Implications for theory and practice

The findings discussed above, together with those of other studies reviewed earlier, strongly suggest that any comprehensive theory of delinquency should explicitly consider the role of guilt and shame in offending. In this book, I have shown how anticipated or prospective feelings of guilt and shame can be integrated into differential social control theory, a symbolic interactionist theory of delinquency based on Mead's theory of the self and role-taking. However, this does not mean that guilt and shame cannot be integrated in other theories as well. The present work has several implications for existing theory and further theoretical development.

In situational action theory (SAT), internalised moral rules and the associated emotions of guilt and shame are together considered as the main components of an individual's morality (Wikström, 2010; Wikström et al., 2012). SAT assumes that all action (including acts of crime) ultimately results from a two-stage perception-choice process in which individuals first perceive one or more action alternatives and then choose which option they will pursue. According to SAT, individuals with a strong law-relevant morality do not *choose* to refrain from crime because of the perceived costs and risks; they simply do not *perceive* crime as a possible action alternative to begin with. That is, their moral beliefs and moral emotions preclude them from even considering the possibility of engaging in an offense. Thus, in the framework of SAT, guilt and shame do not operate to *inhibit* an individual's desire to commit crime. Rather, they *filter* an individual's perception in such a way that they do not see crime as an option and do not experience a desire to offend in the first place (Barton-Crosby, 2022).[50]

Apart from the fact that the precise workings of the moral filtering process remain somewhat unclear (Brauer & Tittle, 2017), SAT's understanding of the role of guilt and shame is too narrow. In particular, the theory fails to acknowledge the inhibitory role that guilt and shame may play when individuals *do* consider crime as an option for choice. SAT recognises that even individuals with a strong law-relevant morality may sometimes perceive crime as a possible action alternative when they find themselves in 'criminogenic settings' (i.e. contexts in which the prevailing norms encourage acts of crime). Perhaps the best example here is that of an adolescent who holds that stealing is wrong but who is encouraged by a group of friends to join a shoplifting expedition. This adolescent, perhaps because of a desire to 'fit in' or 'look cool' among friends, may feel tempted to shoplift. SAT argues that in such situations individuals need to exercise self-control in order to withstand the temptation and act in accordance with their moral beliefs (Wikström & Treiber, 2007). However, though SAT highlights the importance of *self-control capacity* (i.e. an individual's cognitive abilities), the theory pays little attention to *self-control motivation*. Following the symbolic interactionist perspective outlined in this book, prospective guilt and shame could be integrated in SAT as factors that can motivate and make meaningful a person's effort to exercise self-control in the face of deviant temptations. More generally, it is proposed that guilt and shame may not only operate as a 'moral filter' in the perception process but also function as 'barriers' to offending in the subsequent process of choice.

According to rational choice and deterrence theories, moral emotions do necessarily preclude individuals from becoming motivated to offend. Rather, in contemplating an act of crime, prospective offenders consider whether they would feel guilty or ashamed for it, a potential cost then weighed along with other potential costs and benefits in an instrumental calculus (Grasmick & Bursik, 1990; Tibbetts, 1997b). Hence, if the perceived benefits are high enough, individuals may be willing to incur guilt and shame in order to commit an offense.

One problem with rational choice and deterrence theories is their narrow conceptualisation of guilt and shame. Specifically, these theories only deal with *anticipated* feelings of guilt and shame, which are essentially cognitive beliefs about future emotional states that are themselves devoid of any affective content (van Gelder, Elffers, et al., 2014).

50 In a lengthy discussion on the role of morality in SAT, Barton-Crosby (2022, p. 1430) writes that 'if a person thinks it is wrong to break a particular rule and anticipates that he or she would feel guilt and/or shame if he or she did break the rule, it is unlikely that rule-breaking will be perceived as an action alternative.' However, one may wonder why a person who does not even perceive rule-breaking as an action alternative would anticipate feelings of guilt and shame. Mentally anticipating the future consequences of a moral transgression, and being *influenced* by these anticipated future consequences, seems to presuppose that one first considers committing the transgression.

Rational choice and deterrence theories assume that people *dispassionately* weigh future guilt and shame states against other potential costs and benefits associated with offending. By comparison, the symbolic interactionist conception of prospective guilt and shame that is advanced in this research is broader and allows for including not only *anticipated* but also *felt* guilt and shame states. Indeed, individuals who contemplate committing a moral transgression may not simply expect to feel guilty or ashamed in the future; they may already experience a 'hint' or 'foretaste' of these emotions in the present (i.e. at the mere thought of committing the transgression). Moral emotions that are both anticipated *and* pre-felt are likely to be more compelling – and therefore have stronger inhibitory effects – than moral emotions that are merely anticipated. In fact, the latter may lack the necessary motivational force required to inhibit deviant desires and impulses.

Emotions that are already experienced during the decision-making process are difficult to integrate into traditional rational choice models because they are not expected consequences of the decision to offend; rather, those emotions are factors that affect *the state of mind* in which these consequences are perceived and evaluated. A more comprehensive model of offender decision-making may be developed by integrating conceptions of decision-making based on role-taking and rational choice. Such a model can incorporate interaction effects between role-taking processes (e.g. views of the self and self-conscious emotions) and externally imposed consequences (e.g. the threat of formal sanctions) (e.g. Matsueda et al., 2020). For example, it may be hypothesised that prospective guilt and shame *condition* the effect of instrumental incentives, so that the effect of sanction threats on delinquency is less important for individuals who are already strongly inhibited by guilt and shame.

In addition to the above, the symbolic interactionist analysis presented in this book furthers our theoretical understanding of the social embeddedness of guilt and shame. Indeed, feelings of guilt and shame do not merely reflect an individual's view of themselves but also their perception of how others (would) view them. Some researchers have proposed to use Hirschi's social control theory as a framework for understanding how social bonds to conventional society may affect delinquent behaviour through prospective guilt and shame (Clay-Warner, 2014; Svensson, 2004). However, a symbolic interactionist approach based on Mead's theory of the self and role-taking can offer a more comprehensive explanation of how significant others and reference groups may shape these emotions. At least two distinctive features of this approach can be identified.

First, rather than simply assuming that society is characterised by a single moral order, a symbolic interactionist perspective allows for heterogeneity in the normative orientations of people's reference groups. Hence, whether role-taking will increase or decrease prospective guilt and shame for engaging in delinquency depends on the specific normative orientations of the reference group whose perspective the individual adopts. For example, adolescents who frequently associate with delinquent friends, and who see themselves through the eyes of these friends, may anticipate pride rather than guilt or shame for committing delinquent acts. In general, and compared to classic social control theory, the concept of role-taking broadens the theoretical lens to include not only the *quality* or *strength* of social bonds but also their *content* or *meaning*.

Second, a symbolic interactionist approach is unique in considering how informal labelling processes might affect delinquency through their influence on prospective guilt and shame. Primary reference groups such as parents, teachers and/or peers may begin to apply labels such as 'troublemaker' or 'rule-violator' to adolescents who do not exhibit the manners that are expected of them. The concept of role-taking provides a theoretical mechanism to explain how such forms of stigmatising shaming can influence an adolescent's self-identity in the form of reflected appraisals (i.e. perceptions of how one is viewed by others). Adolescents who believe that others see them as troublemakers are less likely to anticipate feelings of guilt and shame for engaging in delinquency (because such behaviour poses less of a threat to their identity; in fact, it is consistent with the deviant identity ascribed to them). In general, and compared to classic social control theory, a symbolic interactionist approach widens the theoretical scope by considering the importance of informal reactions to delinquency and labelling processes.

Although it was not an objective of this study to make recommendations for policy or practice, the results do have some implications which should be considered by juvenile justice practitioners, youth workers, teachers and parents. The research literature strongly suggests that prospective guilt and shame can restrain adolescents from engaging in delinquent behaviour. Crucially, however, this does not imply that *directly* inducing guilt and shame will necessarily be effective in preventing or reducing delinquency. Prospective guilt and shame are by-products of something else, namely our sense of self in relation to others. If anything, the present study suggests that these emotions should be cultivated *indirectly*, by giving young people the opportunity to develop, negotiate and sustain a positive and respectable self-identity through social bonds with others in conventional reference groups (e.g. the family, the school, the religious community, non-delinquent friendship networks etc.). It is only because adolescents are positively committed to such an identity that they will anticipate feelings of guilt and shame for violating the normative expectations attached to it. Obviously, communicating disapproval of moral transgressions is necessary, but stigmatising forms of shaming and labelling should be avoided at all costs because they can damage young people's identity formation. Indeed, the present study found that levels of prospective guilt and shame for engaging in delinquency are *lower* among adolescents who feel that significant others see them as 'troublemakers', even when taking into account prior offending.

8.3 LIMITATIONS

The present study has several important limitations which should be considered when interpreting the findings. Perhaps the most important limitation is its cross-sectional and observational design, preventing any causal interpretation of the results. Nonetheless, another recent study with a longitudinal design also found that changes in parent-, school- and peer-related factors are associated with changes in anticipated guilt and shame for engaging in delinquency (Svensson et al., 2016). These results corroborate those of the present study and lend further credence to the hypothesis that social factors contribute to differences in prospective guilt and shame among adolescents. At the same time, it should be noted that an interactionist perspective would predict bidirectional relationships between social bonds and the role-taking emotions of guilt and shame. Indeed, anticipated guilt and shame are as much a product of one's engagements with others as a factor that prevents one from doing things that threaten these engagements. Future longitudinal studies are needed to further examine these dynamic relationships.

A second limitation derives from the sample, which included mostly older adolescents (around three-quarter of the sample was aged 17 and older). As a consequence, the results cannot be generalised to the whole period of adolescence. The relatively small effect of the parent-adolescent relationship on prospective shame-guilt, and the null effect of perceived parental labelling, may be partly explained by the age of the sample. In a meta-analysis of the relationship between parenting and delinquency, Hoeve and colleagues (2009) found evidence to suggest that parental influences on delinquency are stronger in early adolescence than in late adolescence. The same may be true for parental influences on prospective guilt and shame.

A third limitation concerns the measurement of prospective guilt and shame. Only two relatively straightforward items were used to assess each emotional response. In retrospect, it may have been preferable to include more items targeting the distinct phenomenological features of guilt and shame (as described in the literature). This would have allowed a more rigorous test of the dimensionality of the prospective shame-guilt construct. Although numerous studies (including the present one) have found that measures of guilt and shame are very highly correlated, this does not necessarily imply that guilt and shame occur as a single emotion; nor does it imply that they are indistinguishable in the mind of the respondents. On the other hand, it could be argued that the relatively subtle differences between guilt and shame

> may not be apparent when people consider how they would feel in the future as opposed to how they actually do feel now, or how they did in the past. (Hynie et al., 2006, p. 1074)

In addition, it would have been interesting to measure anticipated or prospective feelings of guilt and shame in two conditions: with public exposure and without public exposure of the transgression in question. This would have allowed a test of the assumption that prospective guilt and shame do not require public exposure. Nevertheless, based on previous research, it can be argued that this assumption is valid (e.g. Smith et al., 2002).

A fourth limitation of this study concerns the measurement of traditional gender role attitudes using the Gender Ideology Scale of Vermeersch et al. (2010). More specifically, some of the scale's items reflecting traditional femininity were found to have relatively low factor loadings (e.g. the item about the prioritisation of motherhood over career). A recent psychometric study examining the validity of Vermeersch et al.'s scale also reported low factor loadings for these items and concluded that they may be outdated (Halimi et al., 2018). Therefore, the results regarding the effects of adherence to traditional femininity on prospective shame-guilt should be considered preliminary and further studies with better measures are needed to obtain stronger conclusions.

Several other measurement limitations stem from the fact that the design of the survey and the data collection took place before the theoretical framework was fully developed. As a consequence, some of the theoretical constructs of interest were only partially or indirectly measured or not measured at all. The strength or closeness of the parent-adolescent relationship was only measured indirectly, through items reflecting adolescents' perceptions of parental knowledge about their whereabouts and companions. Although several studies have found that parental knowledge is closely associated with the quality of the parent-adolescent relationship (e.g. Kapetanovic et al., 2019; Walters, 2016), a direct measure would have been preferable. This is especially true for the older adolescents in the sample, as parental knowledge (i.e. monitoring knowledge) tends to decrease in late adolescence (Keijsers & Poulin, 2013). Furthermore, religiosity was only measured by a relatively crude measure of religious affiliation and religious behaviour. The study would have benefited from including additional, more detailed measures that directly target the social dimensions of religiosity, such as participation in religious meetings and activities, perceived pressure for religious conformity, and interpersonal relationships with fellow believers. This would have allowed a better test of the moral community hypothesis (according to which the normative force of religion derives not so much from individual religious beliefs and behaviours but from the embeddedness of religious individuals in social groups).

The survey did not include items measuring the perceived normative attitudes of significant others and reference groups towards shoplifting and retaliatory violence. Instead, it was simply assumed that adolescents perceive parents and teachers as unambiguously disapproving and delinquent friends as unambiguously approving of such behaviour. However, significant others and reference groups may vary in the extent to which they approve or disapprove of specific delinquent acts. From a symbolic interactionist perspective, these normative orientations are important in shaping the role-taking emotions of guilt and shame. Assessing them would have enabled a better test of the predictions of the theoretical model. It would have been particularly interesting, for instance, to measure perceived parental disapproval of retaliatory violence and to examine whether this variable modifies the association between the parent-adolescent relationship and prospective shame-guilt. Having closer relationships with parents should increase prospective shame-guilt among those who perceive their parents as strongly disapproving of (retaliatory) violence but not necessarily among those who see their parents as having permissive views about (retaliatory) violence.

A final limitation of this study is that the analyses only focused on two types of delinquency: theft and violence. Moreover, only one specific form of theft (shoplifting) and one specific form of violence (retaliatory violence) were examined. Research by Thomas (2018) has shown that attitudes towards theft and violence are too complex to be assessed with single-item measures. Especially attitudes towards violence can vary substantially depending on the circumstances. Individuals who approve of fighting under specific conditions (e.g. in response to threats or insults) do not necessarily approve of fighting more generally. Hence, interpersonal and social factors that have little or no influence on prospective shame-guilt for engaging in retaliatory violence may still influence prospective shame-guilt for engaging in other types of violence. Future studies should replicate the analyses including other types of delinquency.

8.4 Avenues for future research

All in all, the social factors of interest in this study could only explain a small portion of the observed gender difference in prospective shame-guilt, suggesting that other more important factors need to be investigated. Fortunately, several other potentially explanatory factors can be identified for future research.

First, as mentioned earlier, the present study did not include measures of anticipated disapproval from parents, teachers and friends for involvement in shoplifting and retaliatory violence. Yet, there are reasons to suggest that female adolescents may anticipate stronger disapproval from significant others than male adolescents, especially when it comes to violent delinquency (Heimer, 1996). Future studies would do well to examine the extent to which anticipated social disapproval mediates gender differences in prospective shame-guilt.

A second factor to consider is adolescents' acceptance of 'neutralisations', that is, their acceptance of excuses or justifications for actions that violate normative expectations (Maruna & Copes, 2005; Sykes & Matza, 1957). If individuals can excuse or justify their intended actions in advance, they are free to commit them without serious damage to their moral self-image. One of the mechanisms by which neutralisations may facilitate delinquency is by alleviating or even eliminating (prospective) guilt and shame. Although gender differences in adolescents' use of neutralisation techniques have not been widely studied, one study found that male adolescents were more likely to accept neutralisations for delinquency than female adolescents (Topalli et al., 2013). Whether gender differences in the acceptance of neutralisation techniques are related to gender differences in prospective shame-guilt is an open question that deserves further study.

A third potentially important factor is suggested by the work of Trivedi-Bateman (2019). She proposes that a strong ability to exercise empathy increases the potential to experience shame and guilt at the thought of committing a (violent) offence. Although empathy is not a necessary precursor to guilt or shame, being able to understand and feel what a victim would feel might help one to understand that an intended action is wrong and, thereby, intensify prospective guilt and shame (Miceli & Castelfranchi, 1998; Prinz, 2011).[51] Several studies have found gender differences in empathic abilities more generally and empathic responses to others' pain in particular (Christov-Moore et al., 2014; Derntl et al., 2010; Singer et al., 2006). Hence, examining the role of empathy in explaining gender differences in prospective shame-guilt may prove a fruitful avenue for future research. It is interesting to note in this respect that the observed gender differences in the present study were larger in the case of retaliatory violence (an overt act involving direct confrontation with a victim) than in the case of shoplifting (a covert act not involving direct confrontation with a victim), an observation which suggests that empathy might play a role.

A fourth avenue for further research is the examination of other emotions that may override prospective guilt and shame. Anger, for example, may interfere with guilt and shame because it shifts attention away from the self towards the other who is perceived as causing the anger (van Gelder, Reynald, et al., 2014). Anger may be especially relevant in potentially provocative situations, such as the retaliatory violence scenario used in this study. Another relevant emotion to consider is pride, a role-taking emotion typically seen as the opposite of shame (Shott, 1979). Some studies have found that (minor) delinquency is associated with higher popularity among peers (e.g. Rebellon et al., 2019; Weerman & Bijleveld, 2007). The prospect of gaining popularity or prestige may lead adolescents to anticipate pride rather than guilt or shame for engaging in delinquency. Anticipated pride may be especially relevant in situations that involve risk-taking, such as the shoplifting scenario used in this study. Future research could examine whether gender differences in prospective guilt and shame may reflect males' greater susceptibility to anger and pride.

---

51 Although empathy requires perspective-taking, it is different from role-taking as defined in the symbolic interactionist tradition. Role-taking is reflexive; the focus is ultimately on the self (how it would appear from the perspective of another). In empathy, the focus is entirely on the situation of the other. Put differently, empathy requires the capacity not only to take the perspective of the other but also to detach oneself from one's own perspective.

Finally, the link between retrospective and prospective forms of guilt and shame needs to be examined. Prospective emotions (directed towards future events) are likely to be shaped, nourished and informed by previous emotional experiences (Baumeister et al., 2007). Failing to recognise and acknowledge guilt and shame for past wrongs may diminish one's capacity or inclination to anticipate and pre-feel guilt and shame when considering future offences. Investigating gender differences in feelings of guilt and shame experienced *after* moral transgressions (and gender differences in the management of these feelings), then, can provide valuable information for understanding gender differences in prospective guilt and shame.

Bibliography

Abell, E., & Gecas, V. (1997). Guilt, shame, and family socialization: A retrospective study. *Journal of Family Issues, 18*(2), 99-123. https://doi.org/10.1177/019251397018002001

Aboulafia, M. (1991). Introduction. In M. Aboulafia (Ed.), *Philosophy, social theory, and the thought of George Herbert Mead* (pp. 1-20). State University of New York Press.

Adriaenssen, A., Paoli, L., Karstedt, S., Visschers, J., Greenfield, V. A., & Pleysier, S. (2018). Public perceptions of the seriousness of crime: Weighing the harm and the wrong. *European Journal of Criminology, 17*(2), 127-150. https://doi.org/10.1177/1477370818772768

Agnew, R. (1992). Foundation for a general strain theory of crime and delinquency. *Criminology, 30*(1), 47-87. http://doi.org/10.1111/j.1745-9125.1992.tb01093.x

Agnew, R. (1994). The techniques of neutralization and violence. *Criminology, 32*(4), 555-580. https://doi.org/10.1111/j.1745-9125.1994.tb01165.x

Ahmed, E. (2001). Shame management: Regulating bullying. In E. Ahmed, N. Harris, J. Braithwaite, & V. Braithwaite (Eds.), *Shame management through reintegration* (pp. 209-311). Cambridge University Press.

Ahmed, E., Harris, N., Braithwaite, J., & Braithwaite, V. (2001). *Shame management through reintegration*. Cambridge University Press.

Akers, R. L. (1973). *Deviant behavior: A social learning approach*. Wadsworth.

Akers, R. L. (2009). *Social learning and social structure: A general theory of crime and deviance*. Transaction Publishers.

al-Thakeb, F., & Scott, J. E. (1981). Islamic law: An examination of its revitalisation. *The British Journal of Criminology, 21*(1), 58-69. https://doi.org/10.1093/oxfordjournals.bjc.a047197

Allen, S., Murphy, K., & Bates, L. (2017). What drives compliance? The effect of deterrence and shame emotions on young drivers' compliance with road laws. *Policing and Society, 27*(8), 884-898. https://doi.org/10.1080/10439463.2015.1115502

Anderson, E. (1999). *Code of the street: Decency, violence, and the moral life of the inner city*. Norton.

Andrews, B., Gilbert, P., & Andrews, B. (1998). Methodological and definitional issues in shame research. In *Shame: Interpersonal behavior, psychopathology, and culture* (pp. 39-56). Oxford University Press.

Andrews, B., Qian, M., & Valentine, J. D. (2002). Predicting depressive symptoms with a new measure of shame: The Experience of Shame Scale. *The British Journal of Clinical Psychology, 41*(1), 29-42. https://doi.org/dgjtrt

Andrews, J. L., Ahmed, S. P., & Blakemore, S.-J. (2021). Navigating the social environment in adolescence: The role of social brain development. *Biological Psychiatry*, *89*(2), 109-118. https://doi.org/10.1016/j.biopsych.2020.09.012

Archer, J. (2004). Sex differences in aggression in real-world settings: A meta-analytic review. *Review of General Psychology*, *8*(4), 291-322. https://doi.org/10.1037/1089-2680.8.4.291

Ausubel, D. P. (1955). Relationships between shame and guilt in the socializing process. *Psychological Review*, *62*(5), 378-390. https://doi.org/10.1037/h0042534

Baguley, T. (2009). Standardized or simple effect size: What should be reported? *British Journal of Psychology*, *100*(3), 603-617. https://doi.org/10.1348/000712608X377117

Baier, D. (2014). The influence of religiosity on violent behavior of adolescents: A comparison of Christian and Muslim religiosity. *Journal of Interpersonal Violence*, *29*(1), 102-127. https://doi.org/10.1177/0886260513504646

Baldwin, M. W., & Baccus, J. R. (2004). Maintaining a focus on the social goals underlying self-conscious emotions. *Psychological Inquiry*, *15*(2), 139-144.

Barrett, P. (2007). Structural equation modelling: Adjudging model fit. *Personality and Individual Differences*, *42*(5), 815-824. https://doi.org/10.1016/j.paid.2006.09.018

Barton-Crosby, J. (2022). The nature and role of morality in situational action theory. *European Journal of Criminology*, *19*(6), 1421-1437. https://doi.org/10.1177/1477370820977099

Bartusch, D. J., & Matsueda, R. L. (1996). Gender, reflected appraisals, and labeling: A cross-group test of an interactionist theory of delinquency. *Social Forces*, *75*(1), 145-176. https://doi.org/10.2307/2580760

Batchelor, S. (2005). 'Prove me the bam!': Victimization and agency in the lives of young women who commit violent offences. *Probation Journal*, *52*(4), 358-375. https://doi.org/10.1177/0264550505058034

Baumeister, R. F., Bauer, I. M., & Lloyd, S. A. (2010). Choice, free will, and religion. *Psychology of Religion and Spirituality*, *2*(2), 67-82. https://doi.org/10.1037/a0018455

Baumeister, R. F., Stillwell, A. M., & Heatherton, T. F. (1994). Guilt: An interpersonal approach. *Psychological Bulletin*, *115*(2), 243-267. https://doi.org/10.1037/0033-2909.115.2.243

Baumeister, R. F., Vohs, K. D., Nathan DeWall, C., & Liqing Zhang. (2007). How emotion shapes behavior: Feedback, anticipation, and reflection, rather than direct causation. *Personality and Social Psychology Review*, *11*(2), 167-203. https://doi.org/10.1177/1088868307301033

Becker, G. S. (1968). Crime and punishment: An economic approach. *Journal of Political Economy*, *76*(2), 169-217. https://doi.org/10.1086/259394

Becker, H. S. (1963). *Outsiders: Studies in the sociology of deviance*. The Free Press of Glencoe.

Beedie, C., Terry, P., & Lane, A. (2005). Distinctions between emotion and mood. *Cognition & Emotion, 19*(6), 847-878. https://doi.org/10.1080/02699930541000057

Benedict, R. (1946). *The chrysanthemum and the sword: Patterns of Japanese culture.* Houghton Mifflin.

Ben-Ze'ev, A. (2001). *Subtlety of Emotions.* MIT Press.

Bering, J., & Johnson, D. (2005). 'O Lord ... You Perceive my Thoughts from Afar': Recursiveness and the evolution of supernatural agency. *Journal of Cognition and Culture, 5*(1-2), 118-142. https://doi.org/10.1163/1568537054068679

Bernardi, F., Chakhaia, L., & Leopold, L. (2017). 'Sing Me a Song with Social Significance': The (Mis)use of statistical significance testing in European sociological research. *European Sociological Review, 33*(1), 1-15. https://doi.org/10.1093/esr/jcw047

Blackwell, B. S. (2000). Perceived sanction threats, gender, and crime: A test and elaboration of power-control theory. *Criminology, 38*(2), 439-488. https://doi.org/10.1111/j.1745-9125.2000.tb00896.x

Bollen, K. A. (1995). Apparent and nonapparent significance tests. *Sociological Methodology, 25*, 459-468. https://doi.org/10.2307/271074

Boman, J.H., & Ward, J.T. (2014). Beyond projection: Specifying the types of peer delinquency misperception at the item and scale levels. *Deviant Behavior*, 35, 555-580. https://doi.org/10.1080/01639625.2013.863098

Bottoms, A. (2002). Morality, crime, compliance and public policy. In A. Bottoms & M. Tonry (Eds.), *Ideology, Crime and Criminal Justice* (pp. 20-51). Willan Publishing.

Bradt, L., & Bouverne-De Bie, M. (2014). De schoolbeleving van jongeren in Vlaamse en grootstedelijke secundaire scholen. In L. Bradt, S. Pleysier, J. Put, J. Siongers, & B. Spruyt (Eds.), *Jongeren in cijfers en letters 3. Bevindingen uit de JOP-monitor 3 en de JOP-schoolmonitor 2013* (pp. 40-67). Acco.

Bradt, L., Pleysier, S., Put, J., & Spruyt, B. (Eds.). (2014). *Jongeren in cijfers en letters 3. Bevindingen uit de JOP-monitor 3 en de JOP-schoolmonitor 2013.* Acco.

Braithwaite, J. (1989). *Crime, shame, and reintegration.* Cambridge University Press.

Braithwaite, J. (2018). Minimally sufficient deterrence. *Crime and Justice, 47*(1), 69-118. https://doi.org/10.1086/696043

Braithwaite, J. (2020). Restorative justice and reintegrative shaming. In C. Chouhy, J. C. Cochran, & C. L. Jonson (Eds.), *Criminal justice theory: Explanation and effects* (pp. 281-308). Routledge.

Braithwaite, J., & Braithwaite, V. (2001). Shame, shame management and regulation. In E. Ahmed, N. Harris, J. Braithwaite, & V. Braithwaite (Eds.), *Shame management through reintegration* (pp. 3-69). Cambridge University Press.

Braithwaite, V., & Braithwaite, J. (2001). Creating institutional spaces for shame management. In E. Ahmed, N. Harris, J. Braithwaite, & V. Braithwaite (Eds.), *Shame management through reintegration* (pp. 315-330). Cambridge University Press.

Brauer, J. R., & De Coster, S. (2015). Social relationships and delinquency: Revisiting parent and peer influence during adolescence. *Youth & Society*, *47*(3), 374-394. https://doi.org/10.1177/0044118X12467655

Brauer, J. R., & Tittle, C. R. (2017). When crime is not an option: Inspecting the moral filtering of criminal action alternatives. *Justice Quarterly*, *34*(5), 818-846. https://doi.org/10.1080/07418825.2016.1226937

Brauer, J. R., Tittle, C. R., & Antonaccio, O. (2013). Does religion suppress, socialize, soothe, or support? Exploring religiosity's influence on crime. *Journal for the Scientific Study of Religion*, *52*(4), 753-774. https://doi.org/10.1111/jssr.12063

Brinthaupt, T. M., & Lipka, R. P. (Eds.). (2002). *Understanding early adolescent self and identity: Applications and interventions*. State University of New York Press.

Brody, G. (1982). Contributions of parents and peers to children's moral socialization. *Developmental Review*, *2*(1), 31-75. https://doi.org/10.1016/0273-2297(82)90003-X

Brown, B. B. (2004). Adolescents' relationships with peers. In R. M. Lerner & L. Steinberg (Eds.), *Handbook of adolescent psychology* (pp. 363-394). John Wiley & Sons, Ltd. https://doi.org/10.1002/9780471726746.ch12

Brown, T. A. (2015). *Confirmatory factor analysis for applied research* (2nd ed.). The Guilford Press.

Brownfield, D., & Thompson, K. (2005). Self-concept and delinquency: The effects of reflected appraisals by parent and peers. *Western Criminology Review*, *6*(1), 22-29.

Bullivant, S. (2018). *Europe's young adults and religion: Findings from the European Social Survey (2014-16) to inform the 2018 Synod of Bishops*. Benedict XVI Centre for Religion and Society 2018.

Burke, P. J., & Reitzes, D. C. (1991). An identity theory approach to commitment. *Social Psychology Quarterly*, *54*(3), 239-251. https://doi.org/10.2307/2786653

Calverley, A., & Farrell, S. (2011). The sensual dynamics of processes of personal reform: Desistance from crime and the role of emotions. In S. Karstedt, I. Loader, & H. Strang (Eds.), *Emotions, crime and justice* (pp. 81-100). Hart Publishing.

Campbell, E. Q. (1964). The internalization of moral norms. *Sociometry*, *27*(4), 391-412. https://doi.org/10.2307/2785655

Carmichael, S., & Piquero, A. R. (2004). Sanctions, perceived anger, and criminal offending. *Journal of Quantitative Criminology*, *20*(4), 371-393. https://doi.org/10.1007/s10940-004-5869-y

Carol, S., Peez, F., & Wagner, M. (2020). Delinquency among majority and minority youths in Cologne, Mannheim and Brussels: The role of religion. *Journal of Ethnic and Migration Studies*, *46*(17), 3603-3629. https://doi.org/10.1080/1369183X.2019.1620415

Chandra-Mouli, V., Plesons, M., Adebayo, E., Amin, A., Avni, M., Kraft, J. M., Lane, C., Brundage, C. L., Kreinin, T., Bosworth, E., Garcia-Moreno, C., & Malarcher, S. (2017). Implications of the global early adolescent study's formative research findings for action and for research. *Journal of Adolescent Health*, *61*(4, Supplement), S5-S9. https://doi.org/10.1016/j.jadohealth.2017.07.012

Christov-Moore, L., Simpson, E. A., Coudé, G., Grigaityte, K., Iacoboni, M., & Ferrari, P. F. (2014). Empathy: Gender effects in brain and behavior. *Neuroscience & Biobehavioral Reviews*, *46*(4), 604-627. https://doi.org/10.1016/j.neubiorev.2014.09.001

Cibich, M., Woodyatt, L., & Wenzel, M. (2016). Moving beyond "shame is bad": How a functional emotion can become problematic. *Social and Personality Psychology Compass*, *10*(9), 471-483. https://doi.org/10.1111/spc3.12263

Clay-Warner, J. (2014). Crime and emotions. In J. E. Stets & J. H. Turner (Eds.), *Handbook of the sociology of emotions: Volume II* (pp. 473-493). Springer Netherlands. https://doi.org/10.1007/978-94-017-9130-4_22

Cochran, J. K. (1988). The effect of religiosity on secular and ascetic deviance. *Sociological Focus*, *21*(4), 293-306.

Coenen, E. (2019). Daderschap: Oude en nieuwe vormen. In L. Bradt, S. Pleysier, J. Put, J. Siongers, & B. Spruyt (Eds.), *Jongeren in cijfers en letters 4. Bevindingen uit de JOP-monitor 4, de JOP-kindmonitor en de JOP-schoolmonitor 2.* (pp. 79-102). Acco.

Coenen, E. (2020). Een eerste blik op online delinquentie: Verkennend onderzoek bij Vlaamse jongeren en vergelijking met offline delinquentie. *Tijdschrift Voor Criminologie*, *62*(2-3), 130-152. https://doi.org/10.5553/TvC/0165182X2020062203002

Coffman, D. L., Melde, C., & Esbensen, F.-A. (2014). Gang membership and substance use: Guilt as a gendered causal pathway. *Journal of Experimental Criminology*, *11*(1), 71-95. https://doi.org/10.1007/s11292-014-9220-9

Cohen, T. R., Wolf, S. T., Panter, A. T., & Insko, C. A. (2011). Introducing the GASP scale: A new measure of guilt and shame proneness. *Journal of Personality and Social Psychology*, *100*(5), 947-966. https://doi.org/10.1037/a0022641

Cole, L. M., Cohn, E. S., Rebellon, C. J., & Van Gundy, K. T. (2014). Feeling guilty to remain innocent: The moderating effect of sex on guilt responses to rule-violating behavior in adolescent legal socialization. *Psychology, Crime & Law*, *20*(8), 722-740. https://doi.org/10.1080/1068316X.2013.854794

Connell, R. W., & Messerschmidt, J. W. (2005). Hegemonic masculinity: Rethinking the concept. *Gender & Society*, *19*(6), 829-859. https://doi.org/10.1177/0891243205278639

Consedine, N., Strongman, K., & Magai, C. (2003). Emotions and behaviour: Data from a cross-cultural recognition study. *Cognition & Emotion*, *17*(6), 881-902. https://doi.org/10.1080/02699930244000246

Cook, G. A. (1993). *George Herbert Mead: The making of a social pragmatist*. University of Illinois Press.

Cook, G. A. (2013). Resolving two key problems in Mead's mind, self, and society. In T. F. Burke & K. Skowronski (Eds.), *George Herbert Mead in the twenty-first century* (pp. 95-105). Lexington Books.

Cooley, C. H. (1902). *Human nature and the social order*. Scribner's.

Copeland-Linder, N., Jones, V. C., Haynie, D. L., Simons-Morton, B. G., Wright, J. L., & Cheng, T. L. (2007). Factors associated with retaliatory attitudes among African American adolescents who have been assaulted. *Journal of Pediatric Psychology, 32*(7), 760-770. https://doi.org/10.1093/jpepsy/jsm007

Cops, D. (2014). Criminaliteit en onveiligheidsgevoelens doorheen de tijd. Een analyse op basis van 10 jaar JOP-monitor. In L. Bradt, S. Pleysier, B. Spruyt, J. Siongers, & J. Put (Eds.), *Jongeren in cijfers en letters. Bevindingen uit de JOP-monitor 3 en de JOP-schoolmonitor 2013* (pp. 71-93). Acco.

Cops, D., Pleysier, S., Verdonck, E., & Put, J. (2014). Delinquentie bij Brusselse scholieren van Belgische en niet-Belgische afkomst. *Panopticon, 35*(1), 27-49.

Cornish, D. B., & Clarke, R. V. G. (Eds.). (1986). *The reasoning criminal: Rational choice perspectives on offending*. Springer-Verlag.

Costello, B. J., & Laub, J. H. (2020). Social control theory: The legacy of Travis Hirschi's causes of delinquency. *Annual Review of Criminology, 3*(1), 21-41. https://doi.org/10.1146/annurev-criminol-011419-041527

Cottee, S. (2017). Religion, crime, and violence. In A. Liebling, S. Maruna, & L. McAra (Eds.), *The Oxford handbook of criminology* (pp. 478-500). Oxford University Press.

Crocetti, E., Branje, S., Rubini, M., Koot, H. M., & Meeus, W. (2017). Identity processes and parent-child and sibling relationships in adolescence: A five-wave multi-informant longitudinal study. *Child Development, 88*(1), 210-228. https://doi.org/10.1111/cdev.12547

Crocker, L. D., Haller, M., Norman, S. B., & Angkaw, A. C. (2016). Shame versus trauma-related guilt as mediators of the relationship between PTSD symptoms and aggression among returning veterans. *Psychological Trauma: Theory, Research, Practice, and Policy, 8*(4), 520-527. https://doi.org/10.1037/tra0000151

Curry, T. R. (2014). The benefits and penalties of gender for criminal justice processing out-comes among adults and juveniles. In R. Garther & B. McCarthy (Eds.), *The Oxford hand-book of gender, sex, and crime* (pp. 551-571). Oxford University Press.

Cutrín, O., Gómez-Fraguela, J. A., & Sobral, J. (2017). Two faces of parental support: Risk and protection for antisocial youth depending on parental knowledge. *Journal of Child and Family Studies, 26*(1), 296-305. https://doi.org/10.1007/s10826-016-0559-6

De Boeck, A., Hardyns, W., & Pauwels, L. J. R. (2014). Het probleem van meetinvariantie bij het vergelijken van subgroepen op basis van somscores. *Tijdschrift Voor Criminologie, 56*(1), 42-59.

de Boer, M. S. (2008). *Culturele diversiteit in opvattingen over misdaad en straf onder leerlingen van het VMBO*. Boom.

De Buck, A., & Pauwels, L. J. R. (2019). Intention to shoplift: On the importance of dimensions of propensity in an integrated informal control/lifestyle model. *European*

Journal on Criminal Policy and Research, 25(3), 297-315. https://doi.org/10.1007/s10610-018-9400-7

De Coster, S., & Lutz, J. (2018). Reconsidering labels and primary deviance: False appraisals, reflected appraisals, and delinquency onset. *Journal of Research in Crime and Delinquency, 55*(5), 609-648. https://doi.org/10.1177/0022427818771437

de Hooge, I. E., Breugelmans, S. M., Wagemans, F. M. A., & Zeelenberg, M. (2018). The social side of shame: Approach versus withdrawal. *Cognition & Emotion, 32*(8), 1671-1677. https://doi.org/10.1080/02699931.2017.1422696

de Hooge, I. E., Breugelmans, S. M., & Zeelenberg, M. (2008). Not so ugly after all: When shame acts as a commitment device. *Journal of Personality and Social Psychology, 95*(4), 933-943. https://doi.org/10.1037/a0011991

de Hooge, I. E., Zeelenberg, M., & Breugelmans, S. M. (2010). Restore and protect motivations following shame. *Cognition & Emotion, 24*(1), 111-127. https://doi.org/10.1080/02699930802584466

de Hooge, I. E., Zeelenberg, M., & Breugelmans, S. M. (2011). A functionalist account of shame-induced behaviour. *Cognition & Emotion, 25*(5), 939-946. https://doi.org/10.1080/02699931.2010.516909

Deigh, J. (1983). Shame and self-esteem: A critique. *Ethics, 93*(2), 225-245. https://doi.org/10.2307/2380417

Dempsey, H. (2017). A comparison of the social-adaptive perspective and functionalist perspective on guilt and shame. *Behavioral Sciences, 7*(4), 83. https://doi.org/10.3390/bs7040083

Deonna, J. A., Rodogno, R., & Teroni, F. (2012). *In defense of shame: The faces of an emotion*. Oxford University Press.

Deonna, J. A., & Scherer, K. R. (2010). The case of the disappearing intentional object: Constraints on a definition of emotion. *Emotion Review, 2*(1), 44-52. https://doi.org/10.1177/1754073909345544

Deonna, J., & Teroni, F. (2011). Is shame a social emotion? In A. Konzelmann Ziv, K. Lehrer, & H. B. Schmid (Eds.), *Self-evaluation: Affective and social grounds of intentionality* (pp. 193-212). Springer Netherlands. http://doi.org/10.1007/978-94-007-1266-9_11

Derntl, B., Finkelmeyer, A., Eickhoff, S., Kellermann, T., Falkenberg, D. I., Schneider, F., & Habel, U. (2010). Multidimensional assessment of empathic abilities: Neural correlates and gender differences. *Psychoneuroendocrinology, 35*(1), 67-82. https://doi.org/10.1016/j.psyneuen.2009.10.006

Dippong, J., & Fitch, C. (2017). Emotions in criminological theory: Insights from social psychology. *Sociology Compass, 11*(4), e12473. https://doi.org/10.1111/soc4.12473

Draghi-Lorenz, R., Reddy, V., & Costall, A. (2001). Rethinking the development of "Nonbasic" emotions: A critical review of existing theories. *Developmental Review, 21*(3), 263-304. https://doi.org/10.1006/drev.2000.0524

Durkheim, E. (1951). *Suicide*. The Free Press of Glencoe.

Elis, L. A., & Simpson, S. S. (1995). Informal sanction threats and corporate crime: Additive versus multiplicative models. *Journal of Research in Crime and Delinquency, 32*(4), 399-424. https://doi.org/10.1177/0022427895032004002

Elison, J. (2005). Shame and guilt: A hundred years of apples and oranges. *New Ideas in Psychology, 23*(1), 5-32. https://doi.org/10.1016/j.newideapsych.2005.07.001

Elison, J., Garofalo, C., & Velotti, P. (2014). Shame and aggression: Theoretical considerations. *Aggression and Violent Behavior, 19*(4), 447-453. https://doi.org/10.1016/j.avb.2014.05.002

Elison, J., & Harter, S. (2007). Humiliation. Causes, correlates, and consequences. In J. L. Tracy, R. W. Robins, & J. P. Tangney (Eds.), *The self-conscious emotions. Theory and research* (pp. 310-329). The Guilford Press.

Ellsworth, P. C., & Tong, E. M. W. (2006). What does it mean to be angry at yourself? Categories, appraisals, and the problem of language. *Emotion, 6*(4), 572-586. https://doi.org/10.1037/1528-3542.6.4.572

Else-Quest, N. M., Higgins, A., Allison, C., & Morton, L. C. (2012). Gender differences in self-conscious emotional experience: A meta-analysis. *Psychological Bulletin, 138*(5), 947-981. https://doi.org/10.1037/a0027930

Elshout, M., Nelissen, R. M. A., & van Beest, I. (2017). Conceptualising humiliation. *Cognition & Emotion, 31*(8), 1581-1594. https://doi.org/10.1080/02699931.2016.1249462

Elster, J. (1999). *Alchemies of the mind: Rationality and the emotions*. Cambridge University Press.

Esala, J. J. (2013). Communities of Denial: The co-construction of gendered adolescent violence. *Deviant Behavior, 34*(2), 97-114. https://doi.org/10.1080/01639625.2012.707543

Etzioni, A. (1988). Normative-affective factors: Toward a new decision-making model. *Journal of Economic Psychology, 9*(2), 125-150. https://doi.org/10.1016/0167-4870(88)90048-7

Farmer, E., & Andrews, B. (2009). Shameless yet angry: Shame and its relationship to anger in male young offenders and undergraduate controls. *Journal of Forensic Psychiatry & Psychology, 20*(1), 48-65. https://doi.org/10.1080/14789940802205315

Farrall, S., & Calverley, A. (2006). *Understanding desistance from crime: Emerging theoretical directions in resettlement and rehabilitation*. Open University Press.

Ferguson, T. J. (2010). Like snowflakes and memories: Affective, cognitive, and conative facets of conscience in middle and later childhood. In W. Koops, D. Brugman, T. J.

Ferguson, & A. F. Sanders (Eds.), *The development and structure of conscience* (pp. 69-116). Psychology Press.

Ferguson, T. J., Brugman, D., White, J., & Eyre, H. L. (2007). Shame and guilt as morally warranted experiences. In J. L. Tracy, R. W. Robins, & J. P. Tangney (Eds.), *The self-conscious emotions: Theory and research* (pp. 330-348). Guilford Press.

Ferguson, T. J., & Stegge, H. (1998). Measuring guilt in children: A rose by any other name still has thorns. In J. Bybee (Ed.), *Guilt and children* (pp. 19-74). Academic Press.

Ferguson, T. J., Stegge, H., & Damhuis, I. (1991). Children's understanding of guilt and shame. *Child Development*, *62*(4), 827-839. https://doi.org/10.2307/1131180

Fernández, S., Saguy, T., & Halperin, E. (2015). The paradox of humiliation: The acceptance of an unjust devaluation of the self. *Personality and Social Psychology Bulletin*, *41*(7), 976-988. https://doi.org/10.1177/0146167215586195

Ferwerda, H. B., Leiden, I. M. G. G., Van Arts, N. A. M., & Hauber, A. R. (2006). *Halt: Het alternatief? De effecten van Halt beschreven*. Boom.

Finley, N. J., & Grasmick, H.G. (1985). Gender Roles and Social Control. Sociological Spectrum, 5, 317-30. https://doi.org/10.1080/02732173.1985.9981762

Fisher, M. L., & Exline, J. J. (2006). Self-forgiveness versus excusing: The roles of remorse, effort, and acceptance of responsibility. *Self and Identity*, *5*(2), 127-146. https://doi.org/10.1080/15298860600586123

Fontaine, J. R. J., Luyten, P., De Boeck, P., Corveleyn, J., Fernandez, M., Herrera, D., IttzéS, A., & Tomcsányi, T. (2006). Untying the Gordian knot of guilt and shame: The structure of guilt and shame reactions based on situation and person variation in Belgium, Hungary, and Peru. *Journal of Cross-Cultural Psychology*, *37*(3), 273-292. https://doi.org/10.1177/0022022105284493

Ford, T. E., Stevenson, P. R., Wienir, P. L., & Wait, R. F. (2002). The role of internalization of gender norms in regulating self-evaluations in response to anticipated delinquency. *Social Psychology Quarterly*, *65*(2), 202-212. https://doi.org/10.2307/3090101

Frijda, N. H. (1986). *The emotions*. Cambridge University Press.

Frijda, N. H. (2007). *The laws of emotion*. Erlbaum.

Galambos, N. L., Berenbaum, S. A., & McHale, S. M. (2009). Gender development in adolescence. In R. M. Lerner & L. Steinberg (Eds.), *Handbook of Adolescent Psychology* (pp. 305-357). John Wiley & Sons, Inc. https://doi.org/10.1002/9780470479193.adlpsy001011

Gardner, M., & Steinberg, L. (2005). Peer influence on risk taking, risk preference, and risky decision making in adolescence and adulthood: An experimental study. *Developmental Psychology*, *41*(4), 625-635. https://doi.org/10.1037/0012-1649.41.4.625

Gausel, N., & Leach, C. W. (2011). Concern for self-image and social image in the management of moral failure: Rethinking shame. *European Journal of Social Psychology*, *41*(4), 468-478. https://doi.org/10.1002/ejsp.803

Gausel, N., Vignoles, V. L., & Leach, C. W. (2016). Resolving the paradox of shame: Differentiating among specific appraisal-feeling combinations explains pro-social and self-defensive motivation. *Motivation and Emotion*, *40*(1), 118-139. https://doi.org/10.1007/s11031-015-9513-y

Gecas, V. (2006). The self as a social force. In T. J. Owens, S. Stryker, & T. J. Goodman (Eds.), *Extending self-esteem theory and research sociological and psychological currents* (pp. 85-100). Cambridge University Press.

Gelman, A. (2008). Scaling regression inputs by dividing by two standard deviations. *Statistics in Medicine*, *27*(15), 2865-2873. https://doi.org/10.1002/sim.3107

Gerrans, P., & Kennett, J. (2010). Neurosentimentalism and moral agency. *Mind*, *119*(475), 585-614. https://doi.org/10.1093/mind/fzq037

Gerrans, P., & Kennett, J. (2017). Mental time travel, dynamic evaluation, and moral agency. *Mind*, *126*(501), 259-268. https://doi.org/10.1093/mind/fzv206

Gilbert, P. (1997). The evolution of social attractiveness and its role in shame, humiliation, guilt and therapy. *The British Journal of Medical Psychology*, *70* (Pt 2), 113-147. https://doi.org/10.1111/j.2044-8341.1997.tb01893.x

Gilbert, P. (2003). Evolution, social roles, and the differences in shame and guilt. *Social Research*, *70*(4), 1205-1230. https://doi.org/10.2307/40971967

Gilbert, P., Pehl, J., & Allan, S. (1994). The phenomenology of shame and guilt: An empirical investigation. *British Journal of Medical Psychology*, *67*(1), 23-36. https://doi.org/10.1111/j.2044-8341.1994.tb01768.x

Gilligan, J. (2003). Shame, guilt, and violence. *Social Research*, *70*(4), 1149-1180. https://doi.org/10.2307/40971965

Giner-Sorolla, R. (2001). Guilty pleasures and grim necessities: Affective attitudes in dilemmas of self-control. *Journal of Personality and Social Psychology*, *80*(2), 206-221. https://doi.org/10.1037/0022-3514.80.2.206

Giner-Sorolla, R., & Espinosa, P. (2011). Social cuing of guilt by anger and of shame by disgust. *Psychological Science*, *22*(1), 49-53. https://doi.org/10.1177/0956797610392925

Giner-Sorolla, R., Piazza, J., & Espinosa, P. (2011). What do the TOSCA guilt and shame scales really measure: Affect or action? *Personality and Individual Differences*, *51*(4), 445-450. https://doi.org/10.1016/j.paid.2011.04.010

Gold, J., Sullivan, M. W., & Lewis, M. (2011). The relation between abuse and violent delinquency: The conversion of shame to blame in juvenile offenders. *Child Abuse & Neglect*, *35*(7), 459-467. https://doi.org/10.1016/j.chiabu.2011.02.007

Graham, J., & Haidt, J. (2010). Beyond beliefs: Religions bind individuals into moral communities. *Personality and Social Psychology Review*, *14*(1), 140-150. https://doi.org/10.1177/1088868309353415

Grasmick, H. G., & Bursik, R. J. (1990). Conscience, significant others, and rational choice: Extending the deterrence model. *Law & Society Review, 24*(3), 837-861. https://doi.org/10.2307/3053861

Grasmick, H. G., Bursik, R. J., & Arneklev, B. J. (1993). Reduction in drunk driving as a response to increased threats of shame, embarrassment, and legal sanctions. *Criminology, 31*(1), 41-67. https://doi.org/10.1111/j.1745-9125.1993.tb01121.x

Grasmick, H. G., Bursik, R. J., & Cochran, J. K. (1991). 'Render unto Caesar What Is Caesar's': Religiosity and taxpayers' inclinations to cheat. *The Sociological Quarterly, 32*(2), 251-266. https://doi.org/10.1111/j.1533-8525.1991.tb00356.x

Greenland, S., Senn, S. J., Rothman, K. J., Carlin, J. B., Poole, C., Goodman, S. N., & Altman, D. G. (2016). Statistical tests, P values, confidence intervals, and power: A guide to misinterpretations. *European Journal of Epidemiology, 31*(4), 337-350. https://doi.org/10.1007/s10654-016-0149-3

Gross, N. (2009). A pragmatist theory of social mechanisms. *American Sociological Review, 74*(3), 358-379. https://doi.org/10.1177/000312240907400302

Grusec, J. E., & Hastings, P. D. (Eds.). (2015). *Handbook of socialization: Theory and research* (2nd ed.). The Guilford Press.

Gungor, D., Fleischmann, F., & Phalet, K. (2011). Religious identification, beliefs, and practices among Turkish Belgian and Moroccan Belgian Muslims: Intergenerational continuity and acculturative change. *Journal of Cross-Cultural Psychology, 42*(8), 1356-1374. https://doi.org/10.1177/0022022111412342

Hacker, P. M. S. (2017). *The passions: A study of human nature.* John Wiley & Sons.

Haidt, J. (2003). The moral emotions. In R. J. Davidson, K. R. Scherer, & H. H. Goldsmith (Eds.), *Handbook of affective sciences* (pp. 852-870). Oxford University Press.

Halimi, M., Consuegra, E., Struyven, K., & Engels, N. (2018). A critical examination of the reliability and validity of a gender role attitude scale in Flanders (Belgium): What lessons can be learned? *Sex Roles, 78*(5-6), 423-438. https://doi.org/10.1007/s11199-017-0807-2

Harder, D. H., & Zalma, A. (1990). Two promising shame and guilt scales: A construct validity comparison. *Journal of Personality Assessment, 55*(3-4), 729-745. https://doi.org/10.1080/00223891.1990.9674108

Hardy, S. A., Padilla-Walker, L. M., & Carlo, G. (2008). Parenting dimensions and adolescents' internalisation of moral values. *Journal of Moral Education, 37*(2), 205-223. https://doi.org/10.1080/03057240802009512

Hareli, S., & Parkinson, B. (2008). What's social about social emotions? *Journal for the Theory of Social Behaviour, 38*(2), 131-156. https://doi.org/10.1111/j.1468-5914.2008.00363.x

Harris, N. (2001). Shaming and shame: Regulating drink-driving. In E. Ahmed, N. Harris, J. Braithwaite, & V. Braithwaite (Eds.), *Shame management through reintegration* (pp. 71-207). Cambridge University Press.

Harris, N. (2003). Reassessing the dimensionality of the moral emotions. *British Journal of Psychology, 94*(4), 457-473. https://doi.org/10.1348/000712603322503033

Harris, N. (2006). Reintegrative shaming, shame, and criminal justice. *Journal of Social Issues, 62*(2), 327-346. https://doi.org/10.1111/j.1540-4560.2006.00453.x

Harris, N. (2011). Shame, ethical identity and conformity. In S. Karstedt (Ed.), *Emotions, crime and justice* (pp. 194-209). Hart Publishing.

Harris, N. (2014). Shame in criminological theory. In G. Bruinsma & D. Weisburd (Eds.), *Encyclopedia of criminology and criminal justice* (pp. 4809-4817). Springer. http://doi.org/10.1007/978-1-4614-5690-2_433

Harris, N., Walgrave, L., & Braithwaite, J. (2004). Emotional dynamics in restorative conferences. *Theoretical Criminology, 8*(2), 191-210. https://doi.org/10.1177/1362480604042243

Hayduk, L. A. (2014). Shame for disrespecting evidence: The personal consequences of insufficient respect for structural equation model testing. *BMC Medical Research Methodology, 14*, 124. https://doi.org/10.1186/1471-2288-14-124

Heimer, K. (1996). Gender, interaction, and delinquency: Testing a theory of differential social control. *Social Psychology Quarterly, 59*(1), 39-61. https://doi.org/10.2307/2787118

Heimer, K., De Coster, S., & Unal, H. (2006). Opening the black box: The social psychology of gender and delinquency. In M. Deflem (Ed.), *Sociological Theory and Criminological Research* (Vol. 7, pp. 109-135). Elsevier/JAI Press.

Heimer, K., & Matsueda, R. L. (1994). Role-taking, role commitment, and delinquency: A theory of differential social control. *American Sociological Review, 59*(3), 365-390. https://doi.org/10.2307/2095939

Hejdenberg, J., & Andrews, B. (2011). The relationship between shame and different types of anger: A theory-based investigation. *Personality and Individual Differences, 50*(8), 1278-1282. https://doi.org/10.1016/j.paid.2011.02.024

Herman, S., & Pogarsky, G. (2020). Morality, deterrability, and offender decision making. *Justice Quarterly, 39*(1), 1-25. https://doi.org/10.1080/07418825.2019.1709884

Hirschi, T. (1969). *Causes of delinquency*. University of California Press.

Hirschi, T. (1986). On the compatibility of rational choice and social control theories of crime. In D. B. Cornish & R. V. Clarke (Eds.), *The reasoning criminal: Rational choice perspectives on offending* (pp. 105-118). Springer-Verlag.

Hoeben, E. M., Meldrum, R. C., Walker, D., & Young, J. T. N. (2016). The role of peer delinquency and unstructured socializing in explaining delinquency and substance use: A state-of-the-art review. *Journal of Criminal Justice, 47*, 108-122. https://doi.org/10.1016/j.jcrimjus.2016.08.001

Hoekstra, R., Finch, S., Kiers, H. A. L., & Johnson, A. (2006). Probability as certainty: Dichotomous thinking and the misuse of p values. *Psychonomic Bulletin & Review, 13*(6), 1033-1037. https://doi.org/10.3758/BF03213921

Hoeve, M., Dubas, J. S., Eichelsheim, V. I., van der Laan, P. H., Smeenk, W., & Gerris, J. R. M. (2009). The relationship between parenting and delinquency: A meta-analysis. *Journal of Abnormal Child Psychology, 37*(6), 749-775. https://doi.org/10.1007/s10802-009-9310-8

Holdsworth, C., & Morgan, D. (2007). Revisiting the generalized other: An exploration. *Sociology, 41*(3), 401-417. https://doi.org/10.1177/0038038507076614

Hosser, D., Windzio, M., & Greve, W. (2007). Guilt and shame as predictors of recidivism: A longitudinal study with young prisoners. *Criminal Justice and Behavior, 35*(1), 138-152. https://doi.org/10.1177/0093854807309224

Hu, L., & Bentler, P. M. (1999). Cutoff criteria for fit indexes in covariance structure analysis: Conventional criteria versus new alternatives. *Structural Equation Modeling: A Multidisciplinary Journal, 6*(1), 1-55. https://doi.org/10.1080/10705519909540118

Hynie, M., MacDonald, T. K., & Marques, S. (2006). Self-conscious emotions and self-regulation in the promotion of condom use. *Personality and Social Psychology Bulletin, 32*(8), 1072-1084. https://doi.org/10.1177/0146167206288060

Inbar, Y., Pizarro, D. A., Gilovich, T., & Ariely, D. (2013). Moral masochism: On the connection between guilt and self-punishment. *Emotion, 13*(1), 14-18. https://doi.org/10.1037/a0029749

Jensen, K. D., & Gibbons, S. G. (2002). Shame and religion as factors in the rehabilitation of serious offenders. *Journal of Offender Rehabilitation, 35*(3-4), 209-224. https://doi.org/10.1300/J076v35n03_11

Joas, H. (1985). *G. H. Mead, a contemporary re-examination of his thought*. Polity Press.

Johnston, R., Jones, K., & Manley, D. (2018). Confounding and collinearity in regression analysis: A cautionary tale and an alternative procedure, illustrated by studies of British voting behaviour. *Quality & Quantity, 52*(4), 1957-1976. https://doi.org/10.1007/s11135-017-0584-6

Junger, M., & Polder, W. (1993). Religiosity, religious climate, and delinquency among ethnic groups in the Netherlands. *The British Journal of Criminology, 33*(3), 416-435. https://doi.org/10.1093/oxfordjournals.bjc.a048334

Junger-Tas, J., Marshall, I. H., Enzmann, D., Killias, M., Steketee, M., & Gruszczynska, B. (Eds.). (2010). *Juvenile delinquency in Europe and beyond: Results of the second international self-report delinquency study*. Springer.

Kågesten, A., Gibbs, S., Blum, R. W., Moreau, C., Chandra-Mouli, V., Herbert, A., & Amin, A. (2016). Understanding factors that shape gender attitudes in early adolescence globally: A mixed-methods systematic review. *PLoS One*, *11*(6), e0157805. https://doi.org/10.1371/journal.pone.0157805

Kapetanovic, S., Skoog, T., Bohlin, M., & Gerdner, A. (2019). Aspects of the parent-adolescent relationship and associations with adolescent risk behaviors over time. *Journal of Family Psychology*, *33*(1), 1-11. https://doi.org/10.1037/fam0000436

Karlsson, G., & Sjöberg, L. G. (2009). The experiences of guilt and shame: A phenomenological – psychological study. *Human Studies*, *32*(3), 335-355. https://doi.org/10.1007/s10746-009-9123-3

Katz, J. (1999). *How emotions work*. University of Chicago Press.

Keene, A. C., & Epps, J. (2016). Childhood physical abuse and aggression: Shame and narcissistic vulnerability. *Child Abuse & Neglect*, *51*, 276-283. https://doi.org/10.1016/j.chiabu.2015.09.012

Keijsers, L., & Laird, R. D. (2014). Mother–adolescent monitoring dynamics and the legitimacy of parental authority. *Journal of Adolescence*, *37*(5), 515-524. https://doi.org/10.1016/j.adolescence.2014.04.001

Keijsers, L., & Poulin, F. (2013). Developmental changes in parent–child communication throughout adolescence. *Developmental Psychology*, *49*(12), 2301-2308. https://doi.org/10.1037/a0032217

Kelley, K., & Pornprasertmanit, S. (2016). Confidence intervals for population reliability coefficients: Evaluation of methods, recommendations, and software for composite measures. *Psychological Methods*, *21*(1), 69-92. https://doi.org/10.1037/a0040086

Keltner, D. (1996). Evidence for the distinctness of embarrassment, shame, and guilt: A study of recalled antecedents and facial expressions of emotion. *Cognition & Emotion*, *10*(2), 155-172. https://doi.org/10.1080/026999396380312

Kim, S., Thibodeau, R., & Jorgensen, R. S. (2011). Shame, guilt, and depressive symptoms: A meta-analytic review. *Psychological Bulletin*, *137*(1), 68-96. https://doi.org/10.1037/a0021466

Kivisto, A. J., Kivisto, K. L., Moore, T. M., & Rhatigan, D. L. (2011). Antisociality and intimate partner violence: The facilitating role of shame. *Violence and Victims*, *26*(6), 758-773. https://doi.org/10.1891/0886-6708.26.6.758

Kivivuori, J., Savolainen, J., & Aaltonen, M. (2016). The revenge motive in delinquency: Prevalence and predictors. *Acta Sociologica*, *59*(1), 69-84. https://doi.org/10.1177/0001699315607969

Kleemans, E. R. (2013). Organized crime and the visible hand: A theoretical critique on the economic analysis of organized crime. *Criminology & Criminal Justice*, *13*(5), 615-629. https://doi.org/10.1177/1748895812465296

Klein, D. C. (1991). The humiliation dynamic: An overview. *The Journal of Primary Prevention*, *12*(2), 93-121. https://doi.org/10.1007/BF02015214

Kline, R. B. (2016). *Principles and practice of structural equation modeling* (4th ed.). The Guilford Press.

Knekta, E., Runyon, C., & Eddy, S. (2019). One size doesn't fit all: Using factor analysis to gather validity evidence when using surveys in your research. *CBE – Life Sciences Education, 18*(1), 1-17. https://doi.org/10.1187/cbe.18-04-0064

Kotabe, H. P., Righetti, F., & Hofmann, W. (2019). How anticipated emotions guide self-control judgments. *Frontiers in Psychology, 10*. https://doi.org/10.3389/fpsyg.2019.01614

Kristján Kristjánsson. (2006). *Justifying emotions: Pride and jealously*. Routledge.

Kroneberg, C., Heintze, I., & Mehlkop, G. (2010). The interplay of moral norms and instrumental incentives in crime causation. *Criminology, 48*(1), 259-294. https://doi.org/10.1111/j.1745-9125.2010.00187.x

Kroneberg, C., & Kalter, F. (2012). Rational choice theory and empirical research: Methodological and theoretical contributions in Europe. *Annual Review of Sociology, 38*(1), 73-92. https://doi.org/10.1146/annurev-soc-071811-145441

Lagattuta, K. H., & Thompson, R. A. (2007). The development of self-conscious emotions: Cognitive processes and social influences. In J. L. Tracy, R. W. Robins, & J. P. Tangney (Eds.), *The self-conscious emotions: Theory and research* (pp. 91-113). Guilford Press.

Lam, C. B., McHale, S. M., & Crouter, A. C. (2014). Time with peers from middle childhood to late adolescence: Developmental course and adjustment correlates. *Child Development, 85*(4), 1677-1693. https://doi.org/10.1111/cdev.12235

Larson, R. W., Richards, M. H., Moneta, G., Holmbeck, G., & Duckett, E. (1996). Changes in adolescents' daily interactions with their families from ages 10 to 18: Disengagement and transformation. *Developmental Psychology, 32*(4), 744-754. https://doi.org/10.1037/0012-1649.32.4.744

Leach, C. W., & Cidam, A. (2015). When is shame linked to constructive approach orientation? A meta-analysis. *Journal of Personality and Social Psychology, 109*(6), 983-1002. https://doi.org/10.1037/pspa0000037

LeBel, T. P., Burnett, R., Maruna, S., & Bushway, S. (2008). The `Chicken and Egg' of subjective and social factors in desistance from crime. *European Journal of Criminology, 5*(2), 131-159. https://doi.org/10.1177/1477370807087640

Leclerc, B., & Lindegaard, M. R. (2018). The emotional experience behind sexually offending in context: Affective states before, during, and after crime events. *Journal of Research in Crime and Delinquency, 55*(2), 242-277. https://doi.org/10.1177/0022427817743783

Lee, J. S., Tajima, E. A., Herrenkohl, T. I., & Hong, S. (2017). Effects of formal and informal deviant labels in adolescence on crime in adulthood. *Social Work Research, 41*(2), 97-110. https://doi.org/10.1093/swr/svx003

Leibrich, J. (1996). The role of shame in going straight: A study of former offenders. In B. Galaway & J. Hudson (Eds.), *Restorative justice: International perspectives* (pp. 283-302). Criminal Justice Press.

Leidner, B., Sheikh, H., & Ginges, J. (2012). Affective dimensions of intergroup humiliation. *PLoS One*, *7*(9), e46375. https://doi.org/10.1371/journal.pone.0046375

Lemert, E. M. (1951). *Social pathology: A systematic approach to the theory of sociopathic behavior*. McGraw Hill.

Lewis, H. B. (1971). *Shame and guilt in neurosis*. International Universities Press.

Lewis, M. (2007). Self-conscious emotional development. In J. L. Tracy, R. W. Robins, & J. P. Tangney (Eds.), *The self-conscious emotions: Theory and research* (pp. 134-152). Guilford Press.

Lewis, M. (2016). Self-conscious emotions: Embarrassment, pride, shame, guilt, and hubris. In L. F. Barrett, M. Lewis, & J. Haviland-Jones (Eds.), *Handbook of emotions* (4th ed., pp. 792-814). The Guilford Press.

Li, C.-H. (2016). Confirmatory factor analysis with ordinal data: Comparing robust maximum likelihood and diagonally weighted least squares. *Behavior Research Methods*, *48*(3), 936-949. https://doi.org/10.3758/s13428-015-0619-7

Lickel, B., Kushlev, K., Savalei, V., Matta, S., & Schmader, T. (2014). Shame and the motivation to change the self. *Emotion*, *14*(6), 1049-1061. https://doi.org/10.1037/a0038235

Lindegaard, M. R., Bernasco, W., Jacques, S., & Zevenbergen, B. (2014). Posterior gains and immediate pains: Offender emotions before, during and after robberies. In J.-L. Van Gelder, H. Elffers, D. Nagin, & D. Reynald (Eds.), *Affect and cognition affect and cognition in criminal decision making: Between rational choices and lapses of self-control* (pp. 58-76). Routledge.

Lindsay-Hartz, J. (1984). Contrasting experiences of shame and guilt. *American Behavioral Scientist*, *27*(6), 689-704. https://doi.org/10.1177/000276484027006003

Lindsay-Hartz, J., de Rivera, J., & Mascolo, M. F. (1995). Differentiating guilt and shame and their effects on motivation. In J. P. Tangney & K. W. Fischer (Eds.), *Self-conscious emotions: The psychology of shame, guilt, embarrassment and pride* (pp. 274-300). Guilford Press.

Loewenstein, G., & Lerner, J., S. (2003). The role of affect in decision making. In R. J. Davidson, K. R. Scherer, & H. H. Goldsmith (Eds.), *Handbook of affective sciences* (pp. 619-642). Oxford University Press.

Lucas, K., & Steimel, S. J. (2009). Creating and responding to the gen(d)eralized other: Women miners' community-constructed identities. *Women's Studies in Communication*, *32*(3), 320-347. https://doi.org/10.1080/07491409.2009.10162393

Lumley, T., Diehr, P., Emerson, S., & Chen, L. (2002). The importance of the normality assumption in large public health data sets. *Annual Review of Public Health*, *23*(1), 151-169. https://doi.org/10.1146/annurev.publhealth.23.100901.140546

Luyten, P., Fontaine, J. R. J., & Corveleyn, J. (2002). Does the Test of Self-Conscious Affect (TOSCA) measure maladaptive aspects of guilt and adaptive aspects of shame? An empirical investigation. *Personality and Individual Differences*, *33*(8), 1373-1387. https://doi.org/10.1016/S0191-8869(02)00197-6

Lynch, M. J., Newman, G. R., & Groves, W. B. (1992). Control theory and punishment: Control theory as a penal policy. In F. Adler & W. S. Laufer (Eds.), *New directions in criminological theory. Advances in criminological theory, volume 4* (pp. 337-362). Transaction Publishers.

Mahalik, J. R., Morray, E. B., Coonerty-Femiano, A., Ludlow, L. H., Slattery, S. M., & Smiler, A. (2005).

Development of the Conformity to Feminine Norms Inventory. *Sex Roles*, 52(7-8), 417-435. https://doi.org/10.1007/s11199-005-3709-7

Mann, H., Garcia-Rada, X., Hornuf, L., & Tafurt, J. (2016). What deters crime? Comparing the effectiveness of legal, social, and internal sanctions accross countries. *Frontiers in Psychology*, *7*, 1-13. https://doi.org/10.3389/fpsyg.2016.00085

Martinez, A. G., Stuewig, J., & Tangney, J. P. (2014). Can perspective-taking reduce crime? Examining a pathway through empathic-concern and guilt-proneness. *Personality and Social Psychology Bulletin*, *40*(12), 1659-1667. https://doi.org/10.1177/0146167214554915

Maruna, S., & Copes, H. (2005). What have we learned from five decades of neutralization research? *Crime and Justice*, *32*, 221-320.

Matsuda, K. N., Melde, C., Taylor, T. J., Freng, A., & Esbensen, F.-A. (2013). Gang membership and adherence to the "Code of the Street". *Justice Quarterly*, *30*(3), 440-468. https://doi.org/10.1080/07418825.2012.684432

Matsueda, R. L. (1992). Reflected appraisals, parental labeling, and delinquency: Specifying a symbolic interactionist theory. *American Journal of Sociology*, *97*(6), 1577-1611. https://doi.org/10.1086/229940

Matsueda, R. L. (2001). Differential association theory. In C. D. Bryant (Ed.), *Encyclopedia of criminology and deviant behavior* (Vol. 1, pp. 125-130). Taylor and Francis.

Matsueda, R. L. (2006). Criminological implications of the thought of George Herbert Mead. In M. Deflem (Ed.), *Sociological theory and criminological research: Views from Europe and the United States*. (Vol. 7, pp. 77-108). Elsevier. https://doi.org/10.1016/S1521-6136(06)07005-9

Matsueda, R. L., & Anderson, K. (1998). The dynamics of delinquent peers and delinquent behavior. *Criminology*, *36*(2), 269-308. https://doi.org/10.1111/j.1745-9125.1998.tb01249.x

Matsueda, R. L., O'Neill, K. K., & Kreager, D. A. (2020). Embeddedness, reflected appraisals, and deterrence: A symbolic interactionist theory of adolescent theft. In R. T. Serpe, R. Stryker, & B. Powell (Eds.), *Identity and symbolic interaction: Deepening foundations, building bridges* (pp. 239-271). Springer International Publishing.

Matza, D. (1964). *Delinquency and drift.* John Wiley and Sons.

Matza, D., & Sykes, G. M. (1961). Juvenile delinquency and subterranean values. *American Sociological Review, 26*(5), 712-719. https://doi.org/10.2307/2090200

Maxwell, S. R., Zepeda, A., & Rzotkiewicz, A. (2017). Peers, social control, or guilt? Self-conscious emotions as explanation for antisocial behavior. *Deviant Behavior,* 1-10. https://doi.org/10.1080/01639625.2016.1272970

McCarry, M. (2010). Becoming a 'proper man': Young people's attitudes about interpersonal violence and perceptions of gender. *Gender and Education, 22*(1), 17-30. https://doi.org/10.1080/09540250902749083

McCullough, M. E., & Willoughby, B. L. B. (2009). Religion, self-regulation, and self-control: Associations, explanations, and implications. *Psychological Bulletin, 135*(1), 69-93. https://doi.org/10.1037/a0014213

McGloin, J. M., & Thomas, K. J. (2019). Peer influence and delinquency. *Annual Review of Criminology, 2*(1), 241-264. https://doi.org/10.1146/annurev-criminol-011518-024551

McNeish, D., & Stapleton, L. M. (2016). Modeling clustered data with very few clusters. *Multivariate Behavioral Research, 51*(4), 495-518. https://doi.org/10.1080/00273171.2016.1167008

Mead, G. H. (1932). *The philosophy of the present.* Open Court.

Mead, G. H. (1934). *Mind, self & society from the standpoint of a social behaviorist.* University of Chicago Press.

Mead, M. (Ed.). (1937). *Cooperation and competition among primitive peoples.* McGraw-Hill Book Company.

Mears, D. P., Ploeger, M., & Warr, M. (1998). Explaining the gender gap in delinquency: Peer influence and moral evaluations of behavior. *Journal of Research in Crime and Delinquency, 35*(3), 251-266. https://doi.org/10.1177/0022427898035003001

Melde, C., & Esbensen, F.-A. (2011). Gang membership as a turning point in the life course. *Criminology, 49*(2), 513-552. https://doi.org/10.1111/j.1745-9125.2011.00227.x

Merton, R. K. (1938). Social structure and anomie. *American Sociological Review, 3*(5), 672-682. https://doi.org/10.2307/2084686

Messerschmidt, J. W. (1993). *Masculinities and crime: Critique and reconceptualization of theory.* Rowman & Littlefield.

Messner, S. F., & Rosenfeld, R. (1994). *Crime and the American dream.* Wadsworth.

Messner, S. F. (2012). Morality, markets, and the ASC: 2011 Presidential address to the American Society of Criminology*. *Criminology, 50*(1), 5-25. https://doi.org/10.1111/j.1745-9125.2011.00264.x

Miceli, M., & Castelfranchi, C. (1998). How to silence one's conscience: Cognitive defenses against the feeling of guilt. *Journal for the Theory of Social Behaviour, 28*(3), 287-318. https://doi.org/10.1111/1468-5914.00076

Miceli, M., & Castelfranchi, C. (2015). *Expectancy and emotion.* Oxford University Press.

Miceli, M., & Castelfranchi, C. (2018). Reconsidering the differences between shame and guilt. *Europe's Journal of Psychology, 14*(3), 710-733. https://doi.org/10.5964/ejop.v14i3.1564

Miller, D. L. (1973). *George Herbert Mead: Self, language, and the world.* University of Texas Press.

Milligan, R.-J., & Andrews, B. (2005). Suicidal and other self-harming behaviour in offender women: The role of shame, anger and childhood abuse. *Legal and Criminological Psychology, 10*(1), 13-25. https://doi.org/10.1348/135532504X15439

Montada, L. (1993). Understanding oughts by assessing moral reasoning or moral emotions. In G. G. Noam & T. E. Wren (Eds.), *The moral self* (pp. 292-309). MIT Press.

Montes Sánchez, A. (2014). Intersubjectivity and interaction as crucial for understanding the moral role of shame: A critique of TOSCA-based shame research. *Frontiers in Psychology, 5*, 814. https://doi.org/10.3389/fpsyg.2014.00814

Montes Sánchez, A. (2015). Shame and the internalized other. *Ethics and Politics, 17*(1), 181-200.

Moors, A. (2009). Theories of emotion causation: A review. *Cognition & Emotion, 23*(4), 625-662. https://doi.org/10.1080/02699930802645739

Murphy, K., & Harris, N. (2007). Shaming, shame and recidivism: A test of reintegrative shaming theory in the white-collar crime context. *British Journal of Criminology, 47*(6), 900-917. https://doi.org/10.1093/bjc/azm037

Muthén, L. K., & Muthen, B. O. (1998). *Mplus user's guide* (6th ed.). Muthén & Muthén.

Nagin, D. S., & Paternoster, R. (1993). Enduring individual differences and rational choice theories of crime. *Law & Society Review, 27*(3), 467. https://doi.org/10.2307/3054102

Nelissen, R. M. A. (2012). Guilt-induced self-punishment as a sign of remorse. *Social Psychological and Personality Science,* 3(2), 139-144. https://doi.org/10.1177/1948550611411520

Nelissen, R. M. A., Breugelmans, S. M., & Zeelenberg, M. (2013). Reappraising the moral nature of emotions in decision making: The case of shame and guilt. *Social and Personality Psychology Compass, 7*(6), 355-365. https://doi.org/10.1111/spc3.12030

Nelissen, R. M. A., & Zeelenberg, M. (2009). When guilt evokes self-punishment: Evidence for the existence of a Dobby Effect. *Emotion, 9*(1), 118-122. https://doi.org/10.1037/a0014540

Newburn, T., & Stanko, E. A. (Eds.). (1994). *Just boys doing business? Men, masculinities, and crime.* Routledge.

Niedenthal, P. M., Tangney, J. P., & Gavanski, I. (1994). 'If only I weren't' versus 'If only I hadn't': Distinguishing shame and guilt in conterfactual thinking. *Journal of Personality and Social Psychology*, *67*(4), 585-595. https://doi.org/10.1037/0022-3514.67.4.585

Oberski, D. (2010). *JruleMplus*. https://github.com/daob/JruleMplus/wiki

Obsuth, I., Murray, A. L., Malti, T., Sulger, P., Ribeaud, D., & Sulger, P. (2017). A non-bipartite propensity score analysis of the effects of teacher–student relationships on adolescent problem and prosocial behavior. *Journal of Youth and Adolescence*, 46 (8), 1661-1687. https://doi.org/10.1007/s10964-016-0534-y

Olthof, T., Ferguson, T., Bloemers, E., & Deij, M. (2004). Morality- and identity-related antecedents of children's guilt and shame attributions in events involving physical illness. *Cognition & Emotion*, *18*(3), 383-404. https://doi.org/10.1080/02699930341000077

Olthof, T., Schouten, A., Kuiper, H., Stegge, H., & Jennekens-Schinkel, A. (2000). Shame and guilt in children: Differential situational antecedents and experiential correlates. *British Journal of Developmental Psychology*, *18*(1), 51-64. https://doi.org/10.1348/026151000165562

Op de Beeck, H. (2012). *Strain en jeugddelinquentie: Een dynamische relatie?: een toets van twee centrale verklaringsmechanismen uit Agnews General Strain Theory*. Boom Lemma uitgevers.

Owen, T., & Fox, S. (2011). Experiences of shame and empathy in violent and non-violent young offenders. *The Journal of Forensic Psychiatry & Psychology*, *22*(4), 551-563. https://doi.org/10.1080/14789949.2011.602096

Özbay, Ö., & Özcan, Y. Z. (2006). A test of hirschi's social bonding theory: Juvenile Delinquency in the high schools of Ankara, Turkey. *International Journal of Offender Therapy and Comparative Criminology*, 50(6), 711-726. https://doi.org/10.1177/0306624x05283525

Parkinson, B., & Illingworth, S. (2009). Guilt in response to blame from others. *Cognition & Emotion*, *23*(8), 1589-1614. https://doi.org/10.1080/02699930802591594

Parkinson, B., Totterdell, P., Briner, R. B., & Reynolds, S. (1996). *Changing moods: The psychology of mood and mood regulation*. Addison Wesley Longman.

Parrott, W. G. (2019). Emotions as signals of moral character. In U. Hess & S. Hareli (Eds.), *The social nature of emotion expression: What emotions can tell us about the World* (pp. 161-177). Springer International Publishing. https://doi.org/10.1007/978-3-030-32968-6_9

Parsons, T. (1968). *The structure of social action*. The Free Press of Glencoe.

Paternoster, R., Brame, R., Mazerolle, P., & Piquero, A. (1998). Using the correct statistical test for the equality of regression coefficients. *Criminology*, *36*(4), 859-866. https://doi.org/10.1111/j.1745-9125.1998.tb01268.x

Paternoster, R., & Simpson, S. (1996). Sanction threats and appeals to morality: Testing a rational choice model of corporate crime. *Law & Society Review*, *30*(3), 549. https://doi.org/10.2307/3054128

Pauwels, L. J. R., & Svensson, R. (2015). Schools and child antisocial behavior: In search for mediator effects of school-level disadvantage. *SAGE Open*, *5*(2), 1-13. https://doi.org/10.1177/2158244015592936

Phalet, K., Fleischmann, F., & Hillekens, J. (2018). Religious identity and acculturation of immigrant minority youth: Toward a contextual and developmental approach. *European Psychologist*, *23*(1), 32-43. https://doi.org/10.1027/1016-9040/a000309

Pickett, J. T., Roche, S. P., & Pogarsky, G. (2018). Toward a bifurcated theory of emotional deterrence: Fear and deterrence. *Criminology*, *56*(1), 27-58. https://doi.org/10.1111/1745-9125.12153

Preacher, K. J., & Hayes, A. F. (2008). Asymptotic and resampling strategies for assessing and comparing indirect effects in multiple mediator models. *Behavior Research Methods*, *40*(3), 879-891. https://doi.org/10.3758/BRM.40.3.879

Preacher, K. J., & Kelley, K. (2011). Effect size measures for mediation models: Quantitative strategies for communicating indirect effects. *Psychological Methods*, *16*(2), 93-115. https://doi.org/10.1037/a0022658

Prinz, J. J. (2011). Is empathy necessary for morality? In P. Goldie & A. Coplan (Eds.), *Empathy: Philosophical and psychological perspectives* (pp. 211-229). Oxford University Press.

Proeve, J. (2001). *Remorse: Its description and its interpersonal effects*. Unpublished PhD Thesis, University of South Australia.

Proeve, M., & Tudor, S. (2010). *Remorse: Psychological and jurisprudential perspectives*. Ashgate.

Purzycki, B. G. (2013). The minds of gods: A comparative study of supernatural agency. *Cognition*, *129*(1), 163-179. https://doi.org/10.1016/j.cognition.2013.06.010

Quiles, Z. N., & Bybee, J. (1997). Chronic and predispositional guilt: Relations to mental health, prosocial behavior, and religiosity. *Journal of Personality Assessment*, *69*(1), 104-126. https://doi.org/10.1207/s15327752jpa6901_6

Ray, L., Smith, D., & Wastell, L. (2004). Shame, rage and racist violence. *British Journal of Criminology*, *44*(3), 350-368. https://doi.org/10.1093/bjc/azh022

Rebellon, C. J., Manasse, M. E., Agnew, R., Van Gundy, K. T., & Cohn, E. S. (2016). The relationship between gender and delinquency: Assessing the mediating role of anticipated guilt. *Journal of Criminal Justice*, *44*, 77-88. https://doi.org/10.1016/j.jcrimjus.2015.11.006

Rebellon, C. J., Piquero, N. L., Piquero, A. R., & Tibbetts, S. G. (2010). Anticipated shaming and criminal offending. *Journal of Criminal Justice*, *38*(5), 988-997. https://doi.org/10.1016/j.jcrimjus.2010.06.016

Rebellon, C. J., Trinkner, R., Van Gundy, K. T., & Cohn, E. S. (2019). No guts, no glory: The influence of risk-taking on adolescent popularity. *Deviant Behavior, 40*(12), 1464-1479. https://doi.org/10.1080/01639625.2018.1519128

Rebellon, C. J., Wiesen-Martin, D., Piquero, N. L., Piquero, A. R., & Tibbetts, S. G. (2015). Gender differences in criminal intent: Examining the mediating influence of anticipated shaming. *Deviant Behavior, 36*(1), 17-41. https://doi.org/10.1080/01639625.2014.903755

Reddy, V. (2003). On being the object of attention: Implications for self-other consciousness. *Trends in Cognitive Sciences,* 7(9), 397-402. https://doi.org/10.1016/S1521-6136(06)07005-9

Rhemtulla, M., Brosseau-Liard, P. É., & Savalei, V. (2012). When can categorical variables be treated as continuous? A comparison of robust continuous and categorical SEM estimation methods under suboptimal conditions. *Psychological Methods, 17*(3), 354-373. https://doi.org/10.1037/a0029315

Robbins, B. D., & Parlavecchio, H. (2006). The unwanted exposure of the self: A phenomenological study of embarrassment. *The Humanistic Psychologist, 34*(4), 321-345. https://doi.org/10.1207/s15473333thp3404_3

Robinson, R., Roberts, W. L., Strayer, J., & Koopman, R. (2007). Empathy and emotional responsiveness in delinquent and non-delinquent adolescents. *Social Development, 16*(3), 555-579. https://doi.org/10.1111/j.1467-9507.2007.00396.x

Rochat, P. (2009). *Others in mind: Social origins of self-consciousness.* Cambridge University Press.

Rock, P. (1979). *The making of symbolic interactionism.* Macmillan.

Roggemans, L., Spruyt, B., Droogenbroeck, F. V., & Keppens, G. (2015). Religion and negative attitudes towards homosexuals: An analysis of urban young people and their attitudes towards homosexuality. *Young, 23*(3), 254-276. https://doi.org/10.1177/1103308815586903

Roos, S., Hodges, E. V. E., & Salmivalli, C. (2014). Do guilt- and shame-proneness differentially predict prosocial, aggressive, and withdrawn behaviors during early adolescence? *Developmental Psychology, 50*(3), 941-946. https://doi.org/10.1037/a0033904

Roos, S., Salmivalli, C., & Hodges, E. V. E. (2015). Emotion regulation and negative emotionality moderate the effects of moral (dis)engagement on aggression. *Merrill-Palmer Quarterly, 61*(1), 30-50. https://doi.org/10.13110/merrpalmquar1982.61.1.0030

Ropovik, I. (2015). A cautionary note on testing latent variable models. *Frontiers in Psychology, 6,* 1715. https://doi.org/10.3389/fpsyg.2015.01715

Sabatine, E., Lippold, M., & Kainz, K. (2017). The unique and interactive effects of parent and school bonds on adolescent delinquency. *Journal of Applied Developmental Psychology, 53,* 54-63. https://doi.org/10.1016/j.appdev.2017.09.005

Sabini, J., & Silver, M. (1997). In defense of shame: Shame in the context of guilt and embarrassment. *Journal for the Theory of Social Behaviour, 27*(1), 1-15. https://doi.org/10.1111/1468-5914.00023

Sampson, R. J., & Laub, J. H. (1993). *Crime in the making: Pathways and turning points through life*. Harvard University Press.

Santana, M. C., Raj, A., Decker, M. R., La Marche, A., & Silverman, J. G. (2006). Masculine gender roles associated with increased sexual risk and intimate partner violence perpetration among young adult men. *Journal of Urban Health : Bulletin of the New York Academy of Medicine, 83*(4), 575-585. https://doi.org/10.1007/s11524-006-9061-6

Saris, W. E., Satorra, A., & van der Veld, W. M. (2009). Testing structural equation models or detection of misspecifications? *Structural Equation Modeling: A Multidisciplinary Journal, 16*(4), 561-582. https://doi.org/10.1080/10705510903203433

Scarantino, A. (2016). The philosophy of emotions and its impact on affective science. In L. F. Barrett, M. Lewis, & J. Haviland-Jones (Eds.), *Handbook of emotions* (4th ed., pp. 3-49). The Guilford Press.

Schachter, D., Kleinman, I., & Harvey, W. (2005). Informed consent and adolescents. *The Canadian Journal of Psychiatry, 50*(9), 534-540. https://doi.org/10.1177/070674370505000906

Schalkwijk, F., Stams, G. J., Stegge, H., Dekker, J., & Peen, J. (2016). The conscience as a regulatory function: Empathy, shame, pride, guilt, and moral orientation in delinquent adolescents. *International Journal of Offender Therapy and Comparative Criminology, 60*(6), 675-693. https://doi.org/10.1177/0306624X14561830

Scheff, T. J. (2003). Male emotions/relationships and violence: A case study. *Human Relations, 56*(6), 727-749. https://doi.org/10.1177/00187267030566005

Scheff, T. J., & Retzinger, S. M. (1991). *Emotions and violence: Shame and rage in destructive conflicts*. Lexington Books.

Scherer, K. R. (2005). What are emotions? And how can they be measured? *Social Science Information, 44*(4), 695-729. https://doi.org/10.1177/0539018405058216

Scherer, K. R., & Moors, A. (2019). The emotion process: Event appraisal and component differentiation. *Annual Review of Psychology, 70*(1), 719-745. https://doi.org/10.1146/annurev-psych-122216-011854

Schmader, T., & Lickel, B. (2006). The approach and avoidance function of guilt and shame emotions: Comparing reactions to self-caused and other-caused wrongdoing. *Motivation and Emotion, 30*(1), 42-55. https://doi.org/10.1007/s11031-006-9006-0

Schrock, D., & Schwalbe, M. (2009). Men, Masculinity, and Manhood Acts. *Annual Review of Sociology*, 35, 277-295. https://doi.org/10.1146/annurev-soc-070308-115933

Seddig, D. (2014). Peer group association, the acceptance of norms and violent behaviour: A longitudinal analysis of reciprocal effects. *European Journal of Criminology*, 11(3), 319-339. https://doi.org/10.1177/1477370813496704

Sekowski, M., Gambin, M., Cudo, A., Wozniak-Prus, M., Penner, F., Fonagy, P., & Sharp, C. (2020). The relations between childhood maltreatment, shame, guilt, depression and suicidal ideation in inpatient adolescents. *Journal of Affective Disorders, 276*, 667-677. https://doi.org/10.1016/j.jad.2020.07.056

Serajzadeh, S. H. (2001). Islam and crime: The moral community of Muslims. *Journal of Arabic and Islamic Studies, 4*(0), 111-131. https://doi.org/10.5617/jais.4568

Sheikh, S., & Janoff-Bulman, R. (2010). The "Shoulds" and "Should Nots" of moral emotions: A self-regulatory perspective on shame and guilt. *Personality and Social Psychology Bulletin, 36*(2), 213-224. https://doi.org/10.1177/0146167209356788

Shibutani, T. (1955). Reference groups as perspectives. *American Journal of Sociology, 60*(6), 562-569. https://doi.org/10.1086/221630

Shibutani, T. (1991). On the empirical investigation of self-concepts. In D. R. Maines (Ed.), *Social organization and social process: Essays in honor of Anselm Strauss* (pp. 59-70). Aldine de Gruyter.

Shott, S. (1979). Emotion and social life: A symbolic interactionist analysis. *American Journal of Sociology, 84*(6), 1317-1334.

Sijtsma, K. (2009). On the use, the misuse, and the very limited usefulness of Cronbach's alpha. *Psychometrika, 74*(1), 107-120. https://doi.org/10.1007/s11336-008-9101-0

Silfver-Kuhalampi, M., Figueiredo, A., Sortheix, F., & Fontaine, J. (2015). Humiliated self, bad self or bad behavior? The relations between moral emotional appraisals and moral motivation. *Journal of Moral Education, 44*(2), 213-231. https://doi.org/10.1080/03057240.2015.1043874

Singer, T., Seymour, B., O'Doherty, J. P., Stephan, K. E., Dolan, R. J., & Frith, C. D. (2006). Empathic neural responses are modulated by the perceived fairness of others. *Nature, 439*(7075), 466-469. https://doi.org/10.1038/nature04271

Smith, R. H., Webster, J. M., Parrott, W. G., & Eyre, H. L. (2002). The role of public exposure in moral and nonmoral shame and guilt. *Journal of Personality and Social Psychology, 83*(1), 138-159.

Soenens, B., Vansteenkiste, M., Luyckx, K., & Goossens, L. (2006). Parenting and adolescent problem behavior: An integrated model with adolescent self-disclosure and perceived parental knowledge as intervening variables. *Developmental Psychology, 42*(2), 305-318. https://doi.org/10.1037/0012-1649.42.2.305

Solak, N., Tagar, M. R., Cohen-Chen, S., Saguy, T., & Halperin, E. (2017). Disappointment expression evokes collective guilt and collective action in intergroup conflict: The moderating role of legitimacy perceptions. *Cognition & Emotion, 31*(6), 1112-1126. https://doi.org/10.1080/02699931.2016.1197098

Solomon, B. S., Bradshaw, C. P., Wright, J., & Cheng, T. L. (2008). Youth and parental attitudes toward fighting. *Journal of Interpersonal Violence, 23*(4), 544-560. https://doi.org/10.1177/0886260507312947

Somerville, L. H. (2013). The teenage brain: Sensitivity to social evaluation. *Current Directions in Psychological Science, 22*(2), 121-127. https://doi.org/10.1177/0963721413476512

Spivak, A. L., Fukushima, M., Kelley, M. S., & Jenson, T. S. (2011). Religiosity, delinquency, and the deterrent effects of informal sanctions. *Deviant Behavior, 32*(8), 677-711. https://doi.org/10.1080/01639625.2010.514211

Spruit, A., Schalkwijk, F., van Vugt, E., & Stams, G. J. (2016). The relation between self-conscious emotions and delinquency: A meta-analysis. *Aggression and Violent Behavior, 28*, 12-20. https://doi.org/10.1016/j.avb.2016.03.009

Stark, R. (1996). Religion as context: Hellfire and delinquency one more time. *Sociology of Religion, 57*(2), 163-173. JSTOR. https://doi.org/10.2307/3711948

Stark, R., & Bainbridge, W. S. (1996). *Religion, deviance, and social control.* Routledge.

Stattin, H., & Kerr, M. (2000). Parental monitoring: A reinterpretation. *Child Development, 71*(4), 1072-1085. https://doi.org/10.1111/1467-8624.00210

Stearns, D. C., & Parrott, W. G. (2012). When feeling bad makes you look good: Guilt, shame, and person perception. *Cognition & Emotion, 26*(3), 407-430. https://doi.org/10.1080/02699931.2012.675879

Steffensmeier, D., & Allan, E. (1996). Gender and crime: Toward a gendered theory of female offending. *Annual Review of Sociology, 22*(1), 459-487. https://doi.org/10.1146/annurev.soc.22.1.459

Stuewig, J., & McCloskey, L. A. (2005). The relation of child maltreatment to shame and guilt among adolescents: Psychological routes to depression and delinquency. *Child Maltreatment, 10*(4), 324-336. https://doi.org/10.1177/1077559505279308

Stuewig, J., Tangney, J. P., Heigel, C., Harty, L., & McCloskey, L. (2010). Shaming, blaming, and maiming: Functional links among the moral emotions, externalization of blame, and aggression. *Journal of Research in Personality, 44*(1), 91-102. https://doi.org/10.1016/j.jrp.2009.12.005

Stuewig, J., Tangney, J. P., Kendall, S., Folk, J. B., Meyer, C. R., & Dearing, R. L. (2015). Children's proneness to shame and guilt predict risky and illegal behaviors in young adulthood. *Child Psychiatry & Human Development, 46*(2), 217-227. https://doi.org/10.1007/s10578-014-0467-1

Sumter, M., Wood, F., Whitaker, I., & Berger-Hill, D. (2018). Religion and crime studies: Assessing what has been learned. *Religions, 9*(6), 193. https://doi.org/10.3390/rel9060193

Sunar, D., Tosun, Ö., & Tokus, T. (2016). Self-blaming and other-blaming moral emotions are complementary: Two studies in Turkish culture. In C. Roland-Lévy, P. Denoux, B. Voyer, & W. K. Gabrenya (Eds.), *Unity, diversity and culture: Research and scholarship selected from the 22nd Congress of the International Association for Cross-Cultural Psychology* (pp. 416-420). International Association for Cross-Cultural Psychology.

Sundaram, V. (2016). "You Can Try, But You Won't Stop It. It'll Always Be There": Youth perspectives on violence and prevention in schools. *Journal of Interpersonal Violence, 31*(4), 652-676. https://doi.org/10.1177/0886260514556106

Sussman, D. (2018). Is agent-regret rational? *Ethics, 128*(4), 788-808. https://doi.org/10.1086/697492

Svensson, R. (2003). Gender differences in adolescent drug use: The impact of parental monitoring and peer deviance. *Youth & Society, 34*(3), 300-329. https://doi.org/10.1177/0044118X02250095

Svensson, R. (2004). Shame as a consequence of the parent-child relationship: A study of gender differences in juvenile delinquency. *European Journal of Criminology, 1*(4), 477-504. https://doi.org/10.1177/1477370804045692

Svensson, R., Pauwels, L. J. R., & Weerman, F. M. (2017). The role of moral beliefs, shame and guilt in criminal decision making. An overview of theoretical frameworks and empirical results. In W. Bernasco, J.-L. Van Gelder, & H. Elffers (Eds.), *The Oxford handbook of offender decision making* (pp. 225-245). Oxford University Press.

Svensson, R., Pauwels, L. J. R., Weerman, F. M., & Bruinsma, G. J. N. (2016). Explaining individual changes in moral values and moral emotions among adolescent boys and girls: A fixed-effects analysis. *European Journal of Criminology*. https://doi.org/10.1177/1477370816649626

Svensson, R., Weerman, F. M., Pauwels, L. J. R., Bruinsma, G. J. N., & Bernasco, W. (2013). Moral emotions and offending: Do feelings of anticipated shame and guilt mediate the effect of socialization on offending? *European Journal of Criminology, 10*(1), 22-39. https://doi.org/10.1177/1477370812454393

Sykes, G. M., & Matza, D. (1957). Techniques of neutralization: A theory of delinquency. *American Sociological Review, 22*(6), 664-670. https://doi.org/10.2307/2089195

Tangney, J. P. (1995). Recent advances in the empirical study of shame and guilt. *American Behavioral Scientist, 38*(8), 1132-1145. https://doi.org/10.1177/0002764295038008008

Tangney, J. P. (1996). Conceptual and methodological issues in the assessment of shame and guilt. *Behaviour Research and Therapy, 34*(9), 741-754. https://doi.org/10.1016/0005-7967(96)00034-4

Tangney, J. P., & Dearing, R. L. (2002). *Shame and guilt*. Guilford Press.

Tangney, J. P., Dearing, R. L., Wagner, P. E., & Gramzow, R. (2000). *The Test of Self-Conscious Affect-3 (TOSCA-3)*. George Mason University.

Tangney, J. P., Miller, R. S., Flicker, L., & Barlow, D. H. (1996). Are shame, guilt, and embarrassment distinct emotions? *Journal of Personality and Social Psychology, 70*(6), 1256-1269. https://doi.org/10.1037/0022-3514.70.6.1256

Tangney, J. P., Stuewig, J., & Hafez, L. (2011). Shame, guilt, and remorse: Implications for offender populations. *Journal of Forensic Psychiatry & Psychology, 22*(5), 706-723. https://doi.org/10.1080/14789949.2011.617541

Tangney, J. P., Stuewig, J., & Martinez, A. G. (2014). Two faces of shame: The roles of shame and guilt in predicting recidivism. *Psychological Science, 25*(3), 799-805. https://doi.org/10.1177/0956797613508790

Tangney, J. P., Stuewig, J., Mashek, D., & Hastings, M. (2011). Assessing jail inmates' proneness to shame and guilt: Feeling bad about the behavior or the self? *Criminal Justice and Behavior, 38*(7), 710-734. https://doi.org/10.1177/0093854811405762

Tangney, J. P., Stuewig, J., & Mashek, D. J. (2007). Moral emotions and moral behavior. *Annual Review of Psychology, 58*, 345-372. https://doi.org/10.1146/annurev.psych.56.091103.070145

Tangney, J. P., Wagner, P., Fletcher, C., & Gramzow, R. (1992). Shamed into anger? The relation of shame and guilt to anger and self-reported aggression. *Journal of Personality and Social Psychology, 62*(4), 669-675. https://doi.org/10.1037//0022-3514.62.4.669

Tangney, J. P., Wagner, P. E., Hill-Barlow, D., Marschall, D. E., & Gramzow, R. (1996). Relation of shame and guilt to constructive versus destructive responses to anger across the lifespan. *Journal of Personality and Social Psychology, 70*(4), 797-809. https://doi.org/10.1037//0022-3514.70.4.797

Taylor, G. (1985). *Pride, shame, and guilt: Emotions of self-assessment*. Oxford University Press.

Taylor, G. (1996). Guilt and remorse. In R. Harré & W. G. Parrott (Eds.), *The emotions: Social, cultural and biological dimensions* (pp. 57-73). SAGE Publications Ltd. https://doi.org/10.4135/9781446221952.n5

Taylor, G. (2002). Guilt, shame and shaming. In I. Weijers & A. Duff (Eds.), *Punishing Juveniles. Principle and Critique* (pp. 179-192). Hart Publishing.

Teroni, F., & Bruun, O. (2011). Shame, guilt and morality. *Journal of Moral Philosophy, 8*(2), 223-245. https://doi.org/10.1163/174552411X563574

Teroni, F., & Deonna, J. A. (2008). Differentiating shame from guilt. *Consciousness and Cognition, 17*(3), 725-740. https://doi.org/10.1016/j.concog.2008.02.002

Tharp, A. T., DeGue, S., Valle, L. A., Brookmeyer, K. A., Massetti, G. M., & Matjasko, J. L. (2013). A systematic qualitative review of risk and protective factors for sexual violence perpetration. *Trauma, Violence, & Abuse, 14*(2), 133-167. https://doi.org/10.1177/1524838012470031

Theimann, M. (2016). School as a space of socialization and prevention. *European Journal of Criminology*, 13(1), 67-91. https://doi.org/10.1177/1477370815597254

Thoits, P. A. (1989). The sociology of emotions. *Annual Review of Sociology, 15*(1), 317-342. https://doi.org/10.1146/annurev.so.15.080189.001533

Thoits, P. A., & Virshup, L. K. (1997). Me's and we's: Forms and functions of social identities. In R. D. Ashmore & L. Jussim (Eds.), *Self and identity: Fundamental issues* (pp. 106-133). Oxford University Press.

Thomas, K. J. (2018). Revisiting delinquent attitudes: Measurement, dimensionality and behavioral effects. *Journal of Quantitative Criminology, 34*(1), 313-341. https://doi.org/10.1007/s10940-016-9336-3

Tibbetts, S. G. (1997a). Gender differences in students' rational decisions to cheat. *Deviant Behavior, 18*(4), 393-414. https://doi.org/10.1080/01639625.1997.9968068

Tibbetts, S. G. (1997b). Shame and rational choice in offending decisions. *Criminal Justice and Behavior, 24*(2), 234-255. https://doi.org/10.1177/0093854897024002006

Tibbetts, S. G. (2003). Self-conscious emotions and criminal offending. *Psychological Reports, 93*(1), 101-126. https://doi.org/10.2466/pr0.2003.93.1.101

Tibbetts, S. G. (2014). Traits and states of self-conscious emotions in criminal decision making. In J.-L. Van Gelder, H. Elffers, D. Reynald, & D. Nagin (Eds.), *Affect and cognition in criminal decision making* (pp. 221-238). Routledge.

Tibbetts, S. G., & Herz, D. C. (1996). Gender differences in factors of social control and rational choice. *Deviant Behavior, 17*(2), 183-208. https://doi.org/10.1080/01639625.1996.9968022

Tibbetts, S. G., & Myers, D. L. (1999). Low self-control, rational choice, and student test cheating. *American Journal of Criminal Justice, 23*(2), 179-200. https://doi.org/10.1007/BF02887271

Tignor, S. M., & Colvin, C. R. (2017). The interpersonal adaptiveness of dispositional guilt and shame: A meta-analytic investigation: Adaptiveness guilt shame. *Journal of Personality, 85*(3), 341-363. https://doi.org/10.1111/jopy.12244

Topalli, V., Higgins, G. E., & Copes, H. (2013). A causal model of neutralization acceptance and delinquency: Making the case for an individual difference model. *Criminal Justice and Behavior*. https://doi.org/10.1177/0093854813509076

Tosouni, A., & Connie, I. (2008). Shaming youthful offenders: An empirical test of reintegrative shaming theory. *International Journal of Restorative Justice, 4*(2), 53-79.

Tourangeau, R., & Yan, T. (2007). Sensitive questions in surveys. *Psychological Bulletin, 133*(5), 859-883. https://doi.org/10.1037/0033-2909.133.5.859

Tracy, J. L., & Robins, R. W. (2006). Appraisal antecedents of shame and guilt: Support for a theoretical model. *Personality and Social Psychology Bulletin, 32*(10), 1339-1351. https://doi.org/10.1177/0146167206290212

Trivedi-Bateman, N. (2019). The combined roles of moral emotion and moral rules in explaining acts of violence using a situational action theory perspective. *Journal of Interpersonal Violence, 36*(17-18), 8715-8740. https://doi.org/10.1177/0886260519852634

Turner, J. H. (2009). The sociology of emotions: Basic theoretical arguments. *Emotion Review, 1*(4), 340-354. https://doi.org/10.1177/1754073909338305

Turner, J. H., & Stets, J. E. (2006). Moral emotions. In J. E. Stets & J. H. Turner (Eds.), *Handbook of the sociology of emotions* (pp. 544-566). Springer US. http://doi.org/10.1007/978-0-387-30715-2_24

Turner, R. H. (1956). Role-taking, role standpoint, and reference-group behavior. *American Journal of Sociology*, *61*(4), 316-328. https://doi.org/10.1086/221763

Ulmer, J. T., & Wilson, M. S. (2003). The potential contributions of quantitative research to symbolic interactionism. *Symbolic Interaction*, *26*(4), 531-552. https://doi.org/10.1525/si.2003.26.4.531

Vaisey, S. (2009). Motivation and justification: A dual-process model of culture in action. *American Journal of Sociology*, *114*(6), 1675-1715. https://doi.org/10.1086/597179

Van de Bunt, H., Siegel, D., & Zaitch, D. (2014). The social embeddedness of organized crime. In L. Paoli (Ed.), *The Oxford handbook of organized crime* (pp. 321-339). Oxford University Press. https://doi.org/10.1093/oxfordhb/9780199730445.013.030

van de Schoot, R., Lugtig, P., & Hox, J. (2012). A checklist for testing measurement invariance. *European Journal of Developmental Psychology*, *9*(4), 486-492. https://doi.org/10.1080/17405629.2012.686740

Van Droogenbroeck, F., & Spruyt, B. (2014). Religieuze beleving bij Vlaamse jongeren anno 2013. In L. Bradt, S. Pleysier, J. Put, J. Siongers, & B. Spruyt (Eds.), *Jongeren in cijfers en letters. Bevindingen uit de JOP-monitor 3 en de JOP-schoolmonitor 2013* (pp. 217-242). Acco.

Van Droogenbroeck, F., & Spruyt, B. (2020). Social pressure for religious conformity and anti-gay sentiment among Muslim and Christian youth. *Educational Psychology*, *40*(2), 227-248. https://doi.org/10.1080/01443410.2019.1622651

van Gelder, J.-L., Elffers, H., Reynald, D., & Nagin, D. S. (Eds.). (2014). *Affect and cognition in criminal decision making*. Routledge.

van Gelder, J.-L., Reynald, D., & Elffers, H. (2014). Anticipated emotions and immediate affect in criminal decision making. From shame to anger. In J.-L. Van Gelder, H. Elffers, D. Reynald, & D. S. Nagin (Eds.), *Affect and cognition in criminal decision making* (pp. 161-178). Routledge.

Van Houtte, M., & Stevens, P. A. J. (2015). Tracking and sense of futility: The impact of between-school tracking versus within-school tracking in secondary education in Flanders (Belgium). *British Educational Research Journal*, *41*(5), 782-800. https://doi.org/10.1002/berj.3172

Van Stokkom, B. (2002). Moral emotions in restorative justice conferences: Managing shame, designing empathy. *Theoretical Criminology*, *6*(3), 339-360. https://doi.org/10.1177/136248060200600306

Velotti, P., Garofalo, C., Bottazzi, F., & Caretti, V. (2017). Faces of shame: Implications for self-esteem, emotion regulation, aggression, and well-being. *The Journal of Psychology*, *151*(2), 171-184. https://doi.org/10.1080/00223980.2016.1248809

Verdonck, E. (2017). *De aantrekkelijkheid van geweld. Een onderzoek naar de rol van intrinsieke aspecten in de betekenisgeving en verklaring van fysiek geweld bij jongeren.* KU Leuven.

Verhoeven, M., Poorthuis, A. M. G., & Volman, M. (2019). The role of school in adolescents' identity development. A literature review. *Educational Psychology Review, 31*(1), 35-63. https://doi.org/10.1007/s10648-018-9457-3

Verkuyten, M. (2007). Religious group identification and inter-religious relations: A study among Turkish-Dutch Muslims. *Group Processes & Intergroup Relations, 10*(3), 341-357. https://doi.org/10.1177/1368430207078695

Vermeersch, H., T'Sjoen, G., Kaufman, J. M., Vincke, J., & Van Houtte, M. (2010). Gender ideology, same-sex peer group affiliation and the relationship between testosterone and dominance in adolescent boys and girls. *Journal of Biosocial Science, 42*(04), 463-475. https://doi.org/10.1017/S0021932010000106

Vettenburg, N., Gavray, C., & Born, M. (2010). Belgium. In J. Junger-Tas, I. H. Marshall, D. Enzmann, M. Killias, M. Steketee, & B. Gruszczynska (Eds.), *Juvenile delinquency in Europe and beyond* (pp. 29-46). Springer New York. http://link.springer.com/10.1007/978-0-387-95982-5_3

Voas, D., & Fleischmann, F. (2012). Islam moves west: Religious change in the first and second generations. *Annual Review of Sociology, 38*(1), 525-545. https://doi.org/10.1146/annurev-soc-071811-145455

von Lampe, K., & Ole Johansen, P. (2004). Organized crime and trust: On the conceptualization and empirical relevance of trust in the context of criminal networks. *Global Crime, 6*(2), 159-184. https://doi.org/10.1080/17440570500096734

Wallbott, H. G., & Scherer, K. R. (1995). Cultural determinants in experiencing shame and guilt. In J. P. Tangney & K. W. Fischer (Eds.), *Self-conscious emotions: The psychology of shame, guilt, embarrassment and pride* (pp. 465-487). Guilford Press.

Walters, G. D. (2016). Reflected appraisals and self-view in delinquency development: An analysis of retrospective accounts from members of the Racine birth cohorts. *Journal of Criminal Justice, 47*, 100-107. https://doi.org/10.1016/j.jcrimjus.2016.07.004

Warr, M. (2002). *Companions in crime: The social aspects of criminal conduct.* Cambridge University Press.

Warr, M. (2016). Crime and regret. *Emotion Review, 8*(3), 231-239. https://doi.org/10.1177/1754073915586818

Websdale, N. (2010). *Familicidal hearts: The emotional styles of 211 killers.* Oxford University Press.

Weerman, F. M., Bernasco, W., Bruinsma, G. J. N., & Pauwels, L. J. R. (2016). Gender differences in delinquency and situational action theory: A partial test. *Justice Quarterly, 33*(7), 1182-1209. https://doi.org/10.1080/07418825.2015.1064987

Weerman, F. M., & Bijleveld, C. C. J. H. (2007). Birds of different feathers: School networks of serious delinquent, minor delinquent and non-delinquent boys and girls. *European Journal of Criminology*, *4*(4), 357-383. https://doi.org/10.1177/1477370807080718

Weerman, F. M., & Hoeve, M. (2012). Peers and delinquency among girls and boys: Are sex differences in delinquency explained by peer factors? *European Journal of Criminology*, *9*(3), 228-244. https://doi.org/10.1177/1477370811435736

Wicker, F. W., Payne, G. C., & Morgan, R. D. (1983). Participant descriptions of guilt and shame. *Motivation and Emotion*, *7*(1), 25-39. https://doi.org/10.1007/BF00992963

Wikström, P.-O. H. (2006). Individuals, settings, and acts of crime: Situational mechanisms and the explanation of crime. In P.-O. H. Wikström & R. J. Sampson (Eds.), *The explanation of crime* (pp. 61-107). Cambridge University Press.

Wikström, P.-O. H. (2010). Explaining crime as moral actions. In S. Hitlin & S. Vaisey (Eds.), *Handbook of the sociology of morality* (pp. 211-239). Springer.

Wikström, P.-O. H., Oberwittler, D., Treiber, K., & Hardie, B. (Eds.). (2012). *Breaking rules: The social and situational dynamics of young people's urban crime.* Oxford University Press.

Wikström, P.-O. H., & Sampson, R. J. (2003). Social mechanisms of community influences on crime and pathways in criminality. In B. B. Lahey, T. E. Moffitt, & A. Caspi (Eds.), *Causes of conduct disorder and juvenile delinquency* (pp. 118-148). The Guilford Press.

Wikström, P.-O. H., & Treiber, K. (2007). The role of self-control in crime causation: Beyond Gottfredson and Hirschi's general theory of crime. *European Journal of Criminology*, *4*(2), 237-264. https://doi.org/10.1177/1477370807074858

Wikström, P.-O. H., & Treiber, K. (2017). Beyond risk factors: An analytical approach to crime prevention. In B. Teasdale & M. S. Bradley (Eds.), *Preventing crime and violence* (pp. 73-87). Springer International Publishing.

Williams, B. (1993). *Shame and necessity*. University of California Press.

Williams, M. N., Grajales, C. A. G., & Kurkiewicz, D. (2013). Assumptions of multiple regression: Correcting two misconceptions. *Practical Assessment, Research and Evaluation*, *18*(11), 1-14. https://doi.org/10.7275/55hn-wk47

Worthen, M. G. F. (2011). Gender differences in parent-child bonding: Implications for understanding the gender gap in delinquency. *Journal of Crime and Justice*, *34*(1), 3-23. https://doi.org/10.1080/0735648X.2011.554744

Young, J. T., Barnes, J. C., Meldrum, R. C., & Weerman, F. M. (2011). Assessing and explaining misperceptions of peer delinquency. *Criminology*, 49, 599-630. https://doi.org/10.1111/j.1745-9125.2011.00232.x

Ysseldyk, R., Matheson, K., & Anisman, H. (2010). Religiosity as identity: Toward an understanding of religion from a social identity perspective. *Personality and Social Psychology Review*, 14, 60-71. http://dx.doi.org/10.1177/1088868309349693

Yun, H.-J., Cui, M., & Blair, B. L. (2016). The mediating roles of adolescent disclosure and parental knowledge in the association between parental warmth and delinquency among Korean adolescents. *Journal of Child and Family Studies*, *25*(8), 2395-2404. https://doi.org/10.1007/s10826-016-0425-6

Zahavi, D. (2014). *Self and other: Exploring subjectivity, empathy, and shame*. Oxford University Press.

Zeelenberg, M. (1999). The use of crying over spilled milk: A note on the rationality and functionality of regret. *Philosophical Psychology*, *12*(3), 325-340. https://doi.org/10.1080/095150899105800

Zhang, L. (1997). Informal reactions and delinquency. *Criminal Justice and Behavior*, *24*(1), 129-150. https://doi.org/10.1177/0093854897024001008

www.ingramcontent.com/pod-product-compliance
Lightning Source LLC
Chambersburg PA
CBHW080937240926
51849CB00004BA/481
* 9 7 8 9 0 4 7 3 0 1 6 5 3 *